SEAMS SEWN LONG AGO

The Story of Coats the Threadmakers

Brian Coats

ISBN: 1490408266
ISBN-13: 978-1490408262

In memory of my father,
Sir William Coats, and all
those who came before him.

For future generations,
so they can appreciate
their heritage.

Contents

Acknowledgements

I would firstly like to thank all my colleagues and ex-colleagues who helped me to fill in the gaps in my knowledge of the company history. I much appreciate the time that many people took to send me interesting and amusing anecdotes about the company and particularly my father, few of which have found their way into the final text, but all of which I enjoyed immensely. I am also indebted to those at Coats who gave me access to the largely advertising material in the USA, which is where I started my research. One of the surprising things that emerged from this whole endeavor is the significant role that the USA played in the prosperity of what was after all a Scottish family and business. The company in England was very accommodating in showing me the material they have and in allowing me to use the spool label on the book cover. The old Chain logo on the title page is a trademark of J. & P. Coats and was also used with their kind permission.

Back in Scotland, the patience and perseverance of everyone at the Paisley Central Library was much appreciated. They helped me unearth some fascinating information I would never have found without their help. The Thread Mill Museum in Paisley was also an inspiration. They should be applauded for all the material they have preserved, much of which would have been lost without them. The net proceeds from the sale of this book will go to them.

Next on my list are the various members of the family whose support and knowledge were vital, particularly in piecing together the chapters on philanthropy, spending, and the Coatses who found fame outside the world of sewing thread.

I must mention several people by name: Christine McDerment painstakingly read, critiqued, and in the end improved my first version of the book; my son Andrew helped me design the cover and his partner, Leah Shesky, wrote the blurb; my daughter Julia was my first editor and her partner, John George, gave me legal advice; last, but by no means least, my wife Consuelo pushed me to get the book finished and showed infinite patience during the long hours of research and writing. For all that and so much more, she deserves the most special mention.

Prologue

The Origins of Sewing Thread

A thread will tie an honest man better than a chain a rogue.
Scottish proverb

To tell the Coats story, we must first delve into the distant past of the product that made the family pioneers rich and famous, sewing thread. For they were not inventing anything original—far from it. Their fortune was made, as is so often the case, by being in the right place at the right time and having the intelligence, audacity, and organisation to exploit the situation to its fullest extent.

There is nothing new under the sun, and this is certainly true of thread. Yet any product that could even loosely be said to be sewable had to await the invention of a suitable needle. The earliest one with an eye, vaguely resembling the modern implement, is believed to have dated from about 40,000 years ago. The first definitive example came from the Solutrean culture, which existed in the Mâcon district of eastern France between 19,000 and 15,000 BC. Their tools and techniques allowed them to fashion delicate slivers of flint to make light projectiles and even barbed arrowheads. By extension, they could also produce fine items like sewing needles, which were either made from sharp objects such as thorns or fish bones, or honed from ivory, bone, or horn.

Bronze needles appeared in 2,500 BC, in Crete and Egypt; iron ones date back to the third century BC in what is now Germany, and a complete set was also unearthed in a tomb in China from the Han Dynasty (206 BC to 220 AD), along with the earliest example yet found of a thimble.

Although the spinning of threads is a part of folklore and features in such famous children's stories as *Rumplestiltskin* and *The Sleeping Beauty*, nobody can agree exactly where or when it started. Most scholars concur that it was over 10,000 years ago, and we can be sure that early ropes, sail cloth, bandages of Egyptian mummies, and tapestries all started in a spun form. It is theoretically possible to spin yarn without the aid of utensils, but "hand-spun" yarn was made using a distaff and drop spindle, and by the New Stone Age a spinner was capable of making about half a pound of yarn in a long, long day. The raw material was mostly linen, with sheep's wool being used towards the end of the period. The finished product was rough and uneven.

Clothing is even older than the needle and thread and was probably worn as far back as 100,000 BC. How do we know this? It is when the human body louse, which lodges in our clothing, first turned up.[1] These clothes would have been animal skins or furs, combined with decorative shells and bones, and usually tied or draped. The earliest evidence of sewn skins is from over 30,000 years ago, which broadly matches the dating of the first needles.

The development of sewing thread is intimately related to that of embroidery. It is no coincidence that people attempted embroidery once the basic sewing tools were available, and recognisable forms date back to before 3,000 BC. Its introduction as an art form can be attributed to the Assyrians and Babylonians in biblical times, originating around 1500 BC. Their robes were intricately decorated with

1. Before that date we still had bugs but they made their homes in our heads, where our hair kept them comfortable and nourished.

jewelry as well as woven and embroidered designs, and their interior textiles were elaborately patterned. No actual specimens have survived, but the Old Testament indicates that they had vivid colours, probably similar to those that evolved in Persia and Egypt. It is in the latter country that the earliest physical samples have been found, preserved thanks to the exceptionally dry climate. Their white-on-white needlework, used to decorate the fine linens of the Pharaohs, was marvelous.

It is impossible to explore the origins of embroidery or sewing thread without including silk, which developed in China and was shrouded in secrecy for as long as three millennia afterwards. Ancient legend gives the credit for its discovery to Lady Xi Ling Shi, the fourteen-year-old bride of the mythical Yellow Emperor, Huang Ti. According to Confucius, she was sitting in the garden one day, sipping from a cup of hot tea, when a silk cocoon fell in. The wispy fibers started to unwind in the steaming liquid and she had a flash of insight there and then, conceiving the idea of unravelling them to spin into filaments, thus making a yarn. This is supposed to have taken place in 2640 BC. She is also credited with the introduction of silkworm breeding and the invention of the loom, presumably at some later date. Whether the story is true or not, the earliest examples of spun silk came from China at around this time and she became the Goddess of Silk.

Silk production was introduced to Europe in 550 AD. Two Nestorian Monks smuggled silkworm eggs into Constantinople (now Istanbul) for the Eastern Roman Emperor Justinian I in their hollow bamboo walking sticks. They supervised the hatching of the eggs, the worms spun cocoons, and the Byzantine silk weaving mills were established. The Persians soon discovered the secret, so the Middle East began to compete successfully with the Chinese, but it would be another 600 years before Italy got in on the act, when 200 skilled Byzantine silk weavers were brought over at the time of the Second Crusades.

No further development of raw materials for sewing took place until the 1700s. Mechanisation was limited to the introduction of the spinning wheel into Europe in the fourteenth century, only to be made practically obsolete in 1440, when Leonardo Da Vinci invented a flyer and twister, whereby the yarn was twisted and wound onto a spindle in one operation.

So as we approach the beginning of our story, silk is the medium of choice for embroidery and other finer applications, but basic sewing thread is still a rough, uneven product, largely made from hand-spun linen. That is about to change, in a small town in Scotland called Paisley.

Chapter 1

Witchcraft and Sewing Thread

Apart from cheese and tulips, the main product of Holland is advocaat, a drink made from lawyers.
Alan Coren, English humorist

Our tale opens with an eleven-year-old girl, Christian Shaw, levitating from her bed and flying across her bedroom as if possessed. What this has to do with sewing thread will become clear, but first we must see how she got into such a state. What will unfold is a ghoulish tale of witchcraft, illustrative of the power of religious beliefs and bigotry of the age, the unreliability of eyewitness testimony, and the terrible consequences of playacting that gets out of hand.

Christian was the daughter of John Shaw, the laird of Bargarran, a small estate on the outskirts of Paisley, just to the south of Erskine Castle. She was intelligent, well-educated, and bright, but was also rather a spoilt child who loved to be the centre of attention.

In August 1696, when Christian was eleven years old, she caught one of their maids, Katherine Campbell, drinking milk that belonged to the household and told her mother. When Katherine realised who her accuser was, she turned on the startled child, screaming that she hoped the Devil would drag her soul through Hell, condemning her to eternal damnation. Curses were a serious business in Scotland at the time, and as the family were Godly churchgoers, this outburst would have caused considerable distress.

The next Friday, just before dawn, an elderly widow named Agnes Naesmith came to Bargarran house. Illiterate, sullen, and as unattractive as they come, she lived nearby and would drop by regularly in the hope of some scraps of food. This was not unusual; it was a time of hardship, with very cold winters and poor harvests, so there were plenty of beggars to be found. Many of the larger households would put food aside for those less fortunate than themselves and the Shaws were no exception. Agnes came across Christian in the garden and had a brief, apparently innocent, exchange. It would come back to haunt the old widow.

A few days later, Christian had gone to bed as she normally did, but once asleep she began to cry for help and, according to her parents, rose above the bed and flew at such a speed that she would have killed herself had a woman not come between her and the doorpost. Further alarming symptoms reminiscent of scenes from the film *The Exorcist* followed. Doctors were called, but despite drawing blood and applying poultices, her condition was unchanged. The medical profession was baffled.[1]

She named both Katherine and Agnes as her antagonists, saying that they were brandishing knives and trying to cut her. She was taken to see a distinguished physician, Dr. Brisbane in Glasgow. He diagnosed her condition as Hypochondriac Melancholy and prescribed medicine for her. She remained in Glasgow under his care for a ten-day period, during which her health improved, so she was sent home, ostensibly cured.

1. It is extremely doubtful that her behavior was the result of supernatural forces, but probably a combination of mild epilepsy, attention seeking, and just plain fabrication, encouraged by her family and even the clergy.

However, upon her return to Bargarran, her symptoms came back with a vengeance, and she started to produce a huge variety of objects from her mouth: hair like a cat's fur ball, cinders the size of plums and hot to the touch, straw (mixed with dung), pins, small bones, pieces of wood, feathers, gravel, candle-grease, and eggshells. These items were always dry and seemed to materialise in the back of her throat. She held long conversations with imaginary beings, accurately cited biblical texts to them, and offered prayers of forgiveness. The first serious mutterings about witchcraft began to surface.

Unable to conjure up a cure and unwilling to admit that she was merely a drama queen, the doctors reluctantly agreed that this must be some form of diabolic possession. The prospect terrified her father. Like everyone in Scotland at the end of the seventeenth century, educated or ignorant, he lived in mortal fear of witches. This paranoia had started seriously with King James VI, after bad weather had plagued the travel plans for his wedding to Princess Anne of Denmark and the cause had been traced back to witchcraft. Harassment and torture of all witches followed, and although the last one to be put to death in England was in 1682, the Scots took longer to embrace the Age of Enlightenment and continued to persecute them for another fifty years. Rowan trees grew over the arches at Bargarran; there were elder trees all around the estate and horseshoes over the outhouses and doors, all designed to keep out witches. Superstition was alive and well.

Christian's father was also conscious of a disturbing incident that had befallen the family in the not-too-distant past. His father, John Shaw Sr., had disappeared whilst trying to cross a flooded river during an early winter snowstorm some twenty years before. His body was not found for three months, but turned up in a ditch several hundred yards away, where a search party had already looked the day after he vanished. Moreover, the corpse was almost perfectly preserved, as if freshly dead, but the right hand and genitals had been hacked off. He had not been robbed, as his watch was still on him, and he had money in his pockets.

A rational explanation for this is fairly straightforward if a little grisly. He had drowned and someone had found the corpse, removed the hand and genitals (real trophies from a rich or powerful man) to use in some form of black magic ritual, and had discarded the remains in the ditch. This was why nothing was found during the original search. The winter was a hard one, so the body had been hidden and preserved by the frost and snow, only to be discovered at the first thaw of spring. This was not, however, the conclusion at the time. The mysterious reappearance of the dead man, miraculously conserved but with the missing body parts, could be nothing other than witchcraft.

So now John Shaw, faced with the prospect of this particular horror raising its ugly head within his household again, did the only sensible thing he could think of. He went to the Church for help. Amazingly, they took him seriously and the clergy became deeply involved. Christian was the subject of study by a number of distinguished people from farther afield than Glasgow. At this point there was no turning back, and she continued the charade with renewed vigor for fear of being declared a witch herself. She began to accuse others and see the devil himself.

Campbell heard that she was being named as a witch and tried to flee but was captured and imprisoned. A hairball similar to ones produced earlier by Christian was found near her and was taken as definitive proof of her guilt. Naesmith was questioned and released.

Early in February 1697, a commission of distinguished persons appointed by the Privy Council of Scotland met to examine and report on the whole case. Of the eleven members, nine were Renfrewshire lairds, just like Shaw, with three being directly related to him. The impartiality of this august group was clearly open to question.

Under close questioning, Christian Shaw accused more people, some at random and some suggested by her interrogators. Amongst the unlucky ones to be detained were a notorious drunk and blasphemer, Alexander Anderson, and his seventeen-year-old daughter Elizabeth. She was arrested partly because she was related to him, but mostly through her involvement a year before in a witchcraft hearing at nearby Inchinnan, where she had accused her own grandmother of being a witch. Christian named several others as well.

The final deliberations of the commission as to who was guilty were the subject of heated debate. Elizabeth Anderson gave fantastically detailed testimony for an entire day, recalling a witches' meeting in the orchard, baby sacrifices, broomstick flights, spells, and plots. She had a superb memory for the slightest detail and could name all her fellow sorceresses.

Some of the Commissioners were unconvinced. There was conflicting testimony. Elizabeth's ability to recognise everyone in the dead of night seemed almost uncanny, and many of the accused were beggars or other vagrants who seemed unlikely candidates for scheming and murdering. However, others felt that Elizabeth's naming of two babies who had died suddenly of unexplained causes was sufficient reason to believe her. They formed the majority, and the commission reported on February 18 that there was clear evidence of witchcraft. The list of the accused had grown to twenty-four.

Then Christian suddenly announced to her parents that she was free of demons. It is perhaps not entirely coincidental that this miracle cure happened soon after the release of the above report on the "doings of witches", though she claimed that it was because all her tormentors were safely behind bars.

Within a couple of weeks, a further commission of no less than seventeen judges was formed under Lord Blantyre, to try the accused and decide whether they should be burnt or otherwise executed. This was to be a trial by jury, and fifteen men were sworn in. They all met immediately, along with the witnesses and clergy who were there as advisers, to listen to a sermon entitled "Thou shalt not suffer a witch to live" delivered by the famous witch-hater, James Hutcheson of Killellan. The tone of the trial was set.

They then adjourned for a week to allow time for the clergy to extract further confessions to add to those already obtained. This was regarded as essential, but it is strange to note that although they did get more admissions of guilt, the two that were obtained on the morning the commission reconvened did not lead to the corresponding people being put on trial.

In the end, fifteen of the accused were acquitted, despite a bully of a prosecuting council—the Lord Advocate, Sir James Stewart. Elizabeth Anderson never stood trial, as she had already confessed and repented. It is also probable that she was excused because the judges feared that her testimony would crumble if confronted by an even vaguely competent defense council. Her father died in jail, maintaining that she was lying up to his dying breath.

Seven[2] were convicted. The basis of the convictions was that they were all found to bear witches' marks on their bodies, round moles or blemishes which neither bled nor caused them pain when stabbed with the witch-pricker's pins. Hutcheson had suggested this medieval test, but the proceedings were delayed as no one could find the requisite specialist until an old man was located who had once been taught the art and who had the required set of tools.

2. "The Paisley Seven" or "The Bargarran Witches".

All seven were sentenced to death. One of them, John Reid, a blacksmith, confessed and committed suicide that night by strangling himself. He had spoken at the trial of a black dog leading him to the devil, and so was buried under a stone with a horseshoe embedded in it to prevent his spirit passing through.[3]

The manner of the execution of the other six is not entirely clear. There are some accounts of them being hanged, and others indicating that they were burnt. They probably suffered both fates, being throttled on a gibbet for some minutes and then thrown on a pyre, a common form of public execution. The burning was a way of purifying the bodies and sending a dire warning to the massed spectators.

Whichever it was, Margaret Lang, Margaret Fulton, Katherine Campbell, and Agnes Naesmith,[4] were put to death on Paisley Green on June 10 1697, along with John Lindsay and James Lindsay, both cottars[5] or farmers. This was the last case of legal mass execution of witches in Scotland[6] where the law against witchcraft was finally abolished in 1736.

It is very likely that Christian Shaw was present at the Green that Thursday. Children were often taken to these macabre gatherings, both as a terrible warning of the dire

3. This story had a curious postscript. One night in the early 1800s, a local drunkard, Pate the Pirate, became intoxicated and took the horseshoe from the stone above Reid's tomb. Within days, several local textile workers attempted to commit suicide. This mysterious epidemic continued, much to the bewilderment of all and the alarm of Pate, who was convinced in a moment of sobriety that he had caused the whole thing. He took the offending object to the magistrates, who put it back in its original location. The wave of self-destruction stopped.

4. Agnes put a curse on everyone who saw the execution. For years, any misfortune that befell Paisley was attributed to her.

5. Coincidentally, the presumed origin of the Coats name.

6. It was also the last in all of Western Europe.

consequences of bad behavior and as a special treat. There were always sideshows, pie stalls, and other entertainments, and a good time could be had by all. Those who perhaps had the best time were the seventeen judges, who were each made burgesses of Paisley and lavishly entertained, the whole thing costing fifty pounds, a decent annual wage for most people at the time. Corruption is evidently not just a twenty-first-century phenomenon.

This was far from the end of Christian's notoriety. After her involvement with the devil, everyone was pleased that she had exposed the witches amongst them, but they continued to view her with nervous suspicion for years to come, as she had, after all, been responsible for bringing several law-abiding citizens under scrutiny along with the Devil-worshippers. So although she had completely recovered from her ordeal, she found friends hard to come by and suitors even more so. Her teens and twenties came and went without even the slightest suggestion of marriage.

During this period of social isolation, she had to find things to keep herself occupied. As was the custom for ladies of her social standing, she had taken up spinning yarn for the making of fine lawns and linens. Having a great deal of time on her hands, she became highly proficient at it and would send her yarn out for weaving into bed linens, tablecloths, and other household items. These were put away in the linen chest, awaiting the great day when she would finally meet the man of her dreams.

It was also fashionable to decorate fine garments with embroidery thread, and she cultivated her skills in this area too. The threads used did not come from her spinning wheel in this case, but rather from overseas—Holland, to be precise. She ran out of this thread at one point and decided to try using a strand of linen yarn in its place. The result was an uneven, ugly looking stitch, but it seemed functional enough and set her wondering how the Dutch achieved their smooth finish. This curiosity stayed with her, but a more momentous event intervened and so the solution would have to wait.

Much to Christian's surprise and relief, at the grand old age of 32, Mr. Right came along. A member of the same Presbytery who had been so involved in her infamous witch trials started calling on her and, after a brief courtship, proposed marriage. The Reverend John Miller, minister of Kilmaurs, was neither young nor handsome, but he was no pauper, and his religious background meant that he had few qualms about spending his life with a woman with her history. She duly accepted.

The marriage was a happy but cruelly short one, for he died three years later. It was 1721, and she found herself in the prime of life, with cash in her pocket and free as a bird. She moved back to Bargarran and decided to do the fashionable thing and tour around Europe, accompanied by her mother. But she did not go abroad as most widows do to seek a husband, attend the Opera, or visit pleasure gardens and palaces. She made a beeline for Holland. There, rather than admire the windmills, tulips, and clogs, she gazed in wonder at the beautiful quality of their linens spun by the finest manufacturers in the world. She was so effusive about the aprons and bonnets she saw that she was invited to visit a local Dutch spinner.

This was her chance to witness firsthand the processes and procedures that gave the product from the Netherlands its world renown. She absorbed it all, making notes and sketches of everything she could. The Dutch were very secretive about their processes, but it simply never crossed their minds that their competition would come from the widow of a Scottish clergyman and her elderly mother. As a result, the women had access to all the information they needed and took full advantage. She discovered how the Dutch packaged their thread, determined how the twining machines were built and operated, and learned the numbering system they used to distinguish between different thread thicknesses.

Christian Miller did not see any reason why a Scottish product could not be superior to the one from the Netherlands. The climate in Scotland was better for growing flax, the spinners she knew (including herself) were superior, and she was sure that with a bit of research she could come up with a better bleach than theirs. Moreover, the Scots had a work ethic which, combined with her enthusiasm, would be more than a match for the Dutch. She set out for home with a fire in her belly and a newfound purpose in life.

Before leaving, she somehow procured a twisting machine that she arranged to be shipped back home. She had also acquired, by fair means or foul, a number of other parts that gave the foreign manufacturing its edge. These she smuggled back to Scotland in her baggage, along with her plans, drawings, and notes on starting up a thread making operation. Once they had returned, she and her mother joined forces and set up a small production unit at Bargarran. This was based on the twisting machine, which ran twelve bobbins simultaneously, all turned by hand. She worked on a bleaching formula and, as anticipated, came up with a dazzling white. The end product, for which she is reputed to have performed every operation, was noticeably superior to the Dutch competition. All that was needed now was to market it to the fashion-conscious ladies of Britain. At this point, destiny took a hand.

By one of those coincidences that only happen in real life, Lady Blantyre, the wife of the presiding judge at the infamous witch trial, had been intrigued by the case and in particular by the little girl at the centre of it. She had therefore kept in touch with the family long after it was over and, as she lived close by, was a regular visitor. She couldn't avoid finding out about the small factory, and as it was her custom to take the waters at Bath every year, she volunteered to take samples of the Bargarran yarn with her, to show off to the aristocracy. She did this, not for monetary gain, but rather to proclaim the superiority of all things Scottish. Visitors to the spa town were the trendsetters of the age and if they liked a product, its success was guaranteed; they certainly liked this one. Lady Blantyre then took the thread to a variety of lace makers, who found it ideal for their end use, and Christian Miller's creation became famous, almost overnight.

Now that the thread was so popular, the little production unit became completely inadequate. Christian instructed her sisters and as many other local women as she could find in the art of spinning fine yarns and making thread. She built an expanded twining and bleaching manufactory at Johnstone, just a few miles down the road, and moved there.

The thread they produced was called "ounce" or "nun's thread", and it was sold in hanks of 40 threads[7] each. They quickly gained a name for their superb quality and with it found they could charge a handsome premium. The prestige of the Bargarran creation was such that it not only became the first thread made in Scotland to cross the Tweed, but was soon selling as far south as Devon, as well as in Wales and Ireland. Inevitably, it was impossible to keep all their manufacturing secrets contained within that small area of Scotland. The wagging tongues of the apprentices and hangers-on they needed to keep up with production were soon sharing their knowledge. So, with success came imitation, the sincerest form of flattery. This would be a constant feature of the sewing thread trade throughout its history, and a variety of methods have been used over the years to discourage such dishonesty.

In this particular instance, they fought for their rights by circulating the following advertisement:

> The Lady Bargarran and her daughters having attained to a great perfection in making, whitening, and twisting of Sewing Threed, which is as cheap and white, and known by experience to be much stronger than the Dutch, to prevent people's being imposed upon by other threed,

7. A thread was 36 inches.

> which may be sold under the name of 'Bargarran Threed', the papers in which the Lady Bargarran and her daughters at Bargarran, or Mrs. Miller, her eldest daughter (Christian, now a widow), at Johnstone, do put up their Threed, shall, for direction, have thereupon their Coat of Arms, *azure*, three covered cups, *or[e]*. Those who want the said Threed, which is to be sold from fivepence to six shillings per ounce, may write to the Lady Bargarran at Bargarran, or Mrs. Miller at Johnstone, to the care of the Postmaster at Glasgow: and may call for the same in Edinburgh, at John Seaton, merchant, his shop in the Parliament Close, where they will be served either Wholesale or Retail; and will be served in the same manner at Glasgow, by William Selkirk, merchant, in Trongate.[8]

Despite this, some of their competitors took to making identical copies of the item, including duplicates of their coat of arms. There is evidence that they resorted to the law courts to prevent this kind of fraud, to the point that they provoked one of the first recorded cases of a favourable ruling against trademark piracy in 1742.

Other competition arose of an even more damaging nature. Instead of the 40 threads that Mrs. Miller was offering in her product, they would sell only 30 in an attempt to undercut the Bargarran product. In time, "short" threads of 34 or 35 inches were also introduced, in a further effort to profit from her success. All this dishonesty led to a protracted price war, which was finally ended by the Chamber of Commerce, who devised a way of standardising the product.

With greater customer confidence restored and a proliferation of honest competitors, trade was brisk and grew fast. By 1744, just under 100 thread mills (twisting machines) had started up, and forty years later the business in Paisley

8. From *The Paisley Thread Industry* by Matthew Blair, p 22

alone was worth £64,000,[9] about one-third of the total for Scotland, rising to close to £100,000 by the turn of the century. The tradition of thread making in Paisley had been well established.

As for Christian Miller, she continued to run her business in Johnstone for at least another ten years, with few problems of labour unrest, perhaps due to her earlier reputation as a woman whom you crossed at your peril. She remarried in February 1737, by then a successful businesswoman in her fifties. Her second husband's name was William Livingstone, and he had a prosperous glove venture in Edinburgh. At that point all trace of her is lost, and it is assumed that she had a long and peaceful life, hopefully untroubled by the experiences of her youth.

All this thread manufacturing was still based on hand-turned machines and the workforce numbered over 20,000 women and 5,000 men. The inventions of the Industrial Revolution were just around the corner, leading to the introduction of cotton as a raw material for sewing, so this was the zenith of the linen thread industry, both in turnover and employment. It is also where the Clarks, who were to become the Coats's main rivals, enter the story.

9. It is useful to get a sense of the value of money over time. For the whole of the nineteenth century, through to the inflation of the First World War, £1 then was equivalent to approximately £100 now.

Chapter 2

The Clarks Get Started

Clever men are good, but they are not the best.
Thomas Carlyle, nineteenth century Scottish philosopher

The Clark family had been living at Dykebar, a small settlement less than two miles from the centre of Paisley, for at least sixty years and three generations when disaster struck. William Clark, born in 1710, married to Agnes Bryson at the age of twenty-six and father to six young children, was taken ill and died at the early age of forty-three.

Like his father and grandfather, both of whom were named Allan, William was a farmer. With the help of his oldest son and his own wife, he was able to scrape together a reasonable living from the land, provided Mother Nature treated him kindly. It was a hard life, with long hours and little respite from the physical demands of the daily grind. Their property consisted of a strip of fertile ground called a runrig, surrounded by a fallow area where their animals could graze. The runrig was so named as it was plowed to form a series of runs (furrows) and rigs (ridges). This area was manured courtesy of their animals, and the family's crops grew there. Provided that things went well, as they had done for years, they could eke out a meagre existence from the results of their efforts.

However, things were changing in Scotland. The Enlightenment had started a transformation in farming techniques. Drainage was improving, crop rotation was being introduced, hedges and trees were being planted as windbreaks, and larger areas could be managed successfully. All these factors combined to produce an enormous change in productivity. Many became wealthy, and the small-scale farmers like the Clarks found themselves being squeezed out. With the death of her husband, Agnes tried to get help from his elder brother, (another) Allan, who had a farm nearby, but he had problems of his own and was unable to give more than temporary assistance. Incapable of handling the farm alone, with most of her children still too young to make a meaningful contribution, she moved to the New Town in Paisley to look for a job.

Although their initial move to the town was tough, there was at least the prospect of employment for all of them, for Paisley was beginning to prosper from the general boom in textile production in the west of Scotland. The local specialities were fine lawns and cambrics, and silk gauze. The silks in particular were about to make a name for themselves as their production was introduced from Spitalfields, and the transfer of several master weavers from the South meant that a number of firms had moved to Paisley by 1773. At this point the Scottish woven product was said to more than rival the English one, and the merchants and manufacturers of the area learnt that by concentrating on high-end creations that were hard to duplicate, they could protect and grow their business. Imports of exceptionally fine yarns from France and Belgium were also a boost to the high quality weaving industry.

And we should not forget the linen sewing thread trade that had been started earlier by Christian Miller. Besides the 100 thread mills she had spawned, the Carlile family had by this time built the first Paisley thread manufactory at the Sneddon, on the north side of town.

So, with the Industrial Revolution still to come and plenty of labour-intensive textile production in the district, the Clarks had little trouble finding work, however menial and poorly paid. Given their tradition of toil from dawn to dusk and a gritty determination to succeed, they all rose to the challenge, and the youngster of the brood eventually went on to triumph to a degree the family could never have imagined as they trudged from Dykebar to Paisley with their few possessions and uncertain prospects.

The children ranged in ages from Allan, who was 16, down to wee James, who was only 5. As child labour was an accepted norm at the time, it was possible to find them all positions, with Allan becoming a weaver's apprentice along with his younger brother John and the smaller ones starting as weavers' drawboys. Even James found himself at this arduous task soon after his sixth birthday.

In the days before the Jacquard loom, intricate designs were woven on draw looms, including the famous Paisley pattern that is indeed named after the town. These were large devices operated by two workers, the master weaver and the drawboy. The weaver handled the threading of warp and weft threads,[1] so that the woven rows were laid out to form the desired motif. The drawboy raised or lowered the warps' reeds, according to instructions from the weaver, who would decide which of the reeds needed lifting, depending on whether he wanted the warp or weft threads uppermost on the cloth. As the cloth progressed, a pattern would emerge.

A master weaver with a good drawboy might produce two rows per minute, or 200 square inches of patterned silk cloth a day. Drawboys had to stand on top of the loom while lifting the reeds, and as the space was limited, adults couldn't fit, so children were used. They worked six to eight

1. In weaving, a loom interlaces two sets of threads at right angles to each other: the warp, which runs longitudinally, and the weft, which crosses it.

hours a day in a horrendous working environment, lifting 30 pounds of reeds at a time on every call. Given the sanitary conditions and the lack of nutrition afforded the children who undertook this work, it is easy to understand why they were often ill and sometimes crippled. Jacquard himself started out as a drawboy and hated it so much that he dedicated his life to automating these looms, a classic case of good coming out of evil.

James, it appears, was quiet and was often bullied by the lads where he worked. The apprentices gave him the nickname "tippence" partly due to his small stature, but mostly because he could neither afford nor had the head for the stronger fourpenny ale, which they all drank.[2] His master protected him from the worst of the taunts and took the time to teach him the weaver's trade. Although James had had no formal education, he was obviously a good learner and eventually graduated to become a master weaver in his own right.

All the while, his mother Agnes struggled on, spinning flax on a hand loom at home to earn a few extra pennies, whilst keeping the house in shape and feeding six hungry boys. They had all made similar progress to that of James, so she eventually found herself able to retire with the sure knowledge that she would be supported by her children, now grown up. One by one they left the nest and set up house, with wives and children of their own.

When James turned twenty-one, in 1768, he fell in love with and married seventeen-year-old Margaret Campbell, and they settled into a new home at 10 Cotton Street. There he started a family and a small business as a handloom weaver. Being a thrifty Scot, he prepared his own heddle twine rather than buying it from someone else. This twine is formed into loops, and these connect the necessary warp

2. It is doubtful that they could manage this beer either, as it had just over 12% alcohol by volume!

threads to the heddle, which is lifted to form the cloth pattern as the weave progresses. As the warp threads must slip through these loops, the thread has to be strong but very smooth. Silk was the raw material used.

As his business progressed and his family grew to what would eventually become fourteen children, he found himself pressed for time and decided to employ others to prepare the heddle twine. Soon he found he had the capacity to sell the product to his fellow weavers as well. He then added other accessories to his line and in due course stopped weaving and became a full-time weaver's furnisher. He gradually built up a solid portfolio of customers and a regular demand for the paraphernalia of the weaver's trade.

Whilst his business was developing, his brothers John and Patrick[3] had also become weavers, and William had turned his hand, literally, to cotton spinning. As Patrick was living just around the corner from him in New Sneddon Street, James convinced him that they should join forces and become partners. His sons also joined the business, but as he made them dedicate time to schooling in an attempt to give them a better education than he himself had experienced, they could not commit themselves as wholeheartedly as he had from such an early age.

3. It is strange that Patrick Clark, of whom very little has been written, is referred to as Patrick on some occasions and Peter on others. There is no doubt from the archives that his real name was Patrick, and as his part in this account will shortly be over, he will remain Patrick for the remainder of the story. Nobody seems to know why he had two names, but there appear to be three possibilities. The first is that the Peter was simply a mistake, as it was a more common name than Patrick. The second is that he was christened Patrick Peter and he decided on one rather than the other. The third brings to mind a much later tale of the Coatses. Mark Alistair Coats was Managing Director of Coats Fabra in Spain from the 1950s to the 1980s. Everyone knew him as Tim, despite his real name(s). This was because he liked and adopted "Tim" (rather than Mark or Alistair) as his name when he was a small child, and it stuck. It is possible that Patrick Clark had a similar quirk and went for the simpler Peter. We will never know.

Patrick was patently the inventive one, always tinkering with the items they sold and trying to conceive of improvements. James (from now on referred to as James Senior) was the steady hand on the tiller, the consummate businessman. By 1790 his children had all learnt the skills of the weaver and were lending a real hand in the enterprise. James Junior was selling linen sewing thread for them and working in his father's six-loom workshop, alongside William and Andrew (and a certain Alexander Wilson, who went on to become the father of American ornithology).[4]

The business entered the new century with optimism. James Jr.'s linen sewing thread trade was brisk, and the Treaty of Amiens meant peace with France. The French Revolution and the deaths of Louis XVI and Marie Antoinette at the guillotine had horrified the constitutional monarchies of the rest of Europe, particularly the Austrian Empire, which was ruled by Marie's family. In 1792, Great Britain, Austria, and Prussia declared war on the French Republic with the objective of restoring their royal family. France was at a disadvantage, as the excesses of the period immediately following the Revolution had driven off or killed most of the decent generals, so the army was little more than an unruly mob led by inexperienced officers.

Into this scenario stepped a young Napoleon Bonaparte, who, through a minor victory at Toulon, became a Brigadier General at a youthful twenty-four years old. Within a few

4. A Paisley poet with a political slant, Wilson worked for the Clarks as a weaver to make ends meet. After a few of his poems were published, he produced a scathing satirical attack on a Paisley master weaver that went too far. He was incarcerated and forced to burn his work at the crossroads of Paisley. Mortified by this and heartbroken by the collapse of a love affair with a certain Matilda (the subject of more poems), he left for America, where he befriended an ornithologist, William Bartram, who became his mentor. Reborn, he travelled extensively and went on to publish a nine-volume American Ornithology, which included 268 types of bird, 26 of them never previously described. He died of dysentery in 1836, having achieved all the renown he craved. How cruel that he never lived to see his statue erected in the grounds of Paisley Abbey.

short years he had quashed a Royalist insurrection in Paris and was made Commander of the Interior and of the army in Italy. That campaign was followed by another in Egypt, and his resulting popularity and some political manipulation got him elected First Consul, the most powerful man in France. Within a short time he would declare himself Emperor. More battles in Italy and Bavaria led up to the above peace treaty with Britain, which was signed at Amiens in March 1802. This was the basis for the Clarks' optimism at the turn of the century.

Unfortunately for them, the truce was short-lived. A whole series of conditions for peace were not fulfilled by either side, and Napoleon's disposal of one of the Royalist leaders without trial caused outrage. A coalition of Britain, Russia, Austria, and Sweden declared war. He now formed the greatest army in the world, one that would subjugate the rest of Europe for years to come. He set out to invade Britain, but his French/Spanish fleet was brilliantly defeated by Nelson at Trafalgar in 1805. This led the allied forces to believe that they could attack the French and conquer them, but Napoleon had secretly moved his army. In a series of battles, culminating at Austerlitz, he vanquished the combined Austrian and Russian armies, despite being outnumbered. The coalition was defeated.

Although Napoleon had overcome the British, he feared their maritime supremacy and knew that this would not be the end of it, so he decided to wage an economic war against them. His hope was that they would be so financially crippled that they could no longer fund another war with France. On November 20, 1806, he issued the Berlin Decree. This introduced the so-called Continental system, which effectively meant economic sanctions against Britain. It was not as effective as he had hoped. The good citizens of Europe did not want to do without the luxuries that came from a Britain in the throes of the Industrial Revolution and her colonies. Smuggling became the order of the day, and those willing to risk it grew rich.

The Clarks were not amongst them. The flow of goods into Scotland was severely curtailed, and one such product was silk, which the brothers imported from Hamburg to make their heddle twine. There were other goods as well, but these had substitutes available from England. As silk yarn was a very important part of their business, and a large number of local weavers were dependent on them for their supplies, a substitute needed to be found quickly as their stocks were dwindling.

Patrick started to experiment. He quickly realised that cotton was his only real alternative, as flax was too rough, and wool would not spin fine enough. However, cotton was known to be too weak and not smooth enough. At least that was the conventional wisdom.

The Industrial Revolution and in particular Crompton's Mule had introduced a vast improvement in the strength and smoothness of cotton yarn. When Kay invented the flying shuttle in 1733, cotton yarn was still being hand spun. Hargreaves's Spinning Jenny and Arkwright's Water Frame had started the mechanisation of the process, but it was Samuel Crompton's machine, which was a vast improvement on both of these, that paved the way for Patrick's success.

Crompton was born in 1753, and after his father died at only thirty-seven, he was brought up by his mother, who ruled with an iron fist. Charles Dickens Jr. wrote in his weekly journal, *All The Year Round*, of June 16 1883, that "His mother, a strict taskmistress, exacts the daily tale of work, and he often has to grieve over the bad yarn that keeps him from his books and from the violin, that is his great friend." He was put to work at the newly invented Spinning Jenny from an early age, but he was a curious teenager and became intrigued with the idea of improving the machine. He toiled away for five years behind closed doors, in an empty room of their rather palatial house outside town. He financed his contraption through his other interest, music, by getting a job with the orchestra of the Bolton Theatre for the princely sum of eighteen pence a night. He used every penny he saved in developing his invention, and in 1779 he succeeded. The Mule was born.

His machine was a revolution. It could spin an extremely fine cotton yarn, and with water power it could do it quickly and with minimal labour. The principle of the moving carriage was the secret of his success, with the spindle bank going back and forward to maintain the tension while the twist was inserted. It soon dawned on him that he could prosper by selling yarn rather than machines and, as he could spin cotton much finer than anything seen in Britain before,[5] he became an exclusive source, with the finest yarns yielding a price of £2/10/- [6] a pound, the equivalent of over £250 nowadays!

He had the makings of a fortune in his hands, but like other inventors before him, he had to defend himself from those eager to copy his gadget. Word had spread quickly, bringing scores of curious visitors interested in buying the yarn and, more ominously, in getting a look at how it was made. He needed to do something fast to protect himself.

The way Arkwright's patent (which was subsequently rescinded but was still valid at the time) was written, Samuel realised he would never be able to get good copyright protection, so he hit upon a plan which ended in disaster for him, but gave the textile industry a fabulous bequest and

5. This was an English 80s count, which would only have had 60 or 70 fibers in its cross section. Cotton thread thickness, linear density, or size was measured using the English Cotton count (Ne.) system, whereby the count is the number of 840 yard hanks in 1 lb. of thread. This is an inverted system, in that a high number or count means a fine thread and vice versa. Suffice it to say that Ne. 60 and finer is fine, and Ne. 20 and coarser is coarse.

6. Before Feb 15 1971, British currency was different. Pounds still existed, and the symbol for a pound was £. But £1 consisted of 20 shillings or 20/-. One Shilling was made up of 12 pennies or 12d., so 4 pounds 12 shillings and sixpence was written £4/12/6d., (or £4.62½p now).

paved the way for cotton sewing thread. Sam decided to offer the design to everyone, in return for which they would contribute to a subscription list, which would show what each had given, for the right to use it. This seemed like an ideal solution, but he had not bargained with the penny-pinching nature of his customers. The total amount paid from all subscribers was £60, just enough for him to build a slightly larger machine than his original. As he spent all his money on that machine, he really emerged with very little to show for his brilliance.

In 1811, just before the Clarks came to prominence, Samuel Crompton petitioned parliament for financial aid. Cartwright, the inventor of the power loom, had just been awarded £10,000, and Samuel was expecting a similar amount. His research had indicated that over 80% of the five million spinning spindles operating in Britain were based on his Mule. He only got half as much and used this money to set up in business, first as a bleacher and then as a cotton merchant and spinner. Sadly, he was no entrepreneur, and these were doomed to failure. By the time he died in 1827, he was living off an annuity of £63, which some friends had secretly bought him.

Patrick Clark was therefore tackling the problem of how to make heddle twine at a time (1807) when cotton yarn manufacturing was in the process of a step change. Yarn could be spun smoother, more regularly, cheaper, and finer than even thirty years before. He was aware of the cabling process whereby ropes were strengthened but remained smooth enough to slide quite effectively without snagging, so he knew it had to be a folded or twisted product. He reasoned that warp thread used in weaving cotton muslins would be a good starting point since it was stronger than the weft. Patrick twisted this on the same machine he used for silk twine, starting with two yarns, just as it was done for the silk product. Testing was slow because any change in the yarn meant waiting for a new sample to be spun and sent over. He first tried to get as close as he could to the thickness of the silk product, but the result was weak, for silk has a much higher inherent strength than cotton of an equivalent diameter. He spent long days and sleepless nights puzzling over the problem and then waiting for the latest sample to turn up.

He eventually decided that if he increased the yarn twist but also spun a finer yarn, and made three plies instead of two, he could improve both the smoothness and the strength to something similar to silk. In order to spin the product so fine, he also stipulated that the raw cotton be of the Sea Island variety, coming from the Caribbean and the coast of the southern states of America. This made the strongest cotton yarn available, having the longest and finest cotton fibers. The resulting thread was strong, but terribly lively,[7] so further experimentation was needed. Finally, by a combination of balancing the twists and the application of finish to kill the snarls, he arrived at an acceptably smooth result with sufficient strength, yet inert enough to do the job.

This solved the Clarks' immediate problem, and with a little tinkering, they established a way of making the product in bulk, ordered the required yarn, and breathed a collective sigh of relief. Sales were good and the twine was well accepted by the trade, as it not only fulfilled its function, but did so at a price that frankly delighted their customers.

It is remarkable to note that Patrick must have been sixty-five years old at this point, not exactly an age associated with innovation. Moreover, he still wasn't finished.

7. A "lively" yarn will snarl and spiral, usually because it has too much twist. If you take a piece of string and keep twisting it whilst holding it taut between your two hands, and then bring the hands together without letting go of the ends, you can get an idea of the effect.

Chapter 3

Clarks' Thread and Their First Factory

Imagine a World without Thread.
Coats advertising slogan

James Jr. and Patrick were talking one evening some weeks later, and the conversation got round to the similarity between heddle twine and sewing thread. They agreed that it stood to reason that if they could make one out of cotton, the other must be susceptible to a similar approach. Patrick started to work on the idea, and within a relatively short time, James Jr. was selling a cotton version alongside his linen thread, but only to a select few of his "more adventurous" customers who he felt were ready for it.

There had been a number of attempts made in the previous twenty years to produce a cotton sewing thread. The mechanisation of spinning had opened this particular door, and several had tried to step through it. An Indian cotton embroidery thread appeared in Paisley in 1784, but it had very low twist and would not have worked for sewing. Others in Scotland tried without success, so the first cotton sewing thread was actually made in Pawtucket, Rhode Island, in the USA and not in Paisley. The inventor was the wife of a famous Englishman, Samuel Slater.

Slater was born in 1768, the son of a farmer with a small freeholding in Derbyshire, England. Like so many in this story, he went to work as an apprentice, this time in a cotton mill in Belper, where he rose through the ranks to become a superintendent, all the while learning the processes and machinery based on Arkwright's and Crompton's designs, including the use of water power to drive the factory. He also learnt how to organise a labour force subject to this new technology.

Under British law, he was not allowed to share what he had learned or take it abroad. However, he had plans to make his fortune in the USA, so, having memorised the necessary technical details, he made a clandestine departure, passing himself off as a farm labourer. Not even his family knew he had gone. He ended up in New York in 1789 ready to use his knowledge to build a textile empire, provided he could find a sponsor. He befriended a Quaker merchant, Moses Brown, and with his financial support constructed a cotton spinning mill in Pawtucket, Rhode Island. By the end of 1791, this was up and running, powered by a waterwheel.

That same year he married Hannah Wilkinson, who bore him six children and died in 1812, but not before she had staked her claim to fame. She was very involved in the mill, and it has even been hinted that she was the real power behind its development. She is said to have taken the yarn that they had developed over the previous couple of years and twisted it on her spinning wheel, thus creating the first cotton sewing thread. For this, she received a patent in 1793, the first ever given to an American woman.[1]

1. It is interesting that many history books incorrectly ascribe this honor to Mary Kies of Connecticut, for "a method to weave straw with silk and thread", but this was sixteen years later, in 1809. See: pbs.org/opb/historydetectives_old/investigations/202_inventors.html

A commercial production method seems to have eluded the Slaters, for their future expansion was largely based on high-quality cotton yarn for weaving, with sewing thread taking a very minor role.[2] Also, although the product may have worked, it was made from Surinam cotton and was only two ply[3] and therefore inferior to what came later.

Back in Britain, there were others who were tinkering with cotton sewing thread in the early 1800s. Jonas Brook of Meltham, a cotton manufacturer who will feature later on, claimed to be making an acceptable product in 1802, but this only reappeared as a commercial proposition some years later and in a modified form. There is evidence of a number of cotton threads being sold from 1805 onwards, but all apparently too weak to challenge the linen equivalent. At least, that was the opinion of Alexander Carlile, who was making and selling the latter product at the time, so he may have had a vested interest in the failure of cotton.

So the Clarks were the first ones to make a cotton sewing thread that could be successfully mass-produced. As is so often the case, they stumbled upon it when looking for something else—everyone else was looking to substitute linen as a raw material, not silk.

Their second stroke of genius came from James Jr. The Clarks' heddle twine was sold in skeins, or hanks, as was their sewing thread. The housewife would wind off the amount she needed into little balls, in the same way as with wool products. It doesn't take much imagination to realise that this must have been a really finicky process, particularly at the end of the day by candlelight.

2. Slater went on to be named the "father of American manufactures" by Andrew Jackson, the US President at the time. He was also the founder of the Sunday school system in the USA. He died in 1836.

3. Ply refers to the number of yarns in a thread. Three ply threads are made up of three yarns twisted together.

Some manufacturers started to use Balling machines to automate this procedure, making the handling of the finished product much easier. Unfortunately, although these balls of thread were neat and beautiful when new, they became almost completely unmanageable towards their end, so the amount of thread wasted in their use was a source of deep dissatisfaction.

James Jr. hit on the idea of improving this step by offering to wind any skein bought from him onto a pirn and from there onto a wooden spool or reel, a far more manageable prospect than a tangle of threads in a ball. This was literally done on demand as the customer waited. The process (and particularly the spool itself) was expensive, which was perhaps why nobody else had attempted it. The Clarks devised a scheme whereby they charged a halfpenny for the service, which at least covered the cost of the cotton reels.[4]

However, where they were clever was the way they marketed the new product. Appealing to the good Scottish nature of their customers, they gave them their money back for the spool if it was returned empty, so an early form of recycling emerged. The returned spools could then be used to wind up their next order, and this almost guaranteed that they would return to Clark's rather than make their next purchase elsewhere; they had created product loyalty before branding had really developed.

Inevitably, with the thread easily analysed by the competition and machinery readily available, it was not long before the Clarks' competitors started to copy their product. Both silk and linen producers, Thomas Carlile amongst them, started making cotton sewing thread, and in 1812 alone there

4. These were bought for three shillings (now 15 pence) a half gross from Robert Paul, a local wood-turner, whose workshop was located where the Paisley Town Hall now stands. James would carry the order of seventy-two spools home in his coat pocket. He wound them by hand.

were eleven new manufacturers added to the list of Paisley thread makers; but there was little doubt that the Clarks, who had settled on a three ply product, were the clear leaders in both quality and capacity.

At this point, James Sr. decided that the time had come to build a factory capable of serious volume, and to this end he bought an extensive tract of land at Seedhill, at the east end of Paisley, on the River Cart. His plans were on a grand scale, judging by the acreage bought. The initial structure would only cover a small part of the total area.

But before construction could start, war intervened. The British had retaliated when Napoleon created his economic blockade back in 1806, by legislating that all shipments from neutral countries to enemy territories had to call at English ports before continuing to their final destination. The consequent delays and bureaucracy led to US frustration, retaliatory measures and eventually, in 1812, a declaration of war. Shortages of cotton followed, severely restricting production in all areas of manufacturing using that raw material. A punitive UK tax of between 25 and 35% on imports of American cotton followed, and although it was all over when Napoleon was banished to Elba in April 1814, the British had lost trade that would be hard to win back, given the higher cost base.

Even so, by 1815, cotton had largely replaced linen as the raw material of choice for the discerning seamstress. Not only was it cheaper, but it also sewed better, with a more flexible and softer handle and a tendency to bed into the seam, giving improved appearance.

James Sr. had soft-pedaled on the plans for Seedhill, given all these complications, but in 1817 he forged ahead.[5]

5. Almost everyone mistakenly gives the date as 1812, the year the land was bought, but James Balderston's evidence to the Factory Inquiry Commission of 1834 clearly gives the year of construction as 1817.

The mill was steam driven, this becoming the accepted source of industrial power after Watt's patent had expired in 1800. The twisting machines were the longer 48 spindle type. He offered principally white and black, specialising in spooled thread, but the product was still based on yarn purchased from cotton spinners. It would be many years before the Clarks started to spin for themselves.

Two years later he decided to retire and sold the whole thing to his two sons, James Jr. and John, lending them £4,000 to allow them to complete the deal. They, in their turn, formed the company of J. & J. Clark, Thread Manufacturers, in 1820.

The plant was immediately enlarged, the loan paid back, and they expanded their horizons by starting shipments to Europe. They also made their first direct export to the USA in 1821, surprisingly through New Orleans, thread on spools being a novelty for that market. However, as they had established a position as the industry leaders in Britain, they decided that exports were to be given low priority, with any expansion in UK demand often being satisfied by cutting off overseas shipments. This was a policy that they would regret later on.

A further drawback for the Clarks was exemplified by an event that took place just before James Sr.'s retirement. Another John Clark had learned the cotton spinning trade in a mill built by his father, William, who was James and John's cousin. This mill burned to the ground in 1816, not because the fire brigade was late in arriving to attend the fire, but because there was not enough water once they got there. With his inheritance in ashes, John went to Glasgow and built a cotton thread business in the Mile End area, setting up in direct competition to his namesakes. His company, John Clark Jr., went on to moderate prosperity, and he became the first of the family to export thread with that name to the USA, through an agent in New York. As the story unfolds, the confusion caused by a profusion of Clark companies will become apparent, the disunity of the family turning into a real handicap in the fight for thread supremacy.

The number of competitors in the cotton sewing thread market continued to grow. Alexanders opened a cotton thread section in Glasgow, and Arkwright, Ashworth, and Brooks, all North of England cotton spinners, opened thread departments. Chadwicks (of whom more later) included thread in their range of products at Eagley Mill, outside Bolton, but the main thrust of production was centred in Paisley, where Carlile, Kerr, Carswell, and others joined the Clarks, along with Ross & Duncan.

Then, in 1826, another newcomer was added to the list — James Coats.

Chapter 4

James Coats, Senior

To be humble to superiors is duty, to equals courtesy, to inferiors nobleness.
Benjamin Franklin

The Coats family first hit Paisley in 1760 when George tramped into town from his father's farm in Lanarkshire to look for work. He was a couple of years behind the Clarks (this became a Coats tradition), but as reform and modernisation swept through the country, both families faced a gloomy future as agricultural smallholders, so they had to seek alternative ways of making a living.

The Coats name is thought to come from their occupation as cottars back in the fourteenth century. A cottar was "a farm labourer or tenant occupying a cottage in return for labour", and they were quite common in Scotland and Ireland in the Middle Ages. However, this particular provenance is not set in stone, and they may have simply lived in a cot (old English word for cottage) or originate from Cotes in Leicestershire. There were several variations of their name as the use of surnames developed. Their earliest definite ancestor was David Coittis, who lived from 1545 to 1607 and married Katherine Clerk, who was not related to the family thread rivals.

The Coittis family did well for themselves, though this doesn't seem to have rubbed off on David. One of his relatives, also named David, was the Mair of Fee.[1] He served as a city official in the 1560s, and his son Andrew was Marshall of the Regality and Barony, a form of magistrate, in 1582. Several members of other branches of the family entered the church and there were at least three knighthoods – Sir James Coittis was in command of the King's ships in 1507 and again in 1539, Sir Thomas was Prior of Blantyre in 1522, and Sir Robert succeeded him.

David lived in Barnhill, now a district of Glasgow, and had land that he farmed there, as did the next two generations. Then James Coates[2] was transferred property at Dykehead on June 12, 1711 and the family moved farther east to their new Lanarkshire home[3] and remained there until George, who was this James's great grandson, moved to Paisley and became a weaver's apprentice in about 1760.

The Coatses had continued in their farming tradition, so he was exchanging an uncertain future on the land for the exciting possibilities of the world of textiles on the eve of the Industrial Revolution. Paisley was an obvious choice. It was gaining a reputation for the production of fine lawns and muslins, and silk was introduced to Scotland in the year he .

1. Jamieson's *A Dictionary of the Scottish Language* (1846) defines this as "a hereditary officer under the crown, whose power resembled that of a sheriff-substitute". "Mair" comes from the Gaelic Maor, which means an officer of authority.

2. The last name had changed to Coates by then, and became Coats with the next generation. They all used the same first names, usually John or James, much to everyone's confusion.

3. Andrew, James Coats's sixth son, wrote in an account of the family, *From the Cottage to the Castle*, in 1898 that his great grandfather (another James) was a shepherd in the Haddington area, some eighty miles from Paisley. This came from an eighty-year-old cousin, a "nice old gentleman" who remembered following the older James as he tended his flocks. The reliability of his memory must be open to question, and this is most likely incorrect. Andrew is unclear how his grandfather ended up in Paisley.

moved, which led to the most prosperous period ever for the town's weaving trade. The street names such as Lawn, Gauze, Cotton, Silk, and Shuttle, which were added over this period, show its importance to the town. The number of looms was growing fast from about 1,700 when he arrived to over 7,000 by the time the Clarks built their Seedhill mill, so opportunities for employment abounded.

The seventeen-year-old George quickly found a weaver willing to take him under his wing, and he applied himself to learning the trade. He was quick, determined, and worked hard—evidently a family trait—so he had mastered the complexity and intricacies of the job within three short years.

The weavers of the time were highly skilled. They had to develop their own designs and were constantly producing new fabric types and ingenious adaptations of their looms. A successful weaver could work from early morning to lunchtime, taking the rest of the day off for the pursuit of other interests. The intellectual challenge of producing complicated patterns and textures meant that most were highly intelligent. Many were poets, the most famous being Robert Tannahill, who was a great friend of George's son, James, the founding father of J. & P. Coats. Others were painters, ornithologists, botanists, or entomologists, and most were well read and had extensive collections of books. Some were accomplished musicians, and musical events, such as glee and quartette parties, were popular, helping to pass the long evenings. Fishing, bowls, and curling were their chosen sports.

So it is easy to see that the young apprentice, even allowing for the long hours of study needed to become proficient in the weaver's craft so quickly, would have had time for other activities, and it was during these spells of leisure that he met and fell in love with his future wife, Catherine Heywood. She was the daughter of an English master weaver who lived nearby, and as George's master and he were good friends and spent much of their leisure time together, the young man had ample opportunity to be in her company.

Now his independence was tested, as his eagerness to branch out on his own was tempered by his desire to be with her. In the end, as soon as he had gained sufficient command of the weaver's trade and the wherewithal required, they married. He set up a business of his own in a small weaver's cottage at No. 4 North Croft in the Walneuk, just northeast of where Paisley Gilmour St. station would be built.

Their home was typical of Paisley at the time, with the front door opening onto a passageway, the weaving shop and looms in a room on the right hand side, and the family dwelling opposite. George would spend his days at the looms and with his fellow weavers at reading clubs or discussing the hot topics of the day. Catherine would spin yarn or tend to the house.

They set about raising a family almost immediately, but as was so often the case, they had multiple disappointments before finally being blessed with children. Three sons all died whilst infants and although a daughter Rachel survived, they were still eager to hear the patter of tiny male feet. They called the first and third sons George, but subsequently gave up on that name, for fear that the same fate would befall any others so baptised. Finally, in 1772, Jervis was born hale and hearty, and two years later James, the rather spindly but otherwise healthy founder of the Coats Empire, came into the world on October 1, 1774. George and Catherine had one more son who did not survive his first year.

Jervis began his working life as a weaver, but his vision was so poor that he took up curing hams instead and went on to create a grocery business, the initial capital for which was advanced by his brother. He also became famous as the unintended victim of the counterfeit trade. For several years from the mid-eighteenth century, insufficient farthings[4] were

4. A farthing was ¼ of a penny (¼d., or equivalent to about 0.1 pence)

minted, and as a result many fake coins were struck and put into circulation. By the time Jervis set up shop, these were quite easy to detect, but with his limited eyesight he could not tell the difference, so his establishment became renowned as the place to offload them. To solve this problem, the family collected all the counterfeits together and with permission from Edinburgh, he melted them down and minted more easily identified "Coats Farthings" in their place. These had "J. Coats & Sons, 38 Broomlands" in relief on one side and "Ham Curers and Grocers, Paisley" with a picture of a Ham pendant on the reverse. He put 20,000 into circulation and they became accepted as normal currency, such was his reputation for honoring their value.

His son William took over from him and in his turn handed the business on to two of his sons, William[5] and Allan. The company was renamed W. & A. Coats, expanding to cover general groceries and going on to considerable success, not on a par with the scale of the thread business, but enough to give them an affluent lifestyle and the ability to socialise comfortably with their richer cousins. They became known as the "Ham Coats" or more amusingly as the "Petty-Coats" to distinguish them from their relations, the "Threed Coats".

Jervis's brother James grew up in a weaver's household and it was only natural that he should, just like his older sibling, become a weaver at a young age. He had already been studying the craft for some time when he was stopped in the street one day in his late teens by a party of recruiters looking for army volunteers. For reasons that nobody could understand either then or since, he was persuaded to enlist and was soon on his way to join the Third Regiment of Foot Guards in London. He may have felt that the invention of the

5. William's sons, Joseph and George, had distinguished medical careers. Joseph studied under Lord Lister, the pioneer of sterilisation and use of antiseptics to reduce infections from surgery, and went on to become Glasgow University's first Professor of Pathology. George became an eminent London eye surgeon.

power loom and all the other developments of the Industrial Revolution were limiting his future possibilities as a weaver, or he may have simply wanted adventure and travel away from the confines of Paisley. Regardless of his motives, his experience was brief, as he was discharged almost immediately, having been judged unfit to pass the army physical. He therefore found himself out on the streets of London in midwinter with precisely two shillings and sixpence in his pocket and his discharge papers, signed by Col. John Campbell, the Fifth Duke of Argyll, in his hand. As a short coach ride would have cost him over five shillings at the time, and as he wanted to see his home and family again, he had no alternative but to walk to Paisley.

He set out on this 500-mile trip in bitter cold, inadequately shod and poorly clothed. The roads at the time had started to improve, after very little had been done to them since the end of the Roman occupation. The Turnpike act resulted in money being spent to maintain them and the introduction of stone and the methods of Thomas Telford were helping to keep them all from turning into complete quagmires whenever it rained hard. Travel between cities was still uncommon and the condition of the roads was far from consistent, so he trudged through a good deal of mud on his way, facing bitter winds and snow up in the Lake District and eating sparingly, as his meagre wealth did not allow him more. The short days in midwinter afforded him no more than eight hours travel time per day, so a good day was twenty-five miles, even at a fast clip. Nights were dark and cold, and effective shelter was not always at hand. Moreover, coach journeys were done in ten- to fifteen-mile stages, so that any rides that the young James could get were short. He tramped his way slowly homeward and was on the road for over three weeks.

When the exhausted lad reached the Barshaw Hill, he was so worn out and blistered that he felt he could go no further but with his goal—"The Paradise of Scotland"[6]—in sight, he managed one last supreme effort. A bedraggled figure knocked at the door of their home in North Croft and proffered his outstretched hand to his father, expecting at least a warm handshake, if not a heartfelt embrace. However, George, who knew nothing of his plight and thought he must have deserted, asked him, "Nay, Jamie, answer me first, dost thou come wi' honor?" to which his son replied "Yes, father, here is my discharge", after which he was swept up and cared for as was only right for someone so young who had undergone such an ordeal. If he was proud of his son, the head of the household did not show it. These were dour people, not given to demonstrations of either approval or emotion.

James went back to his loom and continued to hone his skills as a weaver, but at the age of twenty had a confrontation with the law that ended up driving him back into military service, this time for six years. He was walking in the grounds of Hawkhead House, near Dykebar, when he was challenged by a servant who worked for the owner, George Boyle, the fourth Earl of Glasgow. Whatever he said in the exchange that followed was sufficiently offensive for him to end up behind bars in the Tollbooth. When word reached the family, his mother set about having him released through the good offices of two of her relations, William and David Young, who had some clout with the authorities.

Brought up in an atmosphere of honor and religious observance, the shame of this incident was clearly too much for young James, and rather than face the disappointment and disapproval of the family, he opted almost immediately to have another shot at army life. Given that Britain was now at war with France, he was accepted into the Ayrshire Fencibles, a cavalry regiment dedicated to defensive duties on the home front. Being a sort of early version of the Home

6. A poetic description of Paisley by Rowland Hill, a well-respected preacher, in his journal of 6/14/1798.

Guard, they were more lenient about the physical exam, which he either fudged or passed.

This time his army experience was a much happier one. The regiment was semiprivate, but with the same principles of discipline as the regular army. James became a competent horseman and a great favourite of his commanding officer, Captain Thomas White, whose friendship lasted until the Captain's death some forty years after James had left the army. White showed great kindness and leniency when James's health failed him, which it did on several occasions. Perhaps the most remarkable of these was when, completely at White's own expense, he sent the young soldier to a farmhouse to recuperate "there to enjoy himself till his health was completely restored".[7] In due course the budding cavalryman was promoted to corporal, and so he continued until the Fencibles were disbanded in 1800.

Standing 5 foot 10 and weighing 170 pounds, James would continue to be somewhat frail and would never enjoy the rudest of health, despite living to the ripe old age of eighty. His lack of physical fitness would influence the direction of his life and career, and the essentials of self-control and integrity which his father had taught him and which he had refined with the regiment, were to serve him well as he returned to his weaving at the age of twenty-six.

7. From Andrew Coates's 1898 account *From the Cottage to the Castle.*

Chapter 5

J. & P. Coats

There is a tide in the affairs of men which, taken at the flood, leads on to fortune.
William Shakespeare (from *Julius Caesar*)

Two events were now to change James's life and start him and his children on the road to prosperity. The first came about by way of the brothers who had rescued him from jail. They ran a linen thread business, W. & D. Young, and when his mother suggested they might be interested in employing him, they invited him over, took a liking to him and put him to work in thread production. He thrived on this and being both disciplined and intelligent, soon found himself earning a decent wage. Given the savings he had accumulated from his army pay and his frugal lifestyle, ingrained in him by his family, he soon accumulated a little capital and could entertain the notion of marriage. This was the second milestone in his life, for he tied the knot in 1802.

His wife was Catherine Mitchell, a delicate woman of some beauty, small but sprightly and strong in every sense of the word. She was the daughter of Peter Mitchell, an optician from Greenock, who had two unique claims to fame. The first was that he had been an apprentice under James Watt, though how that led to a career in eye care will have to remain a mystery. The other arrow in the quiver of this man of eclectic abilities was that he was the only person in Greenock who was qualified to "swing" or adjust a compass; this was no small matter, as Greenock was the busiest port in the west of Scotland.

Catherine was devoutly religious, totally unpretentious, and yearned to help those less fortunate than herself. She lived a hard but happy life, retaining a sense of humor and a love for music that was her constant comfort and joy. It is obvious from her children that she was much loved. She was to have eleven of them over the next nineteen years, known affectionately in the family as the First Eleven.[1] Remarkably, they were ten boys and only one girl, who died at the age of five of croup, a virulent form of laryngitis which affects young children. Of the others, Archibald (number nine) only reached the age of eleven and Robert, the youngest, died in infancy.

Although she was a wonderful mother and tireless housewife, tending to the sick, darning the children's socks, keeping the home impeccable and everyone fed, it was her small business that was, in its own quiet way, the spark that ignited the flame of the Coats empire.

To bolster her husband's income, she employed a few local girls as tambourers (a form of embroidery) and offered the resulting goods for sale. This business was moderately successful, and as James found his health failing, he decided to leave the thread company in 1805 and set up on his own as a producer of sewn muslins, by then the main textile products of Paisley. This allowed him to supplement the tambouring business with other products whilst increasing the work available for the girls already employed by his wife.

1. Thomas Coats, her fourth son, would also have eleven children, six boys and five girls, known naturally as the Second Eleven. Both the Coats and Clark family trees are shown at the end of the book, to help unravel the confusion caused by so many family members with the same names.

The only production he did at home was a small amount of twisting of linen and cotton yarns for embroidery. Everything else was purchased or sent out for processing. He would buy fine woven cambrics, lawns, and muslins, have them bleached locally, and then Catherine would arrange for the tambouring or embroidery to be completed using yarns and threads bought from local spinners and thread makers. He would then take samples around, as most of his customers were locals. Sales went well and in 1808, faced with increased demand and a growing family of three children with another on the way, the Coatses moved out of the Walneuk, which James had taken over from his father, into a two-storey villa which his son Andrew rather poetically described as "about halfway between The Braes o' Gleniffer and The bonny woods o' Craigilee". This places it by the current Royal Alexandra Hospital in Paisley but in practice it was further north, in Ferguslie, standing on the corner of Maxwellton Road and West Lane in a street that was known at the time as Back Row. The house had decent sized grounds, with fruit trees at the front and a small burn at the bottom of the rear garden. This was to be the family home until his death.

Their most profitable markets were Glasgow and London, where they sold through agents, but by 1811 pricing pressure was making things tough, and the lack of demand for expensive products was pushing the spinners and manufacturers who had been working with Sea Island cotton to start spinning coarser, cheaper items. So although he continued to buy and make some luxury items from a few local specialist companies, he began to concentrate on cheaper articles, sewing bonnets with coarser threads. Inevitably his future competitor James Clark became one of his suppliers. Little did the other James realise that they would become bitter rivals within the next twenty years.

The business chugged along in a satisfactory but unremarkable fashion. Then an unrelated incident in 1820 occurred which gives an insight into the quiet determination of the man when asked to take a moral stance and highlights one of the qualities that made him and his family so successful. This was a man of whom it could easily be said, "still waters run deep". He was never given to flamboyancy, being a gentle man of few words but unwavering principles and a firm belief in justice and honesty, with the determination to see an issue through to the bitter end. These qualities were inculcated in all his children and they formed the backbone of the company the family created.

He found himself a juror in a trial for high treason, brought against two Paisley weavers. There were a total of seven who were formally charged, but the others had all fled the country, mostly to America, to avoid the long arm of the law. Only James Speirs from Johnstone and John Lang of Kilbarchan remained to face justice. They pleaded not guilty when arraigned in July 1820, and Speirs was brought to trial on August 1, with the Lord President of the Court, the Lord Justice Clerk, Lord Pitmelly, and the Lord Chief Baron presiding.

The case had its roots in the behavior of revolutionary groups of weavers at various gatherings and had come to a head in the days following April 1. According to a pamphlet produced by the radicals, there was to be a popular uprising, and various groups were to visit the houses of local soldiers and remove their arms, which would then be used to form a provisional government. However, their plans did not work out, as the list of soldiers was never copied, and the original was burnt. Nobody could decide who was to be their leader, and the whole thing petered out. But it was not a complete failure. There was a general work stoppage on April 2, and that night gangs of young radicals, with the ringleaders notably absent, went from house to house collecting arms. They were "received with much kindness" according to Parkhill's *History of Paisley*, but when they reached Foxbar, this all changed, as the laird's son opened fire from an upstairs window, killing one of them and wounding another. A debate as to the wisdom of exacting revenge ensued, but the mob mercifully retired, just before both the cavalry and infantry arrived.

By the next day the military had taken control of the streets, and any further acts of revolution were considered to be suicidal. The leaders all dispersed, so that by the time house-to-house searches were instituted, there were only a handful of arms to be found, and few arrests were made. Speirs was unlucky, as he had fled to Ecclefechan where he was working, but he wrote a letter to a colleague in Johnstone, and when the authorities found out, they sent officers to arrest him and put him in jail.

The case against Speirs attempted to link his actions in endeavoring to stop work in the cotton mills in Johnstone with the declarations in the flyer of April 1. In the indictment there were four counts and in some of these up to nineteen overt acts. Some inferred high treason, carrying the death penalty.

The trial opened at 10:00 a.m. on Tuesday, August 1, 1820 with the prosecution taking all day to parade a series of witnesses in front of the jury. After adjourning at midnight, the proceedings resumed on the Wednesday at 10:00 a.m. with the defense making their case. After a long and exhausting day, the Lord Advocate of the Crown told the jury that he was compelled to ask for a guilty verdict, and they retired at 4:20 a.m. on Thursday morning. They worked long hours in the courts in those days.

In a scene reminiscent of Henry Fonda in the film *Twelve Angry Men*, James Coats and one other juror declared the man to be innocent of treason, with the others all wanting a conviction. The two dissenters argued that the man was guilty only of being present at a public meeting, at the same time causing no direct threat to the King by agitating for strike action. The other ten (and the crowd outside) were all for hanging him as an example, and they attempted to wear the other two down, to no avail. After an hour they returned a verdict of guilty on the fifteenth act of the first count, one that did not involve high treason. They also pleaded for clemency, given the man's previously unblemished record. This was clearly not at all what the Court wanted to hear, and they were summarily despatched, but the same impasse persisted, so they reappeared an hour and a quarter later with a similar finding.

This time it was made plain that they had to either return a guilty or not guilty verdict on the whole of the first count and not just a part. The Lord Chief Baron stated that they must decide whether certain acts were done or not and whether they were treasonable or not, i.e., no cherry-picking. As a further incentive for a speedy conclusion, a message was sent to the jury room that, all-night sitting or not, there would be no refreshment for the twelve good men and true until they reached a verdict.

Upon receiving this last communication, a tired and exhausted James Coats, who had been arguing with his fellow jurors for the best part of two and a half hours, lay down upon a wooden bench by the wall and announced to all that he would stay there and die of thirst or starvation, but that the blood of an innocent man would never be on his head. His ally in the defense of justice was equally resolute, so the jury finally returned a verdict of not guilty at 8:00 a.m., which elicited the rather gentle rebuke from the Court: "Tell the Jury we have no more use of them".

Lang was never brought to trial after this, so both were formally acquitted. The crowd that had bayed for blood now cheered for justice and carried Speirs shoulder high through the streets. A weary but contented James Coats made his way home to catch up on lost sleep and get back to the problems of his business.

He had several of these with which to contend. Sales were lagging, so he started to look for new products and became one of the first to switch his interests to silk shawls, an old trade that he tried to revive. He bought chenille shawls and added embroidery or fringes before selling them, and he had experimented with other materials in a continual quest for improved turnover. He spent more time on the road, visiting potential suppliers and customers as far afield as London, and it was on one of these trips that he found and bought a present for his wife, a beautiful Canton crepe shawl imported from China. When he took it home, he became intrigued by its construction, so the gift was temporarily withheld while he pondered over the structure of both the silk threads and the weave of the piece. He began to experiment.

Frustratingly, the exact specification of the product eluded him, despite countless long days and nights of tinkering. He was discussing his predicament with one of his suppliers of muslins, a Mr. James Whyte, when they discovered they had both made the same purchase with the same intentions and the same results. By pooling their resources, they finally made a highly acceptable equivalent of their sample, and in 1823 they formed a partnership to make and market the first ever British Canton crepe shawls, as well as dresses and other materials. Their monopoly lasted a couple of years, and during this period the business was highly profitable.

While all this was going on, Catherine was becoming extremely concerned at the bottleneck created by the twisting of silk for her embroiderers. They had missed a series of selling opportunities through shortages of this product, and she kept cajoling her husband to get more involved in manufacturing, rather than having to rely on others. As he knew that one of his regular suppliers, Ross & Duncan, were looking for capital to respond to the boom of the early 1820s, he provided the required financing and became a silent partner. No sooner had he done this than the upturn went into sharp reverse, and the company had to look for alternative products to keep their new twisting and winding occupied. One of these was sewing thread, which he had already encountered when working for W. & D. Young.

The year 1825 proved to be a pivotal one for James Coats. His partnership with Ross & Duncan was due to end within the year, and his associate in the shawl business, James Whyte, had expressed his intention to withdraw soon. Coats's confidence in the prospects for this market was evaporating with changes in fashion and the appearance of more and better copies of their shawls. Price pressures were mounting. The twisting of cotton sewing thread with Ross & Duncan had whetted his appetite for this new product line, and as he could see a real future for himself and his family in the production of a high-quality version, he bought a piece of land at Maxwellton, on the other side of the Candren burn from his house, and constructed a three-storey brick mill, twenty-one yards long with a twelve-horsepower steam engine, gas lighting, silk winding, and cotton twisting.

He then brought his eldest son, James, aged twenty-two, in to manage the warehouse. James had tried shawl manufacturing, with little luck, so he knew something about production. He was a man of sizable intellect with a fondness for literature, a gifted public speaker of a solid, if rather serious temperament, and his father leant a great deal on him for advice. They hired about twenty workers and started production in 1826, when James's (who will be referred to as Senior from now on to distinguish him from his eldest son, James) association with Ross & Duncan had expired. The Coats mill in Paisley known as Ferguslie was born.

The new mill was designed to be a state-of-the-art manufacturing facility, and much of the machinery was the best available. The boiler, however, was at best temperamental, breaking down with monotonous regularity about once a week. There was only one man in Paisley who understood the idiosyncrasies of this highly capricious engine. He was known as Saipie Davie, the name deriving from his habit of yelling the phrase "mair saip" (more whisky) from the depths of the mechanism whenever he needed sustenance. Work would then cease until his request had been complied with, at which point he would apply himself with renewed vigour.

The date James Coats Sr. chose to launch his business was a brave one indeed. The year 1826 saw a series of events that were eerily reminiscent of the latter part of the first decade of the 21st century. Everyone was living on credit, some commodity prices had surged through rampant speculation, and the banks found themselves overstretched and suddenly loath to advance loans to those most in need. Confidence collapsed, and panic ensued, leading to recession and extensive unemployment. Paisley was badly affected, and public subscriptions were opened to give relief to the unemployed; these were the dark days long before social security. The looms stopped producing and 15,000 weavers were out of work by midsummer. Some were given jobs improving pathways around town, and although there were riots in the English midlands, the good people of Paisley remained calm and resolute, hoping for better times ahead.

Under these circumstances, it is understandable that James Sr. had worried that his new mill might be too big, but fortunately for him and the unemployed of Paisley, 1827 saw a sharp recovery and although he initially concentrated on silk production for the shawl business, he had a number of useful contracts for sewing products and actively sought more. As a result, he acquired more land the following year and doubled the size of the mill. He was already becoming one of the larger producers in Paisley.

His interest in shawls continued, but with James Whyte's retirement in 1827, James Sr. brought in his London salesman James Grieve as his partner, and the company became Coats, Grieve & Co. He also hired his second son, George, to help with production, but he did not last long, preferring to branch out by starting his own shawl business, with an even more spectacular lack of success than his elder brother had had earlier.[2]

Another recession in 1829 hit the silk business particularly hard and further strengthened James Sr.'s conviction that the switch into cotton sewing thread was the way to go. With the trade recovering a year later, he handed his participation in the shawl concern on to his fifth son, William, taking £8,000 out.

He then hired his third son, Peter, to help with the thread business. He was as staid as his eldest brother, but of a more cheerful demeanor and his background was in finance. After flirting with taking up holy orders, he had joined the Counting House of John Fleming & Co., East India Merchants in Glasgow. One of the partners in this firm, James Watson, was a cousin of the Coatses, and he had taken Peter under his wing and turned him into an excellent accountant and trader, so it was natural that he become the financial controller and commercial expert for the fledgling company.

James Sr. then retired, rented the Ferguslie mill to James and Peter, and made way for the formation of J. & P. Coats on July 1, 1830. However, his hand was still firmly on the tiller of the company. The tradition then was for most sons to follow in their father's footsteps, but there is some evidence

2. George was, unusually for the Coats family, the life and soul of the party and a natural wit. His influence on the thread business would be minimal, though one incident indirectly involving him did affect them. He went into coalmining, as managing partner of a colliery that supplied Ferguslie. There was a mammoth explosion at the Victoria Pit, which was owned by his mining company, in March 1851. This was the largest mining disaster ever in Scotland at the time, and sixty-one people died as a result. It was caused by a ventilation failure, even though their system was supposed to be amongst the best around. Many thought the mine was owned by Coats, which reflected negatively on them for a time, but they were merely customers.

that James Sr. manipulated the ambitions of his children,[3] thereby creating an exceptionally strong, multi-disciplined team to guide the new firm. This ultimately consisted of four individuals: a production and factory organisation specialist of a solid dependable character (James), an accountant and business expert (Peter), a first-class, level-headed mechanical engineer (Thomas), and a lawyer with an independent streak and a flair for entrepreneurship (Andrew). These last two had still to reveal their talents at this point, but their influence would be profound. Although James Sr. had ostensibly stopped working, he was clearly a mentor to them all and helped to steer them in the right direction without serious interference. His children had chosen different specialities but held a common set of values based on kindness, integrity, religious observance, and a strong work ethic. These had all been passed to them by James Sr. and his wife.

He also found time for other things. He took an active interest in politics and was a "strong liberal" and a high-profile member of the Paisley branch of that party. His modesty and shyness meant that he seldom spoke in public, and this may well have been his undoing when he stood for the fifth ward in the local elections of 1833. He only polled fifth, behind the winner, a certain James Clark, who eventually became a Bailie (equivalent to a magistrate) where he dealt with petty theft, drunkenness, and wife-beating alongside Jervis Coats, the grocer. However, James Coats Sr.'s political connections did mean that he was chosen to head the great procession through town in honor of the passage of the Reform Bill in 1832. He had become an active horseman after leaving the Ayrshire Fencibles and had kept a riding horse from the day he could first afford one.

3. A classic example is his sixth son, Andrew, whose decision to become a lawyer seems to have been heavily influenced by James Sr. This conclusion comes from the speech that Henry, Andrew's son, made at his father's funeral. He stated, "It was decided that my father should adopt the legal profession". This doesn't sound like Andrew's independent choice.

On this occasion he was not allowed to ride his own horse but was mounted on a magnificent steed "remarkable alike for its beauty and its action" and proudly lead the parade through town with the military bearing of an old soldier.

He would often ride around town and, with time on his hands, took to visiting his brother Jervis's grocery, both to pass the time of day and to compare notes on how J. & P. were getting on with the thread business, and William with the grocery store. By this time, there was a commercial relationship between the two, as buyer and supplier of soap, and it is certain that James Sr.'s interest in his brother's shop was also sharpened by the fact that he had provided the initial finance.

He had a particular mare called Daisy, who loved these visits almost more than he did, as there was always an oatcake waiting for her when they reached the shop. She soon took this route automatically, whether James Sr. wanted to go there or not, and would stick her nose in through the door and wait for her special treat to appear. Such was her devotion to this habit that Jervis bet his brother 2/6d. (£0.125) that he would never again ride past the shop without the mare stopping. A crowd gathered to watch as he struggled to win the wager, which he eventually managed, but not without a tremendous tussle, much to the delight of the onlookers.

The Coats grocery was not the only business venture that James Sr. supported. He was a shareholder in the first Paisley newspaper, the Paisley Advertiser, which appeared in 1824, costing 7d. and was published once a week on Saturdays.

As was common at the time, he was deeply religious and a strong supporter of the Baptist church. He was compassionate and would often crusade for the less well-off when times were tough. In 1826, he famously espoused the cause of the workers at his end of town, when many were left destitute by the catastrophic combination of a deep recession and a disastrous harvest.

Although no longer directly involved, he promoted an informal atmosphere in the mill, exemplified by an incident that took place early on in Ferguslie. Having once heard some experts who had been invited in to help being addressed as Mr. Young, Mr. Arrol, Mr. Lorimer, etc., he asked that they be referred to as John Young, Thomas Arrol, and David Lorimer, quoting the bible which states you should "call no man master". He always insisted that his boys be called Jamie, Peter, and Tom and that he be referred to as James, to distinguish him from his eldest son. This simple, straightforward way of handling people meant that he was viewed as being easily approachable, so he would often be asked to pronounce on all sorts of matters. One such exchange was said to have taken place with one of the mill employees, who asked him for his views on abstinence from drink, this being a hot topic at the time, due to a temperance campaign. He replied, with a twinkle in his eye, that he viewed teetotalism as a very good thing for anyone under sixty, "but I am above it".

His influence on the business cannot be exaggerated. The way the mill ran, the guarantee of the product, the scrupulous honesty with customers, and the insistence on top quality at all cost created a winning formula for future success.

But the other thing that elevated J. & P. Coats above their rivals was the brilliant family management team he had helped create. His sons trusted each other implicitly, and good business is all about trust. Additionally, they had the drive and determination needed to go out and conquer the world.

The first of the three steps on their path to success was in place.

Chapter 6

Six Cord Thread

... I am worn to a ravelling ... I am undone and worn to a thread-paper, for I have no more twist.
Beatrix Potter (from *The Tailor of Gloucester*)

So how do a bunch of fibers become the product that holds your clothes, amongst other things, together? It takes five years to train a production engineer to make good thread, but an abbreviated version is all that is needed to explain the basics. Like most of the products that we take for granted, it is a little more complicated than you would expect.

Once the cotton has been picked and ginned (the seeds removed) the fibers are compressed into bales for transporting. When these bales are ready for production, they are laid out in large groups, and small amounts of each are fed into processing at a time, guaranteeing a consistent mix. All the large impurities are beaten out of the fiber mass, and then the smaller particles are removed by rotating cylinders with small teeth that gently separate them from the cotton, which forms a very fine sheet. This is collected into a rope-like form with no twist, known as a sliver.

After this, a whole series of processes stretch this sliver

ntil it reaches the thickness required, when it is twisted to give it strength. The end product is called yarn. Most cotton for sewing thread is also combed during the stretching process, which removes the shorter fibers and improves the yarn's strength.

In the days when the Coatses and Clarks started out, they did not have any of this processing at Ferguslie and Seedhill, preferring to buy the yarn in from spinners in England. The sizable capital required for this part of the operation and the problems of dealing with international suppliers of cotton meant that early thread makers avoided this stage altogether. As long as there was plenty of competition between the spinners (who use the same techniques and machinery for high-grade cloth yarn) and the quality was adequate, this continued to be the norm. Once the thread businesses became bigger, they started to integrate backwards.

The second stage of thread production involves putting a certain number of yarns together and twisting them, generally in the opposite direction from the yarn twist. The objective is to make a balanced, smooth, even product, with no spiraling or kinks and as few knots as possible. The number of yarns in the thread defines the ply, so a thread with two yarns twisted together was called two ply. These plied threads were sometimes then placed together again and twisted once more in the opposite direction, becoming known as corded threads. Three two ply threads twisted together is known as six cord. This was Coats's main product in the 1830s.

The third stage of manufacturing is the application of colour and any special finishes the product requires. When Coats started out, the great majority of production was either bleached white or dyed black. Colour lots were small and infrequent, but that would change greatly over time. Mercerisation, which is described later, was still sixty years away.

Polishing, however, was already in use. This was the immersion of the thread into a starch solution, followed by brushing, which stroked the surface fibers into the body of the thread and added a glaze on top, which hardened when dry. It produced a lustrous smooth finish, ideal for sewing tough materials like leather, especially for shoes. It was only with the invention of nylon filament yarn in 1938 that this process began to fall into disuse, though even today it is the best way to make thread for sewing fur pelts. The end product is often called glacé, glazed, or polished thread and is rather stiff and slightly harsh.

Neither the Coatses nor the Clarks did their own bleaching or dyeing in the early days, due in part to the capital required but also because there were plenty of local bleachers and dyers who could perform these processes perfectly adequately and at a reasonable price. The downside of this arrangement was that delays occurred which fell outside their jurisdiction, and quality could be hit-and-miss, just as with the spun yarn they bought in.

The last department in the factory is Finishing, where the thread is wound into a ball or a wooden spool,[1] cut to an exact length, labelled, and boxed for shipment. The wooden spools of yesteryear are no more. Their manufacture was highly inefficient, with up to 90% of the birchwood needed for each support being wasted in the process. Great swathes of Canadian and Finnish forest were saved when plastic moulding made wooden spools obsolete in the 1960s.

Labelling was still in its infancy in the 1820s.[2] There was a very limited range of products, mostly in black and white, so the need for clear identification was less pressing than it

1. Cones, tubes, and more sophisticated supports would appear later.

2. The first spool labels were used by the Clarks, bought on May 9, 1827 from Alex Woodrow, but they merely called the thread "3 Cord" with no trademark or indication of thickness. They bought 189 Gross of labels for £1/17/8½d. The next order was much larger, for 863 Gross of "3 Cord Sterling", in 1829, but again with no indication of the thread size.

would become later. The spools were wrapped in paper parcels of six or twelve, and the outside would be clearly marked.

The development of larger ranges of products, with different finishes, sizes, and lengths was not far away, and with it came all sorts of abuses and fraud. These would trouble the industry forever, but for Coats and to almost the same extent Clark, it was their source of strength, as they were scrupulously honest in describing the ticket number[3] of their product correctly and giving the length of thread they promised. Coats would later brag about their accurate length control by offering thread to the railway companies in reels "warranted to contain 1,760 yards", so they could accurately measure how many miles of track they had laid, whilst one of Clarks' early marketing ploys was to urge customers not to buy unmarked thread with a green ticket bearing no name, explaining that these came from dishonest competitors who did not give full lengths or any of the other guarantees available from a reputable manufacturer.

In the late 1820s, the most common sewing thread was three ply, as developed by J. & J. Clark and several others. This was sold in a variety of different thicknesses and successfully marketed and exported, though the ticketing was not always consistent and was therefore open to abuse and deceit. Clark's reputation for giving full lengths made them natural leaders in the industry.

As latecomers to the market, Coats had to find a way to distinguish themselves. Half their sales were silk when J. & P. Coats was formed, largely for the Canton crepe trade. They had started to make three ply cotton like everyone else, and sold three lengths: 100, 200, and 300 yards, covering all thicknesses, largely in black and white. All the companies

3. Ticket number described the overall thickness of a thread and derived from the English Cotton Count system. See Chapter 2, Note 5, on page 28. For those who are interested, it is (technically) three times the overall English Count of the thread.

charged the same, and although there was some haggling over terms, Coats did not manipulate prices, preferring to negotiate extended contracts as a way of increasing sales.

They hit upon a way of differentiating themselves from their competition—with six cord thread. It is almost certain that it was James Coats Sr. who discovered its virtues and costs,[4] as he had time on his hands to experiment. They correctly reasoned that anyone using a high-quality sewing thread in their clothing will make a better, longer-lasting garment, and as the thread is a very small percentage of the total cost, the premium the customer pays will be compensated several times over.

They had started to make this product in a small way in 1831, but quickly converted nearly all their production, whilst simultaneously putting a heavy marketing effort behind it. They started with the coarser threads, ticket 10 to 40, with the medium counts up to 70 being four cord and finer threads remaining three ply. Later, as spinning techniques improved, they moved everything they could to six cord, finally completing the transformation in the 1860s.

Clarks were making some six cord thread, but did not push it, preferring to sell three ply, where they were the clear market leaders and where the lower cost was attractive to the smaller merchants in the areas they had targeted. They also made a variety of knitting and embroidery threads and offered a wide range of sewing threads as well as heddles, heddle twine, and other textile supplies.

4. He found that if you spun a yarn (A) half as thick as another (B), but then twisted two of A together, the result was the same thickness as B but much stronger. If you then twisted three of these stronger versions together, you got higher strength, evenness, and abrasion resistance than three plies of B twisted together. The downside was the cost, as you had to buy a much finer, more expensive yarn and then put it through two additional processes, doubling and twisting. The two ply/three ply version was called six cord and two ply/two ply, four cord.

In focusing on six cord, Coats stumbled onto something truly remarkable, a full twenty years before it would become important. The direction of twist of sewing thread for hand sewing is not ultra-critical, but when it is put on certain types of sewing machine it becomes crucial. Yarn for weaving has Z twist, i.e., if you hold it vertically, the spirals you can see from the twisted fibers go from top right to bottom left, as in the diagonal of the letter Z. Yarn with S twist does the opposite.

When Patrick Clark made his first sewing thread, he twisted the thread in the opposite direction from the yarn, to balance the end product. As he had bought weaving yarn, the thread twist was in the S direction. Clark's and others' subsequent three ply sewing threads were a copy of this construction.

When thread is used for sewing on a lockstitch machine (of which more later), the needle and hook mechanism insert more twist in the Z direction as sewing proceeds. If Patrick Clark's thread had been put into such a sewing machine, it would have unravelled, frayed, and almost certainly broken.

This was not a problem before the 1840s and the advent of sewing mechanisation. However, when these appliances did start to appear, this was the cause of some of their teething troubles if they used conventional three ply. But six cord and indeed any other corded thread, quite by chance, was twisted twice and the final Z twist direction worked perfectly on any lockstitch machine. As Coats was by then the leader in producing and selling six cord, they held an advantage while the others worked this out and caught up. Nowadays, all sewing threads for apparel have a final Z twist, so when they are used for machine sewing on a lockstitch machine, the twist tightens slightly during the process, and the thread sews beautifully.

So Coats was ahead of their time when they started to concentrate on their famous product, and even though there was an element of luck involved, it again showed the wisdom of James Coats Sr. in always striving for the highest quality. Step two on the road to riches was complete. The first had been managerial and the second technical. The third was geographical and took the company to the dominant position it would not relinquish for nearly a century.

Chapter 7

US Expansion, and Thomas Joins the Team

Everything's bigger in America.
From *Supersize Me* directed by Morgan Spurlock

There may well have been another reason for Coats's preference for six cord. In March 1831, they started to sell the product to a merchant house called Thomas Connah, who in turn exported the vast majority to the USA. Coats had toyed with exports (to Haiti and Valparaiso), but the uncertainties involved and the time and effort required to get paid made the venture unappealing.[1] Sales through an agent, though less profitable, had the attraction of leaving the problems of collections and disputes in someone else's hands.

The sales to Connah were not made as Coats thread, but rather as Connah's or Parsons, for resale to a New York importer, Parsons Canning, and labelled as such in Ferguslie. Their American customers loved the thread, and sales growth was stellar: from £310 in 1831, to £8,500 four years later, a sum which represented over 60% of Coats's total. The recession of 1837-38 hurt, but the US trade still reached £9,370 by 1939, almost exactly 40% of their turnover.

1. A classic case was an order for £75, which was shipped direct to the USA in 1830, before James and Peter took over, but was only settled finally in the summer of 1832.

Although this arrangement suited Coats from the point of view of convenience, allowing them to focus on perfecting their product, it had three distinct disadvantages that eventually became important. One was that any goodwill associated with the thread went to the merchant or importer, rather than to the company. The second was that, with no exclusivity agreement, the merchant was free to buy from any suppler[2] so that Ferguslie came to depend on Connah more than the other way around. The third was that although Parsons were paid the higher US prices, they only paid Coats a lower amount, equivalent to the domestic UK market price.

In the meantime, J. & J. Clark, who had sold thread through both New York and New Orleans as early as 1821, had largely abandoned exports to the USA by the end of the 1830s and concentrated on the home market and some small-scale European business. John Clark Jr. of Mile End, in common with a few other thread producers, had an agent in New York and was selling small amounts of their own branded products into the USA.

The period 1830-36 was largely a boom time for everyone, interrupted briefly by a cholera outbreak in 1832. Although this had little physical effect on the mill personnel and only disrupted trade temporarily, the problems created throughout the country were extensive. 446 people died in Paisley alone.

The epidemic started in India, where it had festered along the Ganges for centuries. It was the traditional Kumbh festival at Haridwar in 1817 that was the source, where pilgrims shared the waters of the river with carriers from lower Bengal over a period of three months and then took the disease home. Ten thousand British troops succumbed, as well as an unknown number of Indians. The pilgrims and traders then spread the disease through the Middle East and

2. As an example of this, Clarks believed that Connah had bought and exported <u>their</u> thread.

on to Russia, eventually reaching Europe, conveyed in contaminated kegs of water on board ships or in the excrement of infected travellers. Steam power was shrinking the world, but sanitation was lagging behind. The disease finally reached the North of England in October 1831. From there, it took less than four months to reach Paisley.

The Paisley Advertiser announced its arrival in the February 18, 1832 edition. The town was ill prepared, despite anti-cholera instructions being issued and meetings held. Their sanitation was similar to most in Scotland, with little or no running water indoors and no clear access to sewers. Not that these would have been much help, as they were just cesspools with an overflow at one end and would remain so until the public health act of 1848. The real horror was that they were cleaned out by hand.

Added to this lack of sanitation, the medical profession maintained that cholera was not contagious, and public health administration was still in its infancy, so clusters of cases were not always picked up. The public, panicked by the speed and virulence of the disease, became mistrustful of the doctors, and rumours of medical experiments and sales of bodies to medical schools sprang up. To counter this gossip, the James Coatses (father and son) both signed a resolution to the Central Board of Health, strongly supporting the selflessness and devotion of the "gentlemen of the Medical Faculty here".

Despite this, a riot ensued when an expedition found an empty coffin, a length of rope, and a hook at Paisley Moss, the place set aside for burying the victims. The mob were now sure that the trafficking of bodies was taking place, so they returned to the town with the empty coffin, attacked the hospital and a cholera van, and smashed the windows of several doctors' houses. They destroyed two surgeries and looted a grocery store (happily not Jervis Coats's establishment) after which the riot act was read, and the military arrived and took control.

The outbreak really only lasted three months, but sporadic cases kept appearing for the rest of the year. Its effects on trade lingered for the same period, as there was a general reluctance to move either people or goods between infected and uncontaminated areas. However, the overall commercial impact was insignificant—a temporary interlude in the growth of trade for the period, which was one of prosperity and progress.

Gas lighting had reached most large towns, including Paisley. The mills were working hard, and Thomas Coats had joined his brothers. He was always destined to be an engineer, but being only twenty-one when James and Peter got together, he had to complete his training before joining them in 1832 and soon became the mechanical genius of the team. He was level-headed, single-minded, unflinching, and optimistic in outlook, always finding the positive in every situation. He was conservative, but receptive to new ideas provided he could see value in them, and he had a gift for adapting new technology before adopting it.

He immediately made his mark by having an identical steam engine installed alongside Saipie Davie's original, which he deemed too unreliable. Despite this, both broke down in 1835, bringing the mill to a complete standstill, so he decided to have a brand new 30HP engine from the St. Rollox Foundry installed for £1,350, in a brand new building, the following year. He also oversaw the installation of the first of their powered spooling machines, which greatly improved the productivity of the girls who had previously turned the spools by hand.

Over the same period, Peter was struggling to find a reliable source of cotton yarn. At the start he had relied on merchants in Glasgow, but with the push for the finer counts required for six cord, he had to go directly to the better quality spinners of Sea Island cotton in Manchester and Bolton, and by the end of the decade he was also buying from Browns Malloch of Johnstone, where Christian Miller had set up shop 90 years before.

There were plenty of mill jobs available, and these were keenly sought. Ferguslie was hiring and ran a night shift for the first time in 1833, even though James Coats Sr., and therefore the rest of the family, was against this way of expanding capacity. They viewed "relays", as they referred to shift work, as an expensive alternative to installing more machinery and hiring more day workers, as the night shift worked fewer hours and therefore cost more. The mill expanded from about 60 in 1830 to 230 by 1839, mostly teenage girls, as the work was considered light and appropriate for them, and they could be trained quickly.

They worked a 69 hour week, 12 hours Monday to Friday and 9 hours on Saturday. Overtime was paid at normal rates and was voluntary, but popular, despite the incredibly long standard work-week. There was no compensation for downtime, whether caused by breakdowns, holidays (usually three or four days a year), or understandably frequent sickness. In Twisting, learners earned 4 shillings a week,[3] and experienced girls got 6 shillings, about a penny an hour; they could make more on piecework and still more on nights. Spooling operators, before the introduction of steam-driven machines, could produce a maximum of 25 spools of 200 yards[4] an hour, being paid 8d. a gross, so the

3. To put wages into context, there are a number of ways that the "worth" of 4 shillings can be calculated, but the fairest is probably average nominal earnings, which gives a 2013 equivalent value of about £150 per week.

4. There is no definitive explanation as to why the thread industry settled on 200 yards as their standard length. Sales were usually measured in gross, and Coats used a gross of 200 yards (or G2Y for short) as a standard measure to record production and other statistics, right up to the mid-1980s (they since went metric). It is surmised that it was the nautical influence from the Clyde area, and the fact that early cotton sewing thread was often described as "cabled", a cable being a measure of distance at sea of 200 yards. The naval theme is further reflected in the Coats and Clark main trademarks, Chain and Anchor.

top workers could take home 8 shillings (£0.40) a week. The men employed in the mill fared considerably better, earning 17 shillings and more in the case of skilled tradesmen.

Coats sometimes gave out coal or spool wood in times of very cold weather and would lend money to workers with financial difficulties. They were considered good, benevolent employers, and Ferguslie jobs, as well as those at Seedhill, were coveted. The tradition of children following their parents into the mills was established early and continued through until their closure in 1982 (Ferguslie) and 1993 (Seedhill).

Coats weathered the crisis of 1837-38 rather better than Clarks, thanks to their concentration on the US market, and they ended the decade as the largest thread maker in Paisley (and possibly the world), with 45% of their sales going to America. Things were about to get a whole lot better.

Chapter 8

Andrew Coat(e)s

It is better to be a mouse in a cat's mouth than a man in a lawyer's hands.
Spanish Proverb

It is at this point that Andrew, James Sr.'s sixth son, enters the story at a rather oblique angle. He had been educated at Paisley Grammar and then joined the Paisley offices of John Dunn as a lawyer's apprentice. Dunn acted for J. & P. Coats, but beyond that, there was no connection between Andrew and Ferguslie. After five years with them, he moved to Edinburgh, where he worked for Bowie & Campbell and attended the University law school in 1834-35. Once qualified as a solicitor, he returned to Paisley, but then declared, after ten years' "connection with the legal profession", that he could see no great future in it. He was twenty-six.

He sailed for the United States in 1839 with nothing more specific in mind than "pushing his fortune". It is quite clear that he had no mandate from James, Peter, or Thomas and that his interest in their business was merely cursory. He obviously knew what they did, probably in some detail, but had no intention, at that moment, of helping them. He was more open-minded than any of them and, being one of the younger sons, had not come under his father's influence to the same extent. His independence, demonstrated by the adventurous nature of his journey, was further reinforced by his decision, shortly after arriving in the USA, to change the way he spelt his name to "Coates" with an *e*. It is claimed by some that this was merely a reversion to the old way of writing the family name. His son Henry wrote in a biographical sketch prepared for his funeral that he simply changed it to the more common spelling in the US to make life easier, but this is too straightforward and uncharacteristic of the man. Deep down, it seems to have been yet another way of expressing his autonomy from the rest of the family, and the fact that he never changed it back when he returned to Scotland much later reinforces this view.

The crossing, which lasted six weeks, was aboard an 800-ton sailing ship, which was owned by its captain and had seen better days. It was a rough passage, but he arrived in New York at the beginning of October to perfect warm weather and the glorious colours of the New England fall, a sight he could never even have imagined. He said that it was what a friend of his had heard described as "A day which makes me thank God that I am a living being". His arrival would in due course make his brothers thank God for Andrew.

To get started, he set up on his own as a small-scale importer of "Scotch goods" through two young Scotsmen, Forrest and Drummond. They were commission merchants in New York and introduced him to a variety of buyers. Through these and other contacts, he soon realised that the Coats contract with Parsons Canning was placing them in a precarious position. Back in Paisley they knew that there was no goodwill accruing to them without their own name on the product, and the agreement did not allow them exclusivity, but they felt that the long runs and the lower risks involved outweighed these disadvantages.

Andrew saw things quite differently. He realised that they were limiting sales almost entirely to the Philadelphia area, and with new markets opening up all the time, early entry would be essential to future growth. He knew that they were already foregoing the two buying seasons in spring and fall in Boston, Charleston, and New Orleans, and really only scratching the surface in New York. With travel being time-consuming and pricey, customers from outside these larger centres would only visit twice a year to make all their purchases, and it was important to establish a presence in each.

He also viewed the dependence on one distributor as dangerous. It made them vulnerable to problems with Parsons, for the wholesalers, who were known as jobbers, could desert them in a highly competitive market and leave Coats stranded. The difficulties with international communications, where mail could take three months and the transatlantic cable was twenty-five years in the future, meant that problems could arise in the US, and by the time they found out in Scotland it would be too late to do anything.

He pleaded with his brothers to send him a trial shipment of thread with the Coats name and was met with a resounding "No". They argued that the introduction of their own brand of thread would be seen as competition by Parsons, who would retaliate by transferring their purchases to other manufacturers, leaving Ferguslie high and dry. He countered that this was the very danger that made it essential that they reduce their dependency on a sole distributor, but he would not have prevailed had there not been rumours in 1840 that Parsons were in trouble. The problems with payments became so bad that James Jr. finally decided to cross the Atlantic to see the situation firsthand and, one suspects, to check up on his maverick brother.

In the meantime, Andrew continued to push for own-label sales on a commission basis, whereby the thread would be sent to American importers, but would belong to Coats until sold, with import duties, expenses, selling costs, and bad debts being for their account. The reward for all this would be the higher US prices. This system, to which the American manufacturers vehemently objected, had already been adopted in a small way by many British companies, including J. & J. Clark, who had retained a New York agent since 1828.

With the Parsons payments faltering and Andrew's persistence, in late 1840 the brothers weakened and told him to go ahead and make the arrangements for an exploratory shipment of Coats Six Cord. They must have realised the risks involved. Establishing a trademark would be hard. Coats did not have the volume to set up their own depots, so they had to depend on the jobbers, who demanded credit terms as long as eight months. On top of this was the risk of bad debt and the time taken to sell the thread, which was at best unpredictable. There was little incentive for the jobbers to push one sewing thread over any other, as pricing was transparent. To put the majority of their business at risk in this way was a brave decision, but mercifully one they would not regret. They were placing great trust in Andrew, who responded with hard work and dedication. He was determined to make the plan work.

He first attempted to place the trade with Forrest and Drummond, but they felt that a fully fledged agency for J. & P. Coats would be too much to take on and that they would not have the capital required. He also tried another Scottish firm, Andrew Mitchell, for he had a letter of introduction from their head office in Glasgow, but they turned him down as they already sold their own brand of thread.

So in desperation he finally turned to Hugh Auchincloss & Sons. Hugh was a native of Paisley, and his sister, a Mrs. Stirling, had given Andrew a glowing letter of introduction before embarking on his voyage. Auchincloss were hesitant. They already handled a large trade in printed cotton dresses, and they were woefully understaffed. Hugh Sr. was largely ornamental, if willing, and Hugh Jr. was too young to be more than superficially involved. Besides a bookkeeper and a porter, the only other person employed by them was the elder son, John, who did the selling, arranged the styles, handled correspondence, and generally ran the show. Although he was, according to Andrew "one of the cleverest and... hardest working men in New York", he also had the problem that, "His hands were full—he could undertake no more".

Their reluctance did not deter him. He offered them a deal whereby if they administered the goods and gave him a list of potential customers, he would do the rest. John, under pressure from his father, grudgingly agreed. So Coats had their agents, who were almost certainly completely unaware of the sagacity of their decision.

This was all in place by the time James Jr. set sail for the USA during the winter of 1840, arriving early the next year. He immediately asked for shipments to Parsons Canning to be consigned to him in New York, from where he forwarded the goods once he was sure that payment would be both forthcoming and timely. This continued for several months until direct shipments resumed later that year. Satisfied with the situation, he toured several large factories in the neighbouring states with Andrew during the summer, and spent one extremely unpleasant journey visiting the jobbers in the New York area. The buyers in the US were more aggressive than he was used to, so he quickly concluded his business and made a beeline for Scotland. He had stayed longer than anticipated and spent £150, which, much to his annoyance, was £50 more than he had budgeted.

Andrew had been visiting retailers to sell the Coats product before it had even arrived, such was his confidence in its future. He now set about his task with a will. He continued to do the rounds of all the retailers, helped by Forrest and Drummond, who sold consigned thread to their contacts who were not covered by Auchincloss. This was a costly undertaking, as travel was expensive in "that country of magnificent distances", and he had to give away a multitude of samples and "modest" gifts to induce the retailers to try the thread. There were a prodigious number of small establishments to cover, which took forever and was tedious, but it was the only way to induce the jobbers to order a specific thread. He managed to get round them all himself or through a series of enthusiastic representatives he hired to help. The speculative sales he made often went unpaid, and although the brothers back in the UK had expressed their faith in him, they became very nervous when they saw the level of expenditure needed to establish themselves and their brand in the US.

There were numerous rivals for the business, mostly selling three ply thread, including Clarks of Mile End, Alexander, Chadwicks, and sundry other UK producers, as well as several merchants with own-brand products. American manufactured threads such as Morse and Sagamore were also vying for a foothold, although much of the local competition would turn out to be short length and/or counterfeit. One of Andrew's most telling arguments against all of them was the superiority of the Coats Six Cord product, with better strength and guaranteed lengths, and this approach paid dividends. Once he had the retailers convinced, the rest was relatively easy, as the jobbers mainly ordered what the retailers asked for; the agents then did the same from the jobbers.

With the New York area secured, Andrew began to forage further afield. He contracted Whiton and March to cover New England and then turned his attention to Parsons Canning, who had again fallen behind with their payments, to the tune of almost £3,000 by the summer of 1843. He persuaded his brothers to consign all remaining shipments to him, entrusting him with the power to make his own arrangements regarding payments and delivery of goods. He then went to the now seriously delinquent Parsons and imposed three conditions on them. There would be no further deterioration in their debt to Coats, they would gradually pay it down, and they would maintain their volume to keep Ferguslie working. He gave no further credit and got the arrears paid off in two years, so that when Parsons finally went bankrupt in 1845, they only owed Coats £34 in interest.

Whilst he dealt with Coats's soon-to-be ex agent, he formed his own firm in Philadelphia with Joseph Bates, the son of a Halifax-based customer of J. & P. Coats in the UK. They had met at dinner on a Cunard steamer from Liverpool to Boston and were reintroduced by Andrew's "only friend in that city of friends", Thomas Mellor. Andrew brought no capital to the deal, but his partner accepted this, with the prospect of the Coats agency being more than sufficient incentive to get started. Their association was to last thirty-four years, and they became lifelong friends.

Bates & Coates, as they were named, initially imported piece goods from Yorkshire, as well as linen thread and some wool products through Andrew's brothers, but he did the rounds of the retailers and built up a demand for cotton thread, which he imported from Ferguslie. The volume sold by his company had reached nearly £14,000 by the time of Parsons' demise, effectively replacing them.

He did not stop there. In the next two years they opened an office in New York and took over the sewing thread volume of Forrest & Drummond, who had decided to withdraw when their two other manufacturers packed up almost simultaneously.

Andrew also got an agent for the smaller but important centre in Charleston, Virginia,[1] and set up in New Orleans by hiring two local firms as agents for the area. An adequate but not very lucrative market developed there over time.

1. Charleston is now in West Virginia, which only came into existence in 1861.

Meanwhile Taylor's, a Liverpool merchant who had been the cotton thread market leader since 1830, went under, their reputation ruined by counterfeit goods. Andrew jumped at the opportunity to get their New York agents, McCall & Strong, to take on J. & P. Coats as a replacement. They had all the Taylor's contacts, and their customer portfolio perfectly complimented that of Auchincloss, who still sold thread as a subordinate product to their printed goods. Importantly, they could also offer longer credit terms. Three agents in New York were deemed to be one too many, so Bates & Coates closed their office, and McCall & Strong became J. & P. Coats's ancillary agent in 1848 and remained so till the Civil War.

Having spent a great deal of time and effort in establishing agencies for Coats thread and the sales of their own label Six Cord, it would have been only fair if Andrew had been allowed a moment to catch his breath and consolidate the business. But the same villainy that had been the death of Taylor's had for some time been the greatest threat to Coats, as their product was becoming better known and therefore an attractive target for the counterfeiters. Cheap copies of better quality threads had grown commonplace, particularly amongst American producers. These were concentrated in New England, where the low humidity made fine spinning and twisting impossible, so none of them had perfected an acceptable six cord thread, which requires a much finer yarn. Their higher labour costs also made the production of six cord expensive. Their solution was simple. Make three ply, but sell it as six cord, preferably with reduced lengths, thus obtaining a higher price and vastly improved margins. In other words, cheat.

Many of the UK importers were affected, but found that the cost and effort required to take on the counterfeiters in the courts was prohibitive, so they suffered in silence. Andrew, however, having spent several years building the Coats name for high quality and guaranteed lengths, as well as forming a solid group of reputable agents, decided that it was time to fight. Bolstered by his legal background, he set about taking them on, one at a time.

His first case was typically frustrating, but his tenacity was to win the day. The crooks were an American manufacturer called MacGregor (run by a drunken Scotsman), who sold their three ply thread as J. & P. Coats Best Six Cord through a commission house in New York called Holbrook, Nelson & Co., whose reputation was supposedly beyond reproach, with one of the partners being a pillar of the church. Despite this, when Andrew first approached them to ask them "as honorable men to discontinue a trade that was a fraud upon the public", they were unmoved. They claimed to be doing nothing wrong, as they sold the goods openly as counterfeit and were deceiving nobody. Faced with such shameless effrontery, he threatened legal action, but they treated the idea with derision and sent him on his way.

So he went to court and got a temporary injunction.

Once Holbrook understood that they were likely to lose the case, they called Andrew back and offered to withdraw the product and come to a settlement. Then, with breathtaking arrogance, they coolly added that the only reason they were doing so was because the trade was unlikely to be profitable and the volume was negligible, so there was little point in continuing. Andrew gently reminded them, with enormous satisfaction, of his parting remark at their previous meeting, when he had clearly told them that once he had had recourse to the law, there would be no turning back and no settlements out of court. He went forward with the case.

Judge Sanford granted a perpetual injunction in July 1845 and denounced the conduct of MacGregor and Holbrook in the strongest possible terms, stating:

> The Defendants told the Jobber truly it was an imitation of Coats' Thread—in short they sold it as a spurious article. But what then? Did they imagine that the Jobber would be equally frank and communicative to the Retail Merchants and Shopkeepers, and that every one of the latter would carefully inform every customer who bought a spool that the thread was an imitation of Coats', made in Jersey, and only three cord instead of six? The idea is preposterous. Trade marks, names, labels etc. are not forged, counterfeited or imitated with any such honest design or expectation.[2]

The case had taken a year, but Andrew was so thrilled with the judge's decision that he printed and circulated a million copies around the USA. It was clearly important, as the ruling was reported in The London Times and as far afield as Liverpool. It seemed to have the desired deterrent effect in that there was a lull in the counterfeit trade for a year or two.

But as the popularity of the Coats product continued to grow, the temptation to copy it was such that eventually all sorts of imitations began to appear. Besides outright exact duplicates of the original six cord labelling, such diverse names surfaced as J. & T. Coats, J. L. Coats, J. P. Coats, and Coates & Co. All contained 100 to 150 yards instead of the regulation 200 and were made with mediocre three ply thread. Andrew followed up with multiple lawsuits, but by mid-1848 it was obvious that the effect of these was not to stop the counterfeiters, but simply to make them stealthier. They began selling to jobbers whose business was in the remotest areas, especially out west, rather than in the big industrial centres in the East. When Andrew tried to catch them red-handed, he was thwarted time and again, so he decided that the only way to put a stop to it was to visit as many retailers as possible and get the names of the crooked intermediaries from them directly.

2. From *Sanford's Chancery Reports* by Lewis Halsey Sanford, published by Gould Banks & Co., New York 1847, "Coats v. Holbrook" p.597.

He spent several months in the West, twenty years before the trans-American rail link was built, when there were no highways, and most of the roads were just dirt tracks which spread out from each settlement, with no specific direction in mind. Travel was difficult, time-consuming, and uncertain, and communication with the business back in the East all but impossible. This was also the start of the California gold rush, so there was plenty of movement over there, though he would have finished his tour before the real mania took hold in 1849.

Despite the hardships, he visited every selling establishment in every town where he stopped, and it was no surprise to him that he found plenty of examples of forgeries. He asked all of these retailers to give him the name of their supplier and a bond for between $2,000 and $5,000 to sell no more imitations of the Coats product. Most of the sellers acquiesced, but when faced with a refusal, he prosecuted and either managed to bring them round to his way of thinking or obtained a perpetual injunction against them. He returned to New York with a pile of bonds and enough evidence to prosecute several jobbers and manufacturers, from whom he extracted the same terms.

On the back of this campaign, the States began to establish more stringent laws against counterfeiters, with New York producing one of the strongest pieces of legislation, much to the company's satisfaction. But the practice continued, so Andrew hired a band of agents to scour the country for evidence in the same way he had done in the West. At the end of a year they had collected enough to prosecute sixteen of the largest jobbers in New York, most of whom were Coats customers.

He sued them all on the same day and, fearing negative publicity, they all settled out of court, giving in to all his demands, one by one. He got each of them to give "heavy" bonds not to sell any article with the Coats name or simulation thereof, unless it was the genuine product; they were to name their suppliers; they would give him, if asked, the exact quantities they had sold; they would destroy all labels, wrappers, and tickets under his or his agent's watchful eye; and they would pay all his expenses.

Once the dust had settled from this unprecedented manoeuvre, Andrew found that there were no less than eight New England manufacturers supplying these illegal goods, and he took similar steps to stop them, obtaining bonds or injunctions against them all. It was only at this point that he could appreciate the volumes involved, which were astonishing in their magnitude. One house alone had sold over 130,000 dozen!

One sad footnote to all this was the involvement of his brother David in this illicit trade. David Coats had from an early age shown his individuality, as exemplified by the story of when he first went to the local church with the rest of family. As Andrew described it in his book:

> He had to stand on the seat at the singing as the very young generally did. When all the people began to sing he thought he ought to sing too. It was all very well till they came to a pause at the end of a verse, and when all was still otherwise—but David's music was not divided into verses—and then his voice sang cheerily through the church, singing 'There's nae luck aboot the house, there's nae luck ata'.

His self-reliance continued. He qualified as a doctor in Glasgow, then as a surgeon in Edinburgh, and immediately went to Paris to study further and attend the hospital. Poor health brought him back to Scotland two years later, but an offer from Dr. Henry Coats, James Sr.'s second cousin, of a job in Rio de Janeiro, Brazil, was too good to pass up; he left for South America. His goal was to take over Henry's practice, which was the largest in the city, but after only two years he realised that the climate was killing him, so he set sail for New York to stay with his brother Andrew. He was so poorly that the friends who waved goodbye to him on the dock were unsure if he would survive the passage. However, the voyage did him good and after a period of recovery he resumed his medical career in North America.

Up to this point, he had absolutely nothing to do with the family business, but a curious case emerged in late 1850 when Andrew was in the heat of battle with the counterfeiters. McCall & Strong found "David Coats Thread" being sold in New York at a discount to the J. & P. Coats Six Cord. The company discovered that this thread had come from Alexanders in Paisley and had been relabelled in the USA, without Alexanders' knowledge or consent. It was unclear whether David had been duped by the agent making the sales into lending his name to the product or if he had participated willingly, but it required extensive negative advertising by both Andrew and Auchincloss to kill the product. Andrew, in the only potential case of family dissent in 100 years, wanted to sue David, but his brothers in the UK persuaded him to go after the agent. This he did, obtaining an injunction, at which point the matter died.

David's health was never robust, and although he lived the rest of his life in New York, he only survived another six years.

He was not the only brother to appear in the US. James Sr.'s fifth son William had taken over Coats, Grieve & Co. from his father, but their shawls had simply stopped selling, so when the business folded, he set out for America, arriving in 1842 and leaving a short time later, when ill health claimed his young life on the boat home, aged thirty-one.

Then John Coats, Andrew's youngest brother, who had spent his early adult life as a carefree sailor, also came to visit and liked the country so much he decided to stay. He married, moved to Detroit, and started a thread selling agency there in 1848, called Jack and Coats. However, he possessed neither the interest nor the ambition of his older sibling, so it never generated notable sales and ceased trading five years later. J. & P. Coats wrote off his debt balance of £1,000, and John bought himself a small islet called Orchard Island, about twelve miles around, in one of the lakes in Michigan, and lived there with his family as the only inhabitants for a number of years, like a Swiss Family Robinson. The place was well-named, for his mother kept a press back in the house at Back Row in Paisley, where she would store the apples he sent her every year.

Unfortunately, the imperatives of schooling meant an end to this idyllic life of isolation, and he took his family back to Scotland, where they lived a more normal life of comfort in Pollockshields, until his death in 1869.

So Andrew had broken the counterfeiters, and the Coats business in the US was well established and strong. When he had left Scotland to seek his fortune, Coats total annual sales were about £24,500, with US exports accounting for 45% of the total. Ten years later, after all Andrew's hard work, the total had nearly tripled to £70,000 with an amazing 80% of this in America. The next five years were to be even more spectacular, the total reaching nearly £170,000, 85% in the US. The third and final rung on their ladder to success was in place, with their dominance of and unerring faith in the American market.

Little did they realise that this was just the start. More dramatic growth was to follow, this time through no brilliant insights from the Coats family, but largely by being in the right place at the right time. Although they were to put in a lot more hard work and would continue to run a great business and sell an excellent product, their remarkable prosperity in the coming years was in no small part due to a nifty new invention, the sewing machine.

Chapter 9

The Development of the Sewing Machine

In Seattle you haven't had enough coffee until you can thread a sewing machine while it's running.
Jeff Bezos, Founder and CEO of Amazon.com

At the end of the eighteenth century, the Industrial Revolution was already underway. Yarn could be produced at a far higher rate than ever imagined, and with the invention of the Jacquard loom in 1801, cloth was spewing out of weaving sheds everywhere. But the conversion of all this material into something useful, be it curtains, sheets, clothing, or whatever, was still at the mercy of hand cutting and sewing. The release of this natural bottleneck would open the market up to a series of improvements in living standards, leading eventually to the world of constantly changing fashions with the multiple clothing seasons we have become accustomed to today. The final stage in the production chain was crying out for mechanisation, so there was no shortage of people in the hunt for the elusive device.

The automation of sewing has been unfairly treated by history. Whenever the important inventions that were the precursors of the Textile Industrial Revolution are mentioned, it is always Hargreaves's Jenny, Arkwright's Water Frame, Crompton's Mule, and Cartwright's Power

Loom that are named as the great innovations. The humble sewing machine,[1] without which the others would have struggled to reach their full potential, is never given its rightful place alongside them, although the historians of the time held the machine in very high regard, giving it the same importance as the electric telegraph and the reaper/mower in the USA. It could be argued that it was the single most important invention of the nineteenth century, being the first mass-marketed home appliance, one which was to improve the quality of life for vast numbers of people and completely transform the textile manufacturing workplace.

Without getting too technical, it is useful to understand the different stitch types and how they are fashioned, before delving into the development of the machines used to construct them. Although there are eight different classes of stitch defined today, there are happily only two to consider when looking at the pioneers of mechanised sewing. They are chain stitch and lockstitch.

A chain stitch is formed by a single thread introduced from one side of the material only. Used for hemming or temporary stitching, it will unravel rapidly if the last stitch in the chain is not secured. In a lockstitch, the needle thread interlaces with a separate underthread, which is on a small bobbin over which the needle thread can pass to lock the stitch in place. This is a much more secure structure.

To put sewing mechanisation into perspective, a skilled seamstress can manage 40 stitches per minute (spm) at full speed. The earliest machines claimed speeds of about 250 spm, Singer's machine in the 1850s could reach 900, and a contemporary domestic machine can do 1,500. Industrial machines will now get up to 10,000 spm and can sew coarse fabrics such as canvas and denim so fast that they will catch fire. A modern Coats thread will continue sewing, despite the flames—it is that good!

1. Or "Iron Needle-Woman" as expressively described by the *New York Times*, Jan 7 1860.

There were numerous attempts to create a device that would sew automatically. More than 700 patents for improvements in sewing technology were lodged in the USA in the nineteenth century, and activity in Europe was no less hectic, particularly in the late 1700s and early 1800s. The real breakthroughs happened in America after 1840, and over 100 inventors contributed in some small way to the evolution of the modern machine. Only a handful were of consequence, making either significant refinements to the mechanics or causing major market changes.

The first invention of any importance was by Charles Weisenthal, who sought a patent in 1755 for "a needle to be used for mechanical sewing". However, this was not the eye-pointed needle which would come some eighty years later, and absolutely no mention was made of a machine, so nobody knows how it was to be applied.

Others followed, but none of them worked, until a patent was awarded to Barthélemy Thimonnier for the first useful sewing machine, constructed entirely of wood, on July 30, 1830. Even though it had no transport mechanism, it produced a very acceptable chain stitch, the cloth being moved forward carefully by hand. He was awarded a contract for eighty machines, which were placed in a Paris factory to produce uniforms for the French army. This was attacked by Luddite-style anti-technology gangs and twice burnt to the ground, Thimonnier only narrowly escaping with his life on one such occasion. He fled to England, but eventually returned to France and opened the first-ever sewing machine factory in 1848, but his timing was poor, and the Paris riots brought it to a stop almost before it had started. His invention never caught on after this, and he died a pauper in 1857.

Real progress came when the technology stopped trying to duplicate human sewing motions. The first lockstitch machine, produced by Walter Hunt in the US, appeared in 1834 and was a fundamental departure from all previous inventions. He placed the thread-hole at the needle point, rather than in the middle, and had an underthread fed from a lower spool to make the lockstitch. It was beginning to resemble the classic machine we know today, though the needle was still curved, and it lacked other refinements, such as a reliable cloth feeder. He never patented his machine or the eye-pointed needle.

Further attempts to crack the secret of automatic sewing were either abandoned or were so unreliable as to be rendered useless. Then an inventor called Elias Howe appeared. In the crisis of 1837, he had lost his job working on hemp carding in Lowell, MA and moved to nearby Cambridge, where he started working in a small machine shop, repairing chronometers and surveying instruments. Howe apparently overheard the proprietor commenting to a group of machinists that they should not be wasting their time on knitting machines, but should "...try something that will pay. Make a Sewing Machine". He did just that.

Without a penny to his name, in 1843 he set out to make such a machine, using all his spare time and obtaining $500 finance from an old school friend, George Fisher, who also gave him board and lodging. He worked on his design off and on for five years, apparently using his wife's sewing motions to guide him. He is said to have fallen asleep at his workbench one night and dreamt his "eureka" moment, giving him the breakthrough he needed to perfect his invention. In his dream, or rather nightmare, he has been captured by cannibals who have him in a cooking pot. As the water starts to boil, he tries to escape, but they poke at him with sharp, needle-like spears to stop him. Upon awakening, he realised that the spears had holes in the points, which is exactly what he needed to simplify his machine and complete the design. On September 10, 1846, he obtained a patent for the first two-thread lockstitch machine.[2]

2. Despite this oft-quoted dream-inspired invention, his model was nothing more than an enhanced version of Hunt's machine, plans of which he had probably seen, so it is doubtful that his idea was original.

The machine did not sell. The $300 price tag probably had a lot to do with this; no single family was likely to lay out the equivalent of six months' wages on a machine to start a small family business, and for the industrialist the investment was hard to justify. Its inability to follow curves and angles was also a deterrent.

Frustrated by his lack of success in the US, Howe left for England with his brother Amasa. His invention also failed to sell there, so Amasa sold it to William F. Thomas of Cheapside, a maker of corsets and umbrellas. He, in turn, filed for a patent (a copy of Howe's in the US), which he obtained on December 1, 1846, effectively stifling further development of sewing mechanisation in Britain, as other inventors feared lawsuits from Thomas.

By 1849, Howe had ended up in debtor's prison and finally cut his losses and returned to Massachusetts, where he soon discovered that the sewing machine had become very popular during his sojourn abroad; most of the designs seemed to bear an uncanny resemblance to his own. He set out on a life of suit and countersuit, through which he became extremely wealthy. Although he contributed nothing technically to the world of sewing after this, he played a vital role in the final shape of the industry after 1850.

Amongst the multiple producers of automated sewing devices that were the targets of Howe's litigation was the man destined to be the greatest of them all, Isaac Merritt Singer.

Singer was the youngest of eight children. His mother left home to become a Quaker when he was ten, and his father remarried, but the boy's relationship with his stepmother never developed, and he was largely neglected by both parents. As a teenager he moved to Rochester, New York and started working as a machinist, an exciting new profession which was developing on the back of the Industrial Revolution. He also took to acting and in

December 1830 married the fifteen-year-old Catharine Maria Haley, who came to see him in Richard III and was captivated by this handsome actor who could recite great chunks of Shakespeare with consummate ease. The responsibilities of marriage meant that Singer needed to get proper work, so he started as a wood turner, then a shop assistant, and finally a machinist's apprentice. He continued to alternate between actor and contract machinist for the next twenty years, travelling extensively and leaving an ever growing family in New York.

He also embarked on a life of polygamy. Soon after marrying, he met Mary Ann Sponslor in Baltimore and persuaded her to join him in a masquerade where they presented themselves as Mr. and Mrs. Merritt until he could arrange a divorce from his first wife. This "bigamy" was to continue for twenty-five years, and his first son by Mary Ann was born in 1837. There would be nine more.

He later took on a third "wife", Mary McGonigal, whom he had met on a trip to San Francisco. She bore him five children during the 1850s and lived in a separate residence in New York, where they were known as Mr. and Mrs. Matthews.

His immoral lifestyle did not interfere with his genius as an inventor. He first developed a rock drilling machine whilst working on a canal project in Chicago and sold the patent (said to be the precursor of the rotary drill press) for a staggering $2,000, but instead of doing something useful with it, he squandered it by forming the Merritt Players of Chicago, who toured for five years with his second "wife" and her brother as lead actors. He ended up penniless in Fredericksburg, Ohio, where he was again forced to find work.

This time he started in a print shop, where he patented a mechanism for carving wood and metal typefaces. He took it to New York, where he found a backer, A. B. Taylor, who erected it on his premises, where it continued to work well for five years, until it was destroyed in a boiler explosion which killed sixty-three of the factory's employees. As Taylor was unwilling to finance a rebuild, Isaac turned to a successful bookseller, George Zeiber, who gave him his entire life savings of $1,700 in return for a full share of the venture. It was a gamble that would dominate the rest of Zeiber's life and ultimately prove to be his downfall.

They set up the newly constructed machine in a room they had rented within the property of Orson C. Phelps at 19 Harvard Place, Boston. Here, Singer became fascinated by the Lerow & Blodgett sewing machines, which Phelps manufactured, sometimes sold, and more frequently repaired. These machines were loosely based on Howe's design, but were, like all the others, very unreliable and in need of constant adjustment.

Phelps suggested that Singer have a look at the machines. Within twenty-four hours he had come up with a modified design, which he claimed would solve most of its design faults. It was immediately obvious to Phelps, a skilled machinist, that the changes suggested had real merit, so he offered his tools, workshop, and labour in exchange for a share in the business, and with additional finance from Zeiber, the three went to work.

They set out to build a machine with a target cost of $40, and it took them eleven days to produce a prototype. Singer slept little until it was done, but even on the last evening it wouldn't work. Singer said he was so nervous and tired at this point that he couldn't get the stitches to tighten. They left for their hotel, but on the way Zeiber brought up the fact that the loose stitches were all on the face of the cloth, at which point it dawned on Singer that he had forgotten to adjust the tension on the needle thread (almost certainly Coats Six Cord). They returned, made the adjustment, and sewed five stitches perfectly, at which point the thread broke, but they had solved the problem. The machine was completed the next day, and Singer took it to New York to apply for a patent.

This patent, number 8294, was awarded to Singer on August 12, 1851. The improvements he had made were all to do with reliability. The needle went straight up and down, leaving much less room for deviation from the intended path. He incorporated automatic feed, the ability to sew on a curve, a compensating spring that allowed for variations in fabric thickness along the seam, and a foot pedal to hold the fabric, thus freeing both hands. The gearing had forced synchronisation, so it could not jam, and the whole thing was constructed of metal with much finer tolerances than any previous machine. It was largely a copy of other ideas, but an incredibly well conceived and engineered one.

It was named after the inventor, the word Singer suggesting fluid, flawless motion, and the three partners set out to make a killing. The initial reaction to their creation was rather lacklustre. The problem was that potential buyers had grown weary of being presented with a whole series of unreliable sewing machines that, even when they were running perfectly, needed an expert to keep them that way. Singer's was seen as just one more in a long line of expensive and exasperating gadgets.

Singer now put his great gift as a showman to good use. He travelled to circuses and fairs to promote his invention and opened a sewing machine showroom, the first of its kind, with elaborate decorations. This was the size of a couple of tennis courts and had rows of dozens of sewing machines, which were demonstrated for the general public by young ladies he had trained personally as sales consultants. His marketing thrust was that if these girls could operate a Singer, then anyone could. The machine began to catch on, and the generally negative attitude to sewing machines softened. Improved versions followed in 1859 and 1865, this last being phenomenally popular.

With success came wealth, but his character and eccentric behavior prevented him from ever entering high society. His immoral lifestyle didn't help much either. He attempted to regularise his conjugal situation by divorcing his first spouse in 1860, but disaster struck that same year when Sponslor spotted him riding in a carriage with McGonigal. There followed a very public altercation, which later continued in private, during which he strangled both Mary Ann and her daughter till they lost consciousness. His "wife" then accused him of frequent beatings, and the public humiliation was such that he left for London in September, accompanied only by McGonigal's nineteen-year-old sister.

He became bored in England, particularly as he no longer had his bevy of beautiful women to keep him entertained, so he moved to Paris, where he met and eventually married Isabella Eugenie Summerville, reputed to be the most beautiful woman in Europe.[3] He finally settled in Paignton, in Devon, England, after fleeing from the approaching Franco-Prussian war in 1870. He died five years later and left his $13 million estate split into no less than sixty parts, for all of his offspring and six of his seven (yes, there were others) common law wives. Sponslor, who had sued him on various occasions to little effect, was left nothing.

Whilst all this unfolded, there was someone else taking the Singer Company on to even greater prosperity. This was Edward S. Clark,[4] who took over the enterprise when Singer relinquished command after being attacked by Elias Howe for patent infringement.

Clark, a lawyer, was contacted by Singer in 1852 when the inventor found himself largely penniless and, like so

3. Upon Singer's death, Isabella became a wealthy widow and went on to enduring fame as the model used by Auguste Bartholdi for the Statue of Liberty.

4. Absolutely no relation of the thread Clarks.

many others, being sued by Howe. Ambrose Jordan, the Senior Partner in the law firm of Jordan, Clark & Company, had helped Singer get his original Sewing Machine patent, but had found the man so obnoxious that he refused to see him when he returned with the Howe problem and asked his colleague to deal with it. Singer had no way of paying for legal advice, but as Phelps had relinquished any interest in the company, Clark offered his services, which included taking almost complete control of commercial operations, in return for a one-third share in the venture.

Zeiber retained the other third, but in late 1852 he fell gravely ill and took to his bed with a very high fever. His old "friend" Isaac appeared at his bedside, saying he had rushed over after talking to the physician who had told him that Zeiber was unlikely to recover. He then asked if he would consider, given the situation, relinquishing his share in their business. The understandably dispirited Zeiber readily agreed and in due course signed over his share for $6,000. The company's assets at the time were worth around $500,000.

Zeiber recovered, but never forgave either Singer or Clark and followed the former around for the rest of his life. Although he eventually managed to obtain menial employment from the company, there was never any offer of compensation for his blatantly immoral treatment.

Clark now introduced a series of brilliant measures which propelled the business from great to world-class. He hired dedicated agents and trained them to not only sell the machines, but repair them as well. They were chosen for their verbal skills and honesty, so they could make convincing and believable presentations. He launched a series of marketing innovations, which included persuading Singer to add gold letters and striping to the largely black machines, giving them a more stylish look and distinguishing them from all their competitors.

Three real masterstrokes followed. The first was to offer trade-ins, not only on older model Singer machines, but also the competitors' models. This established brand loyalty for those who already had a Singer and created an incentive to switch for those who did not. To prevent a market forming for secondhand spares (and machines), he simply had the old ones destroyed.

Then, in late 1856, when the recession began to affect sales, he instituted installment purchasing,[5] with $5 securing a machine, followed by monthly payments of $3 until the whole thing was paid off. This basic scheme was established with variations throughout the world, as the Singer Company had by this time expanded into overseas markets. It cleverly removed the high initial investment as an excuse for postponing a purchase and armed the salesmen with one more tool in their already sizable armory.

Lastly, as Howe had successfully sued almost everyone in the industry for patent infringement, Clark agreed to pay him $15,000 and the $5 license fee for every machine sold by Singer. The fees incurred in settling multiple legal disputes were prohibitive, and it had become common practice for everyone to sue anybody who filed a new patent, accusing them of infringing some earlier one. The court's decision on any one case was largely a lottery, as the patent claims of each side were of equal weight, so costs continued to mount, and the infighting was damaging the reputation of the industry, where Singer was the clear leader. So Clark engineered the Albany Agreement of October 24, 1856, which allowed the four principal players in the market to share their individual patents, but with no restrictions on pricing or other commercial conditions.

5. This is said to have been the progenitor of the modern credit card and the start of America's love affair with debt. Buying on credit was originally introduced in 1807 by the Cowperthwaite furniture store in New York, but remained limited to that industry until Singer's scheme appeared.

Howe went on to collect 33% of the $2 million made from the agreement until 1867, when his patent expired and he was expelled. The balance was divided between the others, with a small amount put aside for expenses. The remaining members continued in peace for another ten years until the last of the patents ran out.

With their legal battles behind them, the leading manufacturers started to expand rapidly, with the combined output topping 250,000 machines in 1870 and over double this seven years later, when Clark delivered his final coup de grace. Without warning, he suddenly halved the price of Singer's New Family domestic machine from $60 to $30. None of his competitors or anyone else could understand this, but what they hadn't realised was that within the year all remaining patent protection would lapse, at which point anyone could enter the market with a clone of the Singer, or any other machine. By this time, Singer, with their bargain basement pricing, had taken the lion's share of the available demand and had established an unassailable position as market leader.

The results for the clothing industry and textile finishing were outstanding. Mass-produced apparel became a reality; almost everyone could (and did) have a sewing machine in their house, and anyone, of whatever ability level, could become a seamstress. Clothing prices were substantially reduced, bringing greater ranges and quantities within the economic reach of a much larger proportion of the population.

What was more important for the Coatses, more clothing being sold to more people meant more sales of thread. If the sewing machine was the nineteenth century equivalent of the personal computer at the end of the twentieth, then Singer was the IBM or Dell of the mid 1800s, and the thread producers were supplying the software, with Coats being the Microsoft equivalent. The company was poised to dominate.

Chapter 10

Coats Grows and the Clarks Multiply

Blood is thicker than water.
Nineteenth Century English Proverb

Keep your eye on Paisley
Benjamin Disraeli, British Prime Minister

While Andrew was forging ahead in the New World, and Isaac Singer was making his fortune, there were big changes in Paisley. Both the Coatses and Clarks found their businesses expanding, but at different rates. There were good reasons for this.

James and Peter Coats had a moderately easy financial life, as James Sr. handled the early financing of J. & P. Coats. He was responsible for all the initial fixed investment and some of the current costs. Interest was paid on all the loans he made to his sons, but at a rate of only 5%, which was lower than that available outside. James and Peter never needed the banks,[1] and this gave them both freedom of action and a level of comfort not available to the Clark clan.

1. The one exception was when they had small loans with their brother William and their Manchester agent in 1837, after the downturn caught them short.

All other Coats company investments came from ploughed-back profits. The two brothers paid themselves modestly, starting at £70 a year each in 1830 rising to £160 in 1839, by which time Thomas had joined them, receiving the same salary. They split the profits evenly between the three of them after 1834, but kept them in the company as "stock", taking 4% interest of the total as further income. Their rate of withdrawal of funds from the company varied, with Thomas being the most frugal and Peter taking larger amounts to help build a house. Of the £6,300 profit made in the decade, £4,700 was left in the company, so they effectively ploughed back 75% for growth. They could have indulged themselves and become quite rich, but instead invested for what would be a very prosperous future.

The three partners in J. & J. Clark, on the other hand, withdrew more than the total Coats profit for the decade in just one year, 1831. James Clark Sr. had died in 1829, so they were not controlled to the same extent by their father and sleeping partner, and their relative profligacy sharply contrasted with the sheer dedication to growth and provident nature of the Coatses.

Both companies flourished during the '30s, with Coats concentrating on the US and, to a lesser extent, the home market. They toyed with other exports, but very half-heartedly, largely due to the difficulties with collections. J. & J. Clark consolidated in the UK, where they were strongest, and expanded into Western Europe, whilst taking a marginal interest in the Americas through agents in Canada and the US. Both Seedhill and Ferguslie grew to handle the increased demand.

Coats management did not change during the decade, with James, Peter, and Thomas working together under the watchful eye of their father. Conversely, changes were positively de rigeur with the Clarks. James and John had earlier taken on an associate, John Stewart, who was James Sr.'s brother-in-law. He retired in 1838 and was replaced by

James Kerr, a member of a local thread manufacturing family, whose son would marry one of John Clark's daughters. Four years later, James and John Balderston also joined. The Clarks had no qualms about taking on partners from outside the immediate family, something the Coatses did not do until the business was floated on the stock exchange in 1891, by which time it was extremely well established.

The 1840s brought their share of setbacks for the Coats family, but despite these they nearly trebled their sales and increased their exports to the US fivefold, thanks largely to the efforts of the indefatigable Andrew. Home sales were flat, and other exports negligible.

Two years after William Coats died on the boat home from the United States, his oldest brother James was taken at the relatively early age of forty-two. James Sr. had leant heavily on his unmarried son as a sounding post in their commercial decisions, and he took the loss with a heavy heart, reputedly exclaiming, on hearing of his passing, "Where is all this wisdom now?"

With James's demise, Thomas took over the running of the company, with growing influence coming from Andrew in the US. James Sr. continued to guide them and help with the financing, so although there was one person fewer in charge, the direction and philosophy remained the same. Any new blood to be introduced would come from the family, but none of their children were old enough at this point to be considered.

The first few years of the period brought a deep recession and misery to the masses in Paisley, with a third of the population of 48,000 unemployed in mid-1842. Queen Victoria ordered seventeen Paisley shawls in the hope of stimulating trade in the town, and there were several donations of over £50 from famous people like Sir Robert Peel, the founder of the British police force, and also from the

Coats and Clark families. Despite all this, 67 of 112 manufacturers in the town went out of business, and both thread companies lost many local customers; but it was not all bad news, as several of the smaller thread makers also disappeared.

J. & J. Clark were not amongst them. Any problems they had with home sales, where they were dominant, were compensated by sales to places as far afield as Sydney, Copenhagen, and Montreal, with occasional exports to the USA via New York. The Clarks overcame the problems of timely payments from international sales by insisting on the debt being lodged with "some respectable house in this country" before the goods were despatched. It allowed them to add machinery at Seedhill and work night shifts almost continuously. Expansion continued for several years, particularly while Coats was having problems with Parsons Canning.

Coats themselves added capacity in three bursts: a mill extension "five windows in length" in 1840 with new machinery and a counting house; further twisting, spooling, and turning (spool-making) machines in the late '40s; and then a new four-storey building, boilers, boiler house, winding, turner's shop, stables, and drying/storage for birchwood and spools, all between 1850 and 1853. They had got the better of the Clarks, who were no longer the dominant thread company.

Clarks had about 500 employees by 1860. Coats, on the other hand, expanded from around 200 in 1840 to 1,100 in 1860 with the wage bill growing from £4,000 to £27,000 over the same period. Their total assets increased tenfold and their profits even more, to a rather impressive £40,000. Productivity was increasing at over 4% annually,[2] so when

2. Improved efficiency came partly from their more experienced workforce, but also from the Weilds spooling machine, which allowed one operator to wind ten spools at a time with far more accuracy than the old hand spoolers.

legislation was introduced to reduce the working week from sixty-nine to sixty hours, they took it in their stride.

Several other developments had a hand in their continuing prosperity. They had started to understand and appreciate the value of staff loyalty and began to buy up houses around the mill for some of their employees. They also invested in coalmining, as fuel was such a vital element in the manufacturing process and a major cost item. Although they continued to buy yarn rather than do their own spinning, the up-and-coming growth of cotton brokering and the futures market helped to smooth the fluctuations in cotton yarn prices and facilitate longer-term contracts, which made budgeting much easier.

Coats did toy with the polishing process to produce some of the cheaper three ply glazed products that had started to become popular in the US in the 1850s, but their main thrust continued to be high-grade six cord thread. Their obsession with quality was such that when confronted with a shortage of their usual Scottish birchwood for spool making in 1851, they imported from America at five times the price, rather than experiment with offers of other woods, fearing issues which might reflect on the reputation of their article. A persistent timber merchant who was trying to push other varieties on them was politely referred to a competitor, R. F. & J. Alexander.

The '50s were not all plain sailing, but the tight-knit family came through with their usual stoicism. The first setback came in 1856 when Peter, who was feeling the pressure of a business growing at breakneck speed, decided to retire to "devote his time to public activities in the town". His place was taken by his eldest son James, who was now twenty-two and had already been working for the company for three years at a salary of £50. He was a tall, handsome man of amiable disposition with a sociable nature and a gift as a great storyteller. He was devoutly religious and would run his house under the strictest observance of the Sabbath, with all secular books and texts put away and replaced by religious material for the day. Whistling was deeply frowned upon. He abhorred waste, which made him a great asset to the family business as it grew.

This transition was effected smoothly, and the finances were sorted out with a minimum of fuss, James[3] taking a £200 salary and a quarter of the profits, with Thomas taking the rest and £300 annually. Peter then sold them his interest in the business, but on condition that they let his second son join when old enough.[4] This was Archibald, who was only sixteen at the time, but was to play a prominent part in the development of the company in the late 1800s.

No sooner had all this happened than James Sr.'s seventh son, David, died in New York. This was followed, a year later, by the death of James's wife, Catherine. She had been feeling poorly for some days, but managed a short walk in the garden the afternoon before she died. At 4:00 p.m. she took to her bed, and three hours later, with her husband at her side trying to cheer her, she fell unconscious, remaining so until she passed away peacefully at 5:00 a.m. the next day. She was a woman of great faith and apparently had little fear of death.

James Sr. never recovered from this blow and only lasted four more months, when a short illness took him on August 24, 1857. By good fortune, Andrew was visiting from the US and sat with him on the last night, when he spoke of no pain

3. James was soon destined to follow his uncle Andrew to America, at which point Peter rejoined the firm. Although this was later on, he is referred to as James (USA) from now on, for clarity.

4. He sold half his interest in the company to Thomas for £55,000 and the other half to James for £65,000, but by way of three loans payable in ten years, for £20,000, £30,000, and £70,000 to Thomas, James, and the company respectively, at 5% interest. He demanded no payment of principal for the period (as long as Coats remained solvent), but also specified that James should transfer "not less than 3/8 and not more than 4/8 of his share and interest in J. & P. Coats to let one of his younger brothers become a partner".

but great weariness and being "happy at the change that awaited him". He talked quietly with Andrew through the small hours, and when George, Peter, and Thomas arrived the next morning, he simply acknowledged their presence and slipped away, with a smile on his face, the expression of a man who reflects on his life as a job well done. He had died with all his surviving family around him, except John, who was still in Michigan.

His death coincided with the financial panic of 1857, which saw the failure of the Ohio Life & Trust Co. in September, immediately followed by suspension of cash payments by banks in Boston, Baltimore, and Philadelphia, as well as sixty-one of the sixty-two banks in New York. The knock-on effect in Britain was swift and severe. Both Dennistoun & Co. and the City of Glasgow Bank suspended payments, and the Western Bank of Scotland failed, all in the space of four days at the beginning of November. Coats held deposits at the Glasgow Bank, but they reopened their doors almost immediately, so no harm was done.

A downturn followed and many factories were forced to reduce working hours. Paisley suffered along with the rest, but as so often in the past, the crisis was short-lived, and life for the thread makers and the town resumed a healthy advance, with Coats definitely at the vanguard.

The concentration of the Coatses on high-quality six cord thread and the US market were major contributors to their emergence as the industry leader. It allowed them longer production runs, a smaller customer base, and all the benefits that come from finding a large, specialised market. They also began to benefit from their superior quality thread, which performed best on the newly developed sewing machines.

The Clarks were less focussed. Their product range was larger and more varied, and they sold into more markets than Coats, but they had one other significant disadvantage: there were too many of them.

As far back as 1816, John Clark, a cousin of J. & J., had built the Mile End mill in Glasgow and had been selling "Clarks" thread for over thirty years. He had been the pioneer in the US, making his first sale there in 1819. There were therefore two Clark companies even before the Coatses started up.

Then in 1851, George A. Clark, the second son of John Clark (of J. & J.), had the audacity to build a larger mill called Linside right next to Seedhill. He had joined forces with Peter Kerr, from another threadmaking family, and they began selling under the name of Kerr & Clark.

The J. & J. Clark partnership had ceased to be a family affair from 1820, with their friend John Stewart involved from the beginning, followed by James Kerr and the Balderston brothers. There was clearly dissension amongst the members when, by 1852, the Jameses (Clark & Kerr) retired and John Balderston had died. Their places were taken by another Kerr (William Pinkerton) and by two younger Clarks, James Jr. (son of the retired James) and James of Camphill, later of Ralston, who was the oldest son of John Clark and now the senior partner.

These changes did nothing to unify the group, and at the end of 1854 James Balderston, John Clark, James Clark Jr., and William Kerr all retired, leaving the other James Clark in charge of everything, including the others' financial stakes in the company. Robert Balderston, James's second son, was made manager of Seedhill, and Stewart Clark, one of James Jr.'s younger brothers, joined the business, but not as a partner.

Now that James Jr. was no longer tied to J. & J. Clark, he formed a partnership with his younger brother, Robert, and bought the Burnside mill on Lonend, just down the road from Seedhill. They began to make and sell sewing thread under the name of J. & R. Clark.

Then George Clark decided to emigrate to America in 1855, with the intention of setting up an agency to sell thread from the Linside mill as well as other products, under his own name. This created a fifth thread company with Clark in the title, all competing with each other and the still unified Coats family. His motives were sound, as his desire was to gather all the Clark companies under one umbrella and direct their attentions to the US, which he could see was an expanding, lucrative market. However, it just created more complications for their customers and strengthened Coats's position.

George's role in the development of the thread trade in the United States was to be pivotal, but before he could make his presence felt, Civil War broke out.

Chapter 11

The US Civil War

Cotton is King.
Senator William H. Seward

The war hit the thread trade hard, for its origins revolved around slavery and, by extension, cotton, as most of the slaves were exploited for cotton growing and particularly harvesting, having progressed from cultivation of tobacco and rice.

Nobody is exactly sure how old cotton is. The earliest known examples were unearthed in a cave in Mexico and have been shown to date from at least 7,000 years ago. Alexander the Great's army introduced cotton (known at the time as "vegetable wool") to Europe in about 330 BC, but it was too expensive for all but the very rich. The name cotton, which is derived from the Arabic *qutn*, came into use at the beginning of the fifteenth Century. The Moors cultivated it in Spain and the East India Company started to import it to England in the early 1700s, against stiff opposition from the wool and linen trades, who managed to have importing and manufacturing cotton goods outlawed. This resistance to the fibre not only slowed up the development of the cotton industry in Britain, but also in the American colonies, where planting began along the James River in Virginia in 1607.

The plant takes about six months from seed to harvest, though this varies by type. The bolls (small green round "fruits") appear after about ten weeks. These contain seeds from which the cotton fibres emerge, and as the plant matures, the fibres grow and thicken, causing the boll to expand until it splits open after about four months, holding the fibres in place while they dry, ready for harvesting some six weeks later. Once the cotton is picked, the fibres, or lint, have to be separated from the seed and the rest of the boll before they can be processed into useful textile products. This process was very laborious. One person (usually a slave) would take a whole day to separate one pound of cotton, until Eli Whitney's invention of the "saw" gin[1] (short for engine), "...with which one man will clean ten times as much cotton as he can in any other way before known".[2] Indeed, he claimed that, turned by a horse, it would do the work of fifty men.

He patented the process in 1794, and set up a manufactory with a partner in New Haven to produce the new machines, but they blundered seriously in their handling of the commercial side of their venture. Rather than sell the gins, they installed them all over the South and charged a fee for every pound of cotton ginned, equivalent to a third of its value and payable in cotton. This was too much for the Georgia farmers. The patent laws at the time were less than rigorous, the machine itself was mechanically simple, and they couldn't keep up with demand, so clones of the device sprang up all over the place. His precious invention became commonplace though he had little to show for it, but it would have profound effects elsewhere.

1. Sea Island cotton had been processed for centuries on a roller gin, or churka. The longer, finer fibres need to be treated far more gently and were relatively easy to separate from the black seeds of this cotton. The fibres from shorter cottons could only be pried loose from their green seeds by hand.

2. From Correspondence of Eli Whitney, in *American Historical Review* (New York, 1898), 111, pp. 99-101.

Before it, the export of eight bales (about 4,000 lbs.) of cotton to England resulted in confiscation by the customs, as it was deemed impossible that such a large amount of cotton could have been produced in the USA! By 1800, only twelve years later, US exports were 18 million pounds a year, and another forty years on, when the Coats family were making serious inroads into the US market, 85% of the world's cotton came from the US.

The introduction of Sea Island cotton to the US only a few years before the invention of the Whitney gin was fortuitous. Although it had been cultivated in Georgia at the beginning of the eighteenth century, it was found to easily exhaust the soil, and as its production was very labour intensive, and prices were poor, it could not compete with other crops such as rice. It was reintroduced on a commercial basis on the Georgia coast in about 1786, and the subsequent massive increase in upland cotton production on the back of Whitney's contraption meant that availability and transport of the longer staple fibre became far easier, allowing more spinners access and improving the pricing. Its sale for cloth was still restricted by the limited quantities available, but thread producers used smaller amounts, so the timing was perfect for the emerging industry.[3]

The other, less fortunate effect of the cotton gin was its contribution to the alarming growth of slavery in the southern states. Whitney had correctly deduced that the labour needed for removing seeds would be vastly reduced, but he did not foresee the huge increase in the numbers required to plant, grow, and pick. The farming of cotton became so profitable once the problem of ginning had been solved, that there was an explosion in the demand for land and consequently for slaves. The six slave States of 1790

3. Other long staple cottons appeared later. The Egyptian variety was introduced by Mohamed Ali Pasha in the nineteenth century and made its mark during the Civil War, when US cotton was unobtainable. American Pima cotton first appeared in the early 1900s, but only took off after 1950. All have had their place in the history of J. & P. Coats.

became fifteen some seventy years later. Although import of slaves was banned from 1808, 80,000 Africans had been shipped to the American South in the previous fifteen years. Plantations got bigger, the work more regimented, and the conditions more cruel and unrelenting. About a third of the population of the South were slaves by 1860, when they numbered over 4 million; there had been only 700,000 in 1790.

The southern aristocracy, which flourished as a result of this expansion in the slave trade, was lazy about developing efficient uses of soil, so the planters found themselves looking farther west for new land to increase production. From 1820 through to the start of the Civil War, an imaginary line running east-west through the United States separated the new states entering the Union as "free" to the north and "slave" to the south, with the plantation owners looking to Arkansas, Texas, and Florida as areas for expansion when these states joined the Union.

At the same time, "white gold", as cotton became known, ruled the US. The southern states' exports were transported on ships from the North. The West and Midwest sold $30 million worth of food to the cotton producers, and the northeastern cloth industry was valued at $100 million, with manufactured goods going south to the tune of $150 million.

The North was experiencing the full effects of the Industrial Revolution, fast expansion of population through immigration, and an increasing birthrate. They sought to protect developing local industries and wanted to do away with slavery, hoping that those freed would drift northwards in search of work, thereby guaranteeing additional manpower, which they needed to fuel the growth of manufacturing.

The South, on the other hand, needed slaves to perpetuate their plantation system. They imported far more than the North and were therefore against any duties on these products. Their influence within the federal government was diminishing, as their population was far more stable than the North, and when Abraham Lincoln, a known opponent of slavery, was elected President, seven of the southern states seceded from the Union, and the Civil War began. They were joined very shortly afterwards by four others, and for three years the Confederacy (as these eleven were known) enjoyed a number of victories and seemed to have the upper hand. But New Orleans fell to the Union in 1862, and defeats at Gettysburg and Vicksburg turned the tide. The Union progressively overcame the enemy army until final surrender in 1865.

During the conflict, cotton supplies were severely curtailed. This was partly due to a Union blockade of the main southern ports, but the Confederacy also restricted shipments. They hoped that they could use cotton as a bargaining chip to obtain British and French backing for their cause, to the extent of getting them to break the blockade. After all, a quarter of the English nation depended on textiles and, therefore, cotton. Although an embargo of cotton shipments to Europe was never officially declared, they stopped them informally and sent emissaries to England, but without success. The combined result was that exports were reduced from about 10 million bales before the start of hostilities, to only 500,000 annually between 1861 and 1865.

The reasons for the lack of response from the Europeans were easy to understand with hindsight. There had been a bumper crop in 1860, and this allowed the spinners to accumulate product and postpone the shortage, which finally hit home in 1862. This gave them time to locate alternative sources principally from Brazil, India, and Egypt. The British were very dependent on wheat from the northern states at a time when supplies from Europe were considerably diminished, so they did not want to rock that particular boat. They were also against slavery, so they would have been unlikely to intervene in any case.

This doesn't mean that the effects of the cotton shortage were negligible. In Lancashire, the "cotton famine" hit home with a vengeance. Mill closures, mass layoffs, and abject poverty followed, with soup kitchens opening in early 1862. Relief funds were set up, and the workforce was offered alternative employment in the woolen industry and even in the Federal army in the US. The Paisley thread makers also felt the pinch, but to a lesser degree. They didn't use as much cotton as the weavers, and, although heavily dependent on the American Sea Island product, they managed to struggle on, relying on supplies from the blockade runners, supplemented by small amounts from the Caribbean. It is also likely that some manufacturers fed Egyptian cotton in as a substitute.

Oddly enough, the first major impact of the war was not on cotton supply, but rather on money. In the US, all contacts between North and South were severed, and the dealers and jobbers in the Confederacy immediately reneged on all their debts. As the customary credit terms were around eight months, this left many of the agents in the North in serious trouble, Bates & Coates amongst them.

Andrew Coates had returned home just before the outbreak of war. His health had deteriorated over the years, due largely to the climate, which is one of marked extremes in the Northeast. There were no such luxuries as air-conditioning or effective central heating, with the radiator having just been invented and even the electric fan still twenty-five years away, so he would have been exposed to the full effects of heat and cold. His tireless work for the company had also meant extensive rather uncomfortable travel. He was "obliged to seek the bracing air of Scotland".

Almost as soon as he reached Scotland, the war broke out, and Bates & Coates found themselves virtually bankrupt, having lost "pretty much all that was owing to them". Andrew's entire fortune from twenty years of work was wiped out, and he was left with debts of £16,000, though his associate Joseph fared better and was still solvent. Andrew had never been a partner in J. & P. Coats, so he never had the opportunities that Peter, Thomas, and now young James had to accumulate capital on the back of the firm's prosperity. However, help was at hand. His brother Thomas got the company to write off much of the agency's assets and loans and lend Andrew enough to keep them from going under. J. & P. Coats also paid him an annual salary of £1,000 until he retired from the business in 1878, when it became Bates & Auchincloss.

There was another silver lining: the crisis effectively did away with the ridiculously long credit terms and cash discounts that had become the norm. So, although almost all of their competitors went broke, Bates & Coates managed to return to profit fairly rapidly, and Andrew paid off the rest of his loans and eliminated his debts. He had always had the intention of returning to the USA, as he looked upon the country as his home and had become very attached to the American way of life. However, it quickly became evident that he was going to need an extended convalescence in Scotland to recover his former vitality, so he settled in Perthshire and went on to live another forty years, taking bracing walks over the moors and reaching the ripe old age of eighty-five. The Scottish air obviously did him some good!

Once he had realised that he would no longer return to the US, he wrote, "...the business was so thoroughly established as to no longer require supervision", which may have been true of the agency, but was certainly not the opinion of Thomas, who despatched James (USA), his nephew, to oversee J. & P. Coats's interests stateside. James was an obvious choice as he knew the business, had already spent time across the Atlantic, and had married Sarah Auchincloss (whose last name is no coincidence) in 1857, so had more than a passing interest in their New York agency. He moved to the US permanently three years later as a sort of replacement for Andrew.

His arrival could have been timed a little better. With the outbreak of war, duties on cotton goods had been raised to 25%, yarn prices rose by a third, and the two sides in the conflict started to print money, usually a prelude to serious inflation. This occasion was no exception, and $1,200 Confederate dollars at the end of the war were equivalent to $1 from the beginning. Inflation in the North was less severe, but still amounted to 75% over the period.

Coats coped better than most in 1861, but even so, their US business was down 55%, and expansion in the UK did little to offset this collapse. J. & J. Clark were even harder hit, unable to expand in Europe due to increased local competition and under attack in the UK by Coats, who were trying to compensate for terrible US sales. They also struggled to find Sea Island cotton yarn supplies, whilst Coats was more proactive about solving their supply problems and invested in two companies as alternative cotton sources, one in Jamaica.

The next year saw a major turnaround. The demand from those states that were still accessible grew strongly, with rapid expansion in ownership and use of sewing machines, and the need for military uniforms and other textile supplies, most of which had traditionally been imported. Longer thread lengths became popular for the same reasons. This improvement and higher prices brought increased activity from US competitors, George A. Clark amongst them, but Coats was the big beneficiary, and with expanded home sales they reintroduced a night shift in Ferguslie towards the end of the year. Most of their competitors went for the cheaper army contracts, selling three ply polished thread and leaving the leaders alone in their traditional short length six cord consumer products market,[4] where their goodwill made them more difficult to dislodge and tariff protection was relatively lower. In any case, Coats preferred to stick with

4. Sold directly to the public through retail outlets, as opposed to Industrial thread, usually longer lengths, sold to factories.

this business, as they knew it would still be around at the end of the war, whereas the military supplies would inevitably dry up. Peter Coats, who had rejoined the business on a part-time basis with James (USA)'s move, was resting in the Hotel Victoria in Nice, when he accurately wrote: "...threads and other staples, war or no war, they will want and must have."

The year 1862 also saw the capture of New Orleans by the Union. This had two important consequences for Coats. First, they could reestablish contact with their customers in the city, an important sales district. Second, and more vital, it opened up a supply line for raw cotton from the American South. This gave them some much needed, if temporary, respite from the hand-to-mouth flow of cotton bales into their yarn spinners, and hence more regular deliveries and better quality yarn to Ferguslie.

Although volumes had improved, US duties on imported threads were raised in 1862 and again two years later, to the point where they were effectively 60%. The indiscriminate printing of banknotes[5] to finance the war, unrelated to the supply of gold, meant that the Sterling exchange rate declined, so that the UK suppliers to the US were being hit three ways: once by the increased tariff, once by increased effective costs in US Dollars, and once by reduced Sterling earnings from their dollar denominated sales. In June 1864, the worst month, Coats was converting their dollar earnings at 298; in other words, their exchange rate to the £1 was $13.23 instead of the normal $4.44. It is hardly surprising that their returns from the US were falling in 1863, zero in 1864, and decidedly negative in 1865.

The improved flow of cotton that had resulted from the taking of New Orleans did not last and, although Coats' volumes and US shipments rose some 15% in 1863, the following year saw the very worst of the cotton famine, with

5. The word Greenback comes from these banknotes, which were dyed green with a secret formula, making them difficult to counterfeit.

severe shortages of raw material and, therefore, yarn. US sales collapsed, and the local American producers, who were less severely restricted, reaped the benefit. With thread prices at the dizzy heights of $1.50 for a dozen 200 yard spools, several new thread companies had entered the market, and some of them were even beginning to make a quite respectable six cord. With the South gradually opening up to commerce and the war nearing an end, Coats saw it as vital that they maintain their market leadership. Almost in desperation, they held their prices at the current unsustainable levels and had Auchincloss mount an advertising offensive in the hope that any recovery would play into their hands, with the massive excess capacity sitting waiting in Ferguslie for just such an eventuality.

As with almost everything that Coats did, this move exasperated George Clark, who wrote that, "Their glory in this hemisphere is departed". He was in the throes of setting up a large manufacturing plant in Newark and obviously wanted better pricing to help him through his initial teething troubles. He was not the only one looking to produce in the USA—James Coats (USA), despite George's affirmation of the company's imminent demise, was rumoured to be looking for a suitable manufacturing site in or around New England. He was apparently scouting in Patterson, New York, about seventy miles north of New York City, and news spread that Coats was to build a large plant there. He even visited his rival, keen to find out how far along the plans with the new Clark plant were progressing, for, as George wrote afterwards to Peter Kerr, "If we succeed, they must either follow or be driven out".

Worse news reached George Clark in early 1865, when the price of cotton finally slumped, as the war was about to end, and demand for war related textiles collapsed. Despite this, longer-term prospects were good, particularly for the more traditional thread products, but dealers were holding off ordering, expecting prices to decrease sharply. This they did, but far harder and faster than expected. By March they had reached $1.30, with Coats offering a 3% cash discount. George was furious, writing to Peter Kerr, "They say they will burst up any makers in the trade, themselves also, rather than let their American trade slip away. This price with gold at 200 is equivalent to 1/5d[6] for six cord. It would not surprise me that they dropped £20,000 this year."

Prices kept dropping, with Coats charging $1.00 with a 5% cash discount. But they had survived, and even though import tariffs increased again, they made a profit of over £17,000 for the year. Part of this came from improved home sales. Aggressive advertising, a new 400 yard "long length" six cord, and the introduction of a less expensive glacé product allowed them to cut into their competitors' markets. They increased their Sterling sales by 120% between the beginning and middle of the decade. J. & J. Clark were certainly one of those most affected, and it is significant that they became more heavily involved in manufacturing and promoting darning thread and crochet products at around this time.

By now the Civil War was over. Slavery had been abolished by the thirteenth amendment. Abraham Lincoln had been reelected at the end of 1864 and assassinated in April of the next year. Hostilities ceased within a month, and Andrew Jackson became President. With peace came renewed prosperity; the stage was set for a new era for the Clarks and the Coatses—manufacturing outside Scotland.

6. About £0.07. The UK average price for 1865 was 1/8d. (£0.083).

Chapter 12

US Competition

Agriculture, manufactures, commerce, and navigation, the four pillars of our prosperity, are the most thriving when left most free to individual enterprise.
Thomas Jefferson

George Aitken Clark arrived in the US some five years before the Civil War started, at the age of thirty-two. Educated at Paisley Grammar School, he was sent away to start his professional life with Kerr & Co. of Paisley, allowing him an early opportunity to spread his wings by travelling to Hamilton, Ontario rather than learning the trade in his hometown. Kerr & Co. were sewing thread makers and friends of the Clarks, so the seventeen-year-old George had the chance to taste life abroad and absorb the essentials of the business well away from the family, only returning to Scotland after celebrating his twenty-first birthday. Following a brief flirtation with shawl making, he joined forces with his brother-in-law, Peter Kerr, who was married to George's younger sister, Margaret. Peter had been producing heddle twine and sewing thread on a modest scale and was an accomplished technical thread maker with two passions in life, literature and whisky. With the latter hobby under control for the time being, he helped his friend build Linside Mill, which was not only right beside Seedhill, but was also appreciably larger than the family's main factory. Their partnership was called Kerr & Clark, and in 1851 they began to produce cotton thread on spools.

George was a gregarious man with a quick mind and a lively sense of humor. He possessed boundless energy and, being a teetotaler and lifelong bachelor, he directed his enthusiasm completely to his business, something he did for his entire life. Like Andrew Coates, he was very much the family rebel, though his relationship with the other Clarks was much less harmonious than Andrew's with his brothers. George believed implicitly in Thomas Jefferson's ten rules for life,[1] and carried a copy with him, often quoting them to his friends and business associates. His one failing was that he saw doom and gloom in any reverse and could not accept that sometimes things just don't go your way.

But above all, he absolutely despised J. & P. Coats.

This coloured his behavior and was in many ways the secret of his success. He was obsessed with making Clarks into a unified company, rather than the ragtag that existed at the time. He was also convinced that the USA was where the company needed to be, very probably because he could see Coats's enormous success there and his own family's reluctance to follow them. Within two years of the start of production, Linside was concentrating on exports to the US, and two years later he left Peter Kerr in charge and set off for the New World.

1. The list is interesting and has some well-known axioms for life:

- Never put off till tomorrow what you can do today.
- Never trouble another for what you can do yourself.
- Never spend your money before you have it.
- Never buy what you do not want, because it is cheap; it will be dear to you.
- Pride costs us more than hunger, thirst, and cold.
- We never repent of having eaten too little.
- Nothing is troublesome that we do willingly.
- How much pain the evils have cost us which have never happened.
- Take things always by their smooth handle.
- When angry, count ten, before you speak; if very angry, an hundred.

On the boat over he met John Frederic Milward,[2] who had been charged with setting up an agency for his family's needle business. They agreed to share an office and set up at 32 Dey Street, New York, not 100 yards away from the site of the future World Trade Center. George was sole agent for both Kerr & Clark and J. & J. Clark, under his own name. American thread sales increased despite the 1857-58 financial crisis, and Linside had to expand. By then they supplied the vast majority of his sales, though he had developed some additional trade for J. & J. Clark. It was around this time that he began to seriously consider producing in the US.

Manufacturing of cotton sewing thread in America began with Samuel Slater's wife in Rhode Island (see page 32), but did not develop there until seventy-five years later. Many producers in New England made a halfhearted attempt at matching the products imported from Scotland in the wake of the Clarks' invention, but success eluded them.

E. J. W. Morse of Dedham, a small town twelve miles southeast of Boston, started an exclusive thread mill in Easton in 1834, but made little progress, as their three ply product was no match for the Coats six cord. The Sagamore Company of Portsmouth, New Hampshire tried to manufacture an equivalent to the superior import, but also found it too difficult (and probably expensive), so they abandoned the attempt.

The first serious challenge to Coats in the US came from Jonas Brook & Bro. in Meltham, which lies between Leeds and Manchester in England. In 1845, they introduced Brooks' Patent Glacé, the forerunner of their famous Goatshead brand. Although it could in no way be said to match the six cord equivalent, it had a smooth finish and one great advantage: it was cheap. The advertising, done by Strong & Smith in New York, described it as combining "the lustre of

2. George Clark took on the Milward agency at a later stage, but this was Milwards' first contact with "Coats", who would eventually acquire the company under the name of Needle Industries, in 1973.

silk with the strength of linen", which was Nirvana as far as any thread user was concerned.

This product got the attention of the American manufacturers, who were all looking for a cost-effective way of competing with Coats. The first to take the plunge was a small outfit in Connecticut called the Willington Thread Co., which had started operating in 1841. Elisha Johnson was the company president, and a first-class thread technician called Origin Hall was working for him. They subsequently bought the rights to manufacture the polished product, and although they only had about 1,000 spindles, they were important because of their association with the next significant player.

This was the Willimantic Linen Co. of Willimantic, Connecticut. Two entrepreneurs, Austin Dunham and Lawson Ives, bought a cotton mill that had originally been built in 1824, with the intention of manufacturing linen fabrics and shoe thread. Their choice of date, 1854, was less than propitious, for no sooner were they ready to produce than their flax supply dried up due to the Crimean War. Faced with a total absence of raw materials, they decided to switch to an alternative niche product, cotton sewing thread.

Their plan was inspired. They lured Gardiner Hall (Origin's brother, another brilliant thread man) away from his own thread business to supervise the conversion of the mill to cotton thread production. They bought the Willington Thread Co. and thus secured the services of both Origin Hall and Timothy Merrick,[3] two more thread experts. They obtained all the rights to make glazed thread in the US, and, finally, they foresaw the devastating effects of the looming Civil War on cotton supply and stashed away large quantities at precisely the right moment. Their growth was impressive, and the company soon acquired the moniker "the Thread City", a name which has lingered even though the factories are now all closed.

3. Merrick was married to Hall's daughter, and would go on to form the highly successful Merrick Thread Company.

Their success did not go unnoticed, and several others entered the market. By 1860 there were seventeen sewing thread concerns in the US—seven in Connecticut and five each in Massachusetts and Rhode Island. Five years later, production for the Civil War and rising prices had attracted twenty more.

One of these, Greene & Daniels of Central Falls, Rhode Island, had progressed from production of coarse yarns for sale to others in 1840, to selling a fully finished polished thread, on spools, by 1855, when they had leased a larger plant. Their Ivory Finish sold 35,000 dozens a week, based on a patented polishing process developed by Daniels.[4]

Willimantic ended the war in a very strong position. The tariff protection afforded them by a government eager to generate funds to finance the war gave them access to Civil War orders, while sellers of imported thread struggled to match their pricing. They joined several other textile manufacturers in the area in lobbying successfully to get a flowage law approved, allowing them rights to cheap water power. Perhaps most telling for the Scottish competition, their investment in highly skilled technicians paid off when they developed a method of controlling humidity in the twisting process using steam. This allowed them to make a very acceptable six cord, which under further tariff protection in 1864 competed effectively with the Coats product. They built a second mill and raised their capital to $1 million.

There was at least one silver lining in all this for George A. Clark and James Coats (USA). Willimantic had disproved the theory that twisting in the northeastern USA was impossible due to an unfavourable climate. Manufacturing in America became a real possibility for the Paisley companies.

4. George A. Clark got quotes from them for US supply of glacé thread at one point, so he must have contemplated local supply and hence manufacture well before he took the plunge.

Chapter 13

George A. Clark in Newark

As a friend, he was sincere, and always ready to perform a friendly act. His genial disposition made him welcome wherever he went, and it might be truly said that none knew him but to love him.
Written about George A. Clark in *The History of Essex and Hudson Counties*, NJ, Volume 1, p 612.

George kept trying to persuade his brothers James (of Camphill) and Stewart, who were in charge of J. & J. Clark, that the future for their business lay with him on the other side of the Atlantic. Unfortunately, they were very wary of the US market and became even more so as the Civil War loomed. George was hopeful that the addition of John Clark (of Gateside) to the board in Paisley in 1860 would help change their world view, but although he was a kindred spirit,[1] his relative youth and inexperience (only thirty-three years old, with a background in shawl making) meant that his more open mind held little sway, at least for the moment.

Given the lack of enthusiasm on the part of his siblings for all things American, George decided to set up an experimental spooling facility on his own in Newark, New Jersey, thereby avoiding paying the higher duty charged on

1. Both were teetotal, lifelong bachelors with a strong work ethic.

spooled thread imports. He brought hanks of thread in from Paisley and finished them locally on thirty hand spoolers in a rented facility that measured only 320 square feet. This was near where the Ballantine Brewery was located at the time, "on Front, Fulton, Rector Streets and the Passaic River".[2] The year was 1860.

His choice of Newark is curious, as most thread manufacturers were in Connecticut, Massachusetts, and Rhode Island at the time. Newark (originally New Ark) had been settled in 1666, when Robert Treat bought it from the Hackensack Indians. Treat was the leader of the New Haven puritans, who moved from Connecticut when the new liberal administration there refused to restrict voting rights exclusively to members of their church. He paid for the land with a wonderfully eclectic collection of items: gunpowder, one hundred bars of lead, twenty axes, twenty coats, guns, pistols, swords, kettles, blankets, knives, beer, and ten pairs of breeches for a total value of $750. He then assessed a percentage on every family that settled there within the first year to cover this cost.

In 1836 it became a city and was a growing centre for leather production, mainly for shoes. Carriages, coaches, lace, and hats were also made there, and the arrival of the Ballantine Brewery from Albany, New York, run by a Scotsman from Ayr, presaged an explosion of the population, growing from 17,300 in 1840 to 105,000 in 1870. The Civil War hit the city hard, but this suited George, as there was plentiful labour available when he was looking to expand. The fast developing railroads, the Morris canal (connecting to the Delaware River), and the Passaic River all meant good access to customers.

No sooner had he established this venture than the Civil War intervened, putting a damper on his ambitions. In 1861,

2. From *Newark The City of Industry*, published under the auspices of the Newark Board of Trade, 1812, p. 168.

his brother Alexander arrived, having been persuaded to join him to help with the expanding business. They opened depots with stock points in Boston and Philadelphia, and this allowed him to take on an additional agency for Milwards Needles, but his main sales continued to be Kerr & Clark's threads, with small amounts for J. & J. Clark, as well as linen thread for Peter Kerr and embroidery braids from John Clark Jr. In 1863 the agency changed its name to George A. Clark & Brother.

A year later, sales had collapsed, despite adding shawls, crochet yarn, and darning cotton to the portfolio. Supplies of cotton and, hence, yarn from the UK were sporadic at best, and yet Coats seemed to be managing fine, which infuriated him. Local competition had made inroads into the market, and import tariffs had been increased. His Paisley rivals were rumoured to be scouting out a site for US manufacture, and on top of all this, his newly named company was in the process of making a loss of $4,161 for the year.

The world seemed to be conspiring against him, and he became discouraged. Alexander did not share his dedication or enthusiasm for the enterprise and, despite being a good salesman, was more fond of the business lunch than the business. Peter Kerr had always been partial to the occasional dram, but had lately allowed the bottle to get in the way of his work. This was a real worry for George, as he was completely dependent on his partner for the smooth running of Linside. His constant exhortations on the value of the US thread market still did not impress J. & J. Clark, even though the newcomer John Clark was at least willing to entertain his ideas. Like Andrew Coates before him, George viewed his brothers at home as a rather conservative and parochial lot. They, in their turn, regarded him as an obsessive empire builder with a one-track mind.

For J. & J. Clark, the US thread market looked like an increasingly competitive one, where the Clark name meant almost nothing, and exchange rate fluctuations made earnings uncertain. It also opened up the chance of severe retaliation if they put Coats's position in America under attack, endangering their own relatively strong position in the UK and Europe, and would also mean diverting expensive resources away from their main markets. Their reluctance was understandable.

This did not interest George, who decided to do something about his plight. He started by expanding the spooling operation. He went across to Scotland, earmarked the spooling machinery he would need, and arranged to bring over trained operatives. He also made a series of visits to local spinners in Lancashire, to view the latest machinery and make a plan for his dream mill back in the US. Whether he sought financing for this project in Scotland or not, he got none, so he returned to Newark eager to get started, independent of his brothers and Peter Kerr.

By the time he returned, tariffs had once again increased, so he accelerated his plans for the spooling plant, having operators and machinery in place by late autumn, despite the terrible market conditions and cotton shortages. He then sat down in his New York office and wrote out a circular, ostensibly for all his colleagues and customers, but really as a challenge to himself. In it, he declared his intention to build a fully integrated American large-scale thread mill "thereby adding in some degree to the permanent resources and capital of the Country", but only if the current plant was a success. He followed this patriotic pronouncement with a campaign to raise the necessary capital for his venture.

His relatives in Scotland were unenthusiastic, but there was a glimmer of hope that this might change, as he wrote at the beginning of 1865 that, "The home market is overdone. John [Clark] writes me doleful letters by every mail. He says between J. & R. [Clark] and Coats he thinks they will be cut out. I am satisfied we can make more money here than at home!" In the meantime, no money was forthcoming from the UK.

He did, however, raise $500,000 from local sources in the US, and together with another quarter million, which he subscribed on behalf of Kerr & Clark, he formed the Passaic Thread Company, capital $750,000, becoming its Treasurer, the equivalent of Managing Director. Alexander was Secretary, and they had two Americans, Henry Sanger and Lewis Coleman of Boston, as President and VP.

At last he had the wherewithal to take on the Coats behemoth and the local manufacturers, whom he appeared to detest almost in equal measure. As he wrote to Peter Kerr in January 1865, "Like you, I am sick, heartily sick, of everything American. I am determined that I will not let the infernal Yankee drive me out of this market if I can help it". For a man who promoted the US as the place to do business, he obviously had little affection for the country.

His little spooling factory continued to do well, and the end of the Civil War meant the resumption of a dependable flow of raw materials and yarn. With plentiful cotton came a price collapse, and the knock-on effect through the supply chain meant that thread values slumped. Lincoln's assassination had few commercial repercussions, and the enormous expansion of sewing machine sales, which had already reached 100,000 a year, but would be five times that a dozen years later, meant that the demand for sewing thread was as buoyant as ever. US immigration and the spread of the population to the West were opening up new markets every day.

George bought a piece of land between Passaic Street and the river of the same name, at the end of what became Clark Street. He started building immediately and used his flair for advertising to publicise its sheer size. A typical example appeared in *Scientific American* from January 1866:

> The Clark Thread Company [by this time he had changed its name] are erecting a new factory at Newark, N.J., comprising six buildings, the largest and most extensive in the country. Four millions of brick will be used. The main

> edifice is to be 323 feet long, 105 feet wide, and five stories high. The foundation of the main building is composed of solid concrete—a firm mass of stone and mortar. The walls are three feet thick at the base, falling off gradually in proportion to the height of the building.

The mill, which was designed to house 50,000 twisting spindles, was a hugely ambitious project[3] considering some of the uncertainties involved. It was supposed to produce about 150,000 dozen of the less expensive glacé three ply thread and 50,000 dozen six cord per month. It included spinning for the first time in any Clark or Coats mill worldwide, so the overall size was greater than the capacity implies. George had a vision of where the American thread market was headed and now had the finance to begin chasing after it.

The company' name change from Passaic to the Clark Thread Company was another way of promoting the good name he was acquiring, and his partners, William Barbour and Abraham Hooley amongst them, agreed to raise the share capital to $1 million if needed. It acquired the plant, machinery, and trademarks of George A. Clark & Bro., as well as the famous Anchor brand, which J. & J. Clark had begun to use in 1864.[4]

George also adopted another trademark to combat the entrenched position of the Coatses as market leaders with their Six Cord. This was the tremendously successful O.N.T. brand, which stands for the remarkably unoriginal "Our

3. About the same capacity as Ferguslie at that time and larger than the Seedhill complex in Paisley.

4. They had originally acquired this brand from an old Paisley thread maker called John McFarlane, who had retired in 1820, the year J. & J. was formed. He had liquidated all his assets to pay off the debt of a friend, for whom he was the guarantor, but the brand had remained, and they willingly took it. It is unclear why they then left the logo dormant for over forty years.

There is no record of where the Coats "Chain" trademark originated. It seems to appear for the first time in the 1860s.

New Thread". It had been registered in its unabbreviated form in Paisley in 1856, and Kerr & Clark first used it for six cord thread two years later. In the US, it reached unimagined pinnacles of success, being so well promoted in its shortened form that there are people within the company to this day who erroneously think it was the Coats group's original corded thread.

In October 1865, not long after its introduction, he advertised it with a letter written by a customer who stated that he had examined all the principal six cord threads sold in the USA and "I find your New Thread very much superior in strength and elasticity to any of the other threads examined. I can, without hesitation, recommend it as the best spool cotton for hand or machine sewing now sold in the US". He also added, "I find that Nos. 50, 60 and 70 of the J. & P. Coats' spool cotton are only 4 cord and their No. 80 three cord". This last statement is ingenuous, as it implies that the Clark versions are all six cord, which they certainly were not. It appears that truth in advertising was no more prevalent 150 years ago than it is now.

The construction of the plant plodded along, slowly falling behind, much to George's frustration. The market was buoyant, and he could not get enough thread, either ready for sale or for spooling in the small finishing plant, now 30% larger than the year before, but still woefully inadequate for the demand. To add insult to injury, Coats, who had always had a policy of keeping high inventory, were making "enormous shipments to New York of nearly 200,000 dozen spools a month". The Clarks in Paisley berated George for not holding stocks in the US, but he politely pointed out that he could not build inventory if they could not supply it.

The troubles with thread from Paisley turned his thoughts to Scotland. He felt he could spare less and less time for Kerr & Clark due to his American commitments, and once the US mill came on stream, he realised that he would no longer need to buy from them, as his intention was for Clark Thread to be self-sufficient. He was also getting "horrible" reports from his brothers about Peter Kerr and his drinking, so he felt that a neat solution would be to sell off his share of their company and hopefully persuade his brothers to absorb Linside into J. & J. Clark. He had hinted at this to John Clark as early as February.

He now decided on more direct action. He told his partner that he wanted to sell his own £18,000 share of the Linside mill to allow him to concentrate 100% on his US business. He then indicated to John Clark that they should find some mechanism to put Linside and Seedhill together, and he set sail for the homeland to see if, by some miracle, he could make this happen. This time his prayers were answered: an agreement was reached to amalgamate J. & J. Clark and Kerr & Clark as of August 10, 1865. His dream of a unified Clark company to compete with the Coatses head-on was taking shape.

He returned to the USA, ready to dedicate himself wholeheartedly to Clark Thread. He had the intention of readying the plant for production by spring of 1866, but this proved impossible. He had quality issues with supplies from the newly enlarged J. & J. Clark (now known as Clark & Co., to add to the confusion) and found it hard to convince them that the Americans wanted only the best, whilst harboring a feeling that they viewed his market as one of quantity over quality. He continued to suffer from supply shortages and was convinced that they were giving priority to the UK, Europe, and even Canada. In desperation he even bought J. & R. Clark's 2,400 yard product directly off the boat, rewinding it to the more traditional 200 yards and selling it as if it were his own. He hated to create trade for his family rivals but saw no alternative.

These problems occupied much time he could ill afford, with the new factory in a critical phase. He had brought over a mill superintendent, coincidentally called William Clark, but no relation, to look after production at the Fulton Street plant in 1864. William was a thread expert who had worked for Peter Kerr from the age of twelve. After twenty years there, he had been moved to Linside in 1851 to help establish the new mill and had remained as a manager until coming to the USA thirteen years later. He was therefore ideally qualified to manage the installation of new machinery. The small spooling plant was running as well as it could with limited thread supplies, so George moved him to oversee the project, but this did little to help, as much of the machinery had not even arrived.

These delays and escalating building costs left the company short of cash, having multiple outlays but no production or inflows. The original share capital of $750,000 had only been 25% paid up. Several calls for more capital were made over the period, and when a particularly hot summer added to the startup woes, he became so desperate for cash that he sold some of his shares in Clark Thread to his brothers in Scotland. Their lack of faith in his abilities is demonstrated by their resale within the year for what he described as a "moiety of his business", i.e., a pittance.

The machinery finally started up in August 1866, and the whole spinning department was running by the end of September. Ring spinning[5] machinery was commercially available by this time from both Whitin and Lowell, and had been adopted by several of his US competitors, notably Willimantic. He did not believe that this modern production method could make best-quality fine yarns, particularly for six cord, so he had gone for mule spinning,[6] based on Crompton's invention, but by now vastly improved.

5. Ring spinning is a continuous process where twist is inserted in the yarn via a spindle that rotates in the centre of a ring. The mass of fibres is pulled by the spindle through a small hoop or "traveller", shaped like a *D*, which is free to rotate on the ring. The action of pulling causes the traveller to rotate, adding twist to the yarn.

6. In mule spinning, the whole spindle carriage moves forward, inserting twist. It then moves back, which wraps the yarn onto the spindles, so the action is intermittent.

The Mules proved troublesome, as the flooring was not perfectly level, and machinery breakdowns and quality problems had caused three complete stoppages by the end of the year. Trained workers were brought over from Paisley but many left for other, better-paid work. Then to cap it all, the SS Britannia, with another group of girls from Paisley on board, went missing and turned up after more than a month on a crossing that would normally last half that time. He passed a "miserable" Christmas, wishing he had never started the whole project and complaining that, "With my eyes open, I sacrificed a life of independence for one of dependence".

At the January 1867 board meeting he had to face his shareholders, who were expecting dividends but got none.

However, all things must pass. George's problems with the new mill eased, and he found himself in the enviable position of having a large amount of "American" capacity which Coats lacked, much less dependence on others for his supplies, and a spanking new mill with a well-trained workforce and a reliable manager. The year 1867 was a good one, with sales of six cord (O.N.T. and Anchor) in excess of a million dozen. The mill made a healthy profit and, as a result, Clark Thread paid a dividend of 10%. His salary was fixed at $10,000, and the sales commission for George A. Clark & Bro. was raised a point to 5%. Alexander had resigned and returned to Scotland in early 1868, and his brother William, who had been over on several occasions to give him support, was now permanently in the US and had become a director of Clark Thread. Life was good.

This moment of euphoria for George arose despite his rather weak position relative to his hated competitor. He was most interested in toppling their position with six cord, using the O.N.T. and, to a lesser extent, Anchor trademarks. The Coats product was better-known, it had more accumulated goodwill, and, although George's advertising was innovative, using the American angle to appeal to a surge in patriotism, it was essentially gimmicky. Sales were going to depend, as usual, on a combination of price, quality, and availability, and Coats had a definite edge.

George's costs were higher, especially in six cord, due to a combination of startup inefficiencies, lack of scale, and high US costs for fine yarns. He complained that Clark & Co. were also charging him too much for thread, but they needed the capacity for home sales, so had to ensure that they made similar returns when producing for the US. This meant that his margins were low, and local competition for polished thread meant meager profits there too.

Coats had more space and could therefore store more inventory than he could. Even if he had the room, he found it very hard to build stocks, as his new mill took several years to reach peak efficiency, demand was buoyant, and he continued to suffer with sporadic delivery performance from Paisley.

In the Coats camp, James (USA) was neither as dynamic nor as able as his Uncle Andrew had been, so Auchincloss ruled the roost as far as sales strategy was concerned. They were conservative, had deeper pockets than the constantly cash-strapped George, and could therefore attack him easily with discounts, credit, and the newly developed thread cabinets,[7] which were particularly important out West. Whilst James Coats (USA) and Ferguslie were probably more relaxed about the man they now considered as their main competitor, their agents had no such notions and were gunning for a fight.

7. These were made of walnut, cherry, mahogany, or maple and had between two and sixteen drawers, full of thread. Most were at the smaller end of this range and sat on top of the store counter with the trademark showing. They were often used as desks, and in fact there were larger models with sloping tops that served this precise purpose.

There is a suggestion in *Pills Petticoats and Plows* by Thomas D. Clark, that Coats invented the thread cabinet, using "by-products of their spool factory" and putting a cabinet making section into their American plant in Pawtucket in 1877. They were probably imported back in the 1860s.

Across the Atlantic, Clark & Co. added J. & R. Clark, who owned the Burnside mill, to their growing empire, further consolidating their position, but despite this addition, there were still an excess of Clarks in the US. Clark of Mile End continued to do solid business, and another one had appeared, the nephew of J. & J., son of their younger brother, Andrew. This company was named J. Clark & Co., and they sold a thread with a £ trademark, which looked exactly like the Anchor at a distance. They luckily only lasted for a dozen years, but were definitely a distraction during this critical period. Another company, run by two more members of the Kerr family, started up in Underwood and began selling thread on both sides of the Atlantic with the ingenuously designed N.M.T. trademark, directly against O.N.T.

Most customers would be forgiven if they were not at least a little confused by all this.

The Coats and the newly enlarged Clarks, whose manufacturing complex of Seedhill, Linside, and Burnside had become known as Anchor Mills, continued to advance in Europe and the UK on the back of surging sewing machine sales. The rise of Singer had been especially beneficial, with their innovative sales and service system, widespread use of hire purchase schemes, and particularly the opening of their Glasgow factory in 1867.

The US market was expanding even faster. Immigration was booming, with an average of 325,000 people arriving every year. The reconstruction of the southern states after the war was at an advanced stage, and the railroads were sweeping across the continent to allow access to the Midwest and the West Coast. The spread to the West was picking up speed, with up to 500 wagons going that way every day, the majority to the Golden State, California.

US thread sales were being boosted by the spread of the sewing machine, just as in Europe, but prices were coming off the wartime highs, and selling was stimulated by the timing of price reductions. Coats was the laggard in this as they held the largest stocks, so they suffered more than others. Over time, their pricing and terms reached parity with Clark & Co. in Scotland, but not with George Clark. He needed to stay price aggressive to push O.N.T. and Anchor six cord threads, and he maintained that neither Clark Thread nor George A. Clark & Bro. had anything to do with the Paisley Clarks. They agreed with him but were concerned that Coats might turn to Clarks' more traditional markets if George continued to take market share from them in America. Coats's encroachment in Europe and the UK in the next two years justified their fears.

Coats suspected that Clark & Co. had as much as a 50% stake in Clark Thread in the US, and, as George was also a partner in the Paisley firm, and most of his unfinished thread came from them, their point of view was understandable. George vehemently denied any such connection, and in January 1869, in response to overtures from Auchincloss, he flatly refused any pricing arrangement suggested, and the Clark Thread Co. unanimously passed the motion:

> Whereas the firm of J. & P. Coats, being a foreign company and the Clark Thread Co., an American or domestic company, having no connection whatever with any Thread firm in Great Britain, therefore resolved: That at this time it is not deemed for the interest of the Clark Thread Co. to make any agreement binding themselves to sell their Six-Cord cotton at the same price and on the same terms that the Agents of J. & P. Coats may adopt for the sale of their Cotton in this Country and that the matter of price and terms be referred to the President and Treasurer with power. [8]

The gloves were off, and price-cutting ensued. Six cord reduced from $1.10 at year-end to 90¢ + 5% discount for cash a month later. Coats cut their home price from 1/9d. to 1/5d.

8. From the Coats papers in the Glasgow University Archives. Also quoted by J.B.K. Hunter in his *History of J. & P. Coats to 1896* p. 69.

and hinted that they would reduce the US price to 50¢ if forced. At this point George threatened to denounce Coats for dumping thread into the US. He was caught between a rock and a hard place: he knew that if he lowered his price further, his adversary would follow, but he also knew that he was unable to compete with the Coats product at an equivalent price. He opted to stand firm unless Coats, "acting like crazy people", lowered the level to 65¢, which was where he feared they might reach. He then persuaded Clark & Co. to get some of their more friendly wholesalers to buy up large quantities of Coats product at these unprofitable levels, but spread out over different areas and in quantities not large enough to get their attention. These were then sold on in other markets, such as Canada, hopefully at a small profit. Although this was highly unethical, George was not always rational when it came to competing with Coats and would do absolutely anything to win.

Costs began to rise, but despite this George knocked off another 5¢, to which Auchincloss predictably responded in kind. At these levels, most of the trade was unsustainable, and there were no further reductions, but it was already too late for one newcomer to the thread business, Hezekiah Conant. However, his misfortune was Coats's gain.

Chapter 14

Hezekiah Conant and Coats in Rhode Island

The two most important requirements for major success are: first, being in the right place at the right time, and second, doing something about it
Ray Kroc, Founder of MacDonald's

Hezekiah Conant was born in Dudley, Massachusetts, on July 27, 1827. He was educated at Nichols Academy, started only a few years before by a wealthy industrialist named Amasa Nichols, who had built a cotton mill there using water power from the local French River and had made his fortune. As was the norm at that time, Hezekiah took his formal lessons during the winter months when it was impossible to cultivate the land, but in summer he worked on his father's farm. Even at this early age, he showed a talent for all things mechanical, so it was no surprise when he was apprenticed to a printing firm, Estey & Evans, who published an antislavery newspaper called the Worcester County Gazette. This publication failed within two years, and he moved on to another paper for a year before getting work in a machine shop.

This was the first turning point in his life, as it allowed him the wherewithal and the time to take further classes at Nichols for a year, as well as to apply himself to independent study of mechanical drafting and engineering. This led to his first invention, in 1852, a pair of lasting pincers, a tool used in shoemaking that a friend had suggested. Despite taking out a patent, this was not a great financial success, and after several more mechanical jobs, including a brief spell in Boston, he ended up in Hartford where he got work in the Colt firearms factory. Here he got to know Christian Sharps, who had invented and later improved the Sharps rifle, the world's first breach loader, which, although it only held one shot, could be primed and fired much quicker than the old musket-loaded flintlock rifles. This could also be achieved lying down, a distinct advantage in war! Whilst doing drawings and helping build machinery for Sharps, he invented an expandable gas check ring for the rifle, which had been shown to leak gas through the breach after prolonged use. Conant's modification solved this problem, and he patented it on April 1, 1856. It was said that Sharps paid him $80,000 for the rights.

In the same year, Samuel Slater (who keeps popping up) asked him to build a machine to sew the selvage of their company's doeskin woolen cloths, which he did, but without registering it for a patent. Whilst working on this, it is likely that he saw Slater tinkering with thread production, and he got the bug for the product, so he next devised both a machine for dressing sewing thread[1] and an automatic winder for 200 yard spools.

He sought a patent for the winder, which brought him to the notice of Willimantic, who sent for him to demonstrate the machine at their stockholders' meeting in January 1859. They were so impressed that they bought half the rights and immediately took him on full-time as their mechanical expert. In this capacity he conceived and built a ticketing machine, which would cut, glue, and apply tickets to both ends of their spools at a rate of one hundred per minute, a production speed unsurpassed till more than a century later.

1. Presumably some form of wax applicator.

After five years with Willimantic, he visited Europe and took in the top spinners in the UK as well as the Ferguslie and Anchor mills, though how Willimantic managed to smuggle him into these two, their main competitors, is a mystery. A year later he became mill superintendent at twice his original starting salary, but after his three-year contract expired, he left with the intention of setting up on his own account. In his nine years with them they had doubled in size.

He moved to Pawtucket, Rhode Island, which gets its name from the Indian word for "the place of the great falls". It remained largely unnoticed until Samuel Slater started the first textile mill and first American factory there in 1793. After that it became a thriving iron working and textile town, and by the time that Conant arrived, it was already home to several small sewing thread producers.

He lost no time in finding partners, arranging finance, and establishing his new enterprise, and in November 1868 he formed the Conant Thread Company with a capital of $30,000. Land was bought from Messrs. Fales, Jenks & Sons (both partners in the original company charter) on the corner of Pine and Potter streets. The latter no longer exists, but the plant was located approximately at the end of what is now Congress Street. The foundations were laid on December 5, during a heavy snowstorm that held up the proceedings for several days. Despite this inauspicious start, a brand new wooden building about 50 feet by 100 feet, on two floors, was finished by March.

Hezekiah could not have timed his new venture much worse. When they broke ground, the price of sewing thread was still at $1.10 and margins were healthy. During January, the exchange between Auchincloss/Coats and George Clark/Clark & Co. took place, and the price immediately fell about 25%. In a masterpiece of understatement, he later explained, "this seemed to check enthusiasm a little", and with the future price picture "somewhat clouded", the partners of Conant Thread realised very quickly that their venture was unlikely to make enough money to sustain itself. An alternative strategy was needed. Conant had met the Coatses in 1864, so he wrote to them on March 1, with the mill only 85% finished, proposing that they might "use the Company's buildings, machinery and capital in their interest."

Timing in life is everything, and Hezekiah was like the cat that falls off the roof and not only lands on all four paws, but right next to an enormous bowl of milk. James Coats (USA), spurred on by both the tariff barriers and George Clark's new establishment, had been trawling around for a suitable US site for Coats to manufacture in America. They wanted to buy a going concern rather than have to start from scratch, as George A. Clark had done, but a suitable candidate had not presented himself until the letter arrived.

A reply was sent off immediately indicating their keen interest in the venture, providing Conant could guarantee a production of 5,000 dozen spools a day—an enormous commitment given that George Clark's mill at Newark was only designed to do about 8,000 when fully operational. They knew Conant, both by reputation and from his earlier visit to Ferguslie, and were obviously in a hurry, as they asked him to communicate with Auchincloss directly, rather than via the slower transatlantic conduit, stating that "If they consider from your reply that there is some likelihood of our making an arrangement we would be glad to have you take a run across to this side at our expense, as a personal interview would be much more satisfactory".

He left for Paisley on May 1, 1869 and was back on a boat from Liverpool before month end, with a contract in his pocket promising him a twelfth of the profits of the company and instructions to build a new, larger mill beside the existing one. Coats put in an extra $70,000, raising the capital to $100,000 and giving them control of the company and ownership of the other half of the patent on the Conant spooler. James Coats (USA) was named company President, with Hezekiah as general manager. The deal was ratified at a hastily convened stockholders' meeting on June 10.

Spooling started immediately in his original building, using Ferguslie thread, but on a very small scale. At the same time, he bought eight acres of land, contracted the required machinery, and started on the foundations of a new building (Mill No. 2) on August 1. This was to dwarf the initial structure, being four storeys high and measuring 70 x 300 feet. The construction was spurred on by the urgency of the Coatses, so that finished thread was already being wound there in April 1870. A bleachworks followed promptly, with the necessary machinery being imported from the UK.

Most of the workforce was recruited from the UK. Coats, in common with other companies setting up for the first time in the US, needed skilled artisans, which in their case meant particularly dyers and colour technicians. Their advertising in local newspapers in and around Paisley and the Lancashire area was designed to lure experienced mill workers over to Pawtucket, with promises of higher wages, subsidised sea passages, and help in finding inexpensive housing. Many came over, including the mill supervisor, the ubiquitously named Scot, James Stewart.

Unlike the Clarks in the US, Coats had decided to start their manufacturing with Conant in the same way as they did it in Scotland, i.e., with yarn brought in from elsewhere to be twisted and finished. However, good yarn from US suppliers proved hard to find, as most concerns there were fully vertically integrated with their own dedicated spinning. Importing was the only answer, but the introduction of further punitive duties on yarn imports put paid to this, so a spinning mill was required. This was built to the north of all the other buildings, a third again as big as Mill No. 2 and holding all the spinning operations, from bale to yarn, with 50,000 spindles.

Coats had never done their own spinning before, and it can be safely assumed that their knowledge of the process and the whole technology of the spinning mill was at best perfunctory. As jealous of their quality as Newark, they also shunned modern ring spinners, preferring the proven technology of self-acting Mules. This may have been a rather unadventurous attitude, as several US companies had introduced the newer process and were making medium and coarser yarns quite effectively that way, but it is difficult to argue with success. They finally introduced ring spinning some fifteen years later, coincidentally at the same time as the Clarks.

There was another reason for their conservatism. Some of the American six cord manufacturers, Willimantic in particular, had started making all but the very finest threads with the true six cord structure, whereas Coats, Clark, and most others made the coarser counts in six cord, the medium ones in four cord, and the very finest in three ply.[2] At Auchincloss's insistence, Coats had introduced a policy of making all of their six cord threads, including the finest, in a true 2 x 3 configuration. The potential quality problems inherent in such a policy meant that the decision about mule spinning was a no-brainer.

They were, however, much more adventurous in the twisting department, where they installed ring twisters rather than the older throstle type already in extensive use in Ferguslie. They were on safer ground here, not only because they knew the process from forty years of experience, but they also had the leading manufacturer of ring twisters on their doorstep, in Pawtucket.

Two floors were added to Mill No. 2 in 1874, and Mill No. 4 followed a year later, bigger than any of its predecessors and largely dedicated to spinning the finest, best quality threads. A dye-house and a box-making section

2. Just as a reminder, six cord is two ply thread twisted back threefold and four cord is 2 x 2.

were built in 1877, and No.5 was completed in 1882, in response to the demand surge of 1879. Twelve years after Hezekiah had started his first building, the total area occupied was nearly 100 times his original, rather modest factory, and similar in size to Ferguslie. By the time of Conant's death, ten years later, it had become one of the largest manufacturing plants in the country, employing about 3,000 people.

Although Hezekiah remained as manager, overseeing the rapid expansion of production, centralised control from Ferguslie meant that nothing new could be tried without thorough testing in Paisley, so he started to work on new inventions, some unrelated to thread production.[3] This did not concern Coats, as they now had a palpable presence in the US and were a viable competitor to George Clark's Newark plant. Sales went from 3.8 to 9.6 million dozens in the 1870s. Once again, they had followed the Clarks and trumped them.

Conant also produced one very useful tool for Coats. A frequent problem with spool tickets was (and still is) that in certain climactic conditions they come unstuck. The thread on the spool is then difficult to identify as to size, colour, and even manufacturer. Hezekiah invented a "knurling" machine that could emboss the necessary information directly on the wooden spool. This was tremendously popular, much copied, and eventually became the subject of a protracted lawsuit with the Merrick Thread Co., which Coats lost.

3 His most famous gadget was a multi-pendulum isochronous regulator—a sophisticated clock with four pendulums. These were connected by an ingenious differential mechanism to a single wheel, which averaged out the inherent errors in a conventional pendulum clock and provided "...a new and improved time measuring instrument which is perfectly isochronal", as described by the man himself in a patent book from August 23, 1887. The first clock, built for the Tiffany Clock Makers, was completed on Feb. 28 of that same year, and an example was exhibited in the Time Museum in Illinois, until the museum was closed. The clock was subsequently sold in 2004.

Chapter 15

The Death of George A. Clark

No one can confidently say that he will still be living tomorrow.
Euripides

While Hezekiah was building, expanding, and inventing, two important events took place. The first was an honor for the Coats family, as Peter was knighted on July 9, 1869. It was said that the new Prime Minister, William Gladstone, had wanted to make him a Lord, but that his son James (USA) had discouraged this, as he did not want to inherit the title whilst working abroad, for fear of embarrassing the company. The title was, as much as anything else, for Peter's contribution to industrial expansion, his generosity to the town of Paisley, and his support of the Liberals.

At almost the same time, Peter Kerr was over in the US visiting his friend and business partner, George Clark. On August 3, a couple of weeks after arriving, whilst taking an afternoon swim in the sea off the New Jersey coast at Long Beach, Peter drowned, despite being a good swimmer. He was only fifty-one and had just built himself a colossal mansion at Gallowhill, on the outskirts of Paisley, but would never occupy it. George was deeply saddened by his passing, for although he had constantly berated him for his excessive drinking and lack of focus on their business, he liked the man, as did everyone, for he was friendly and was renowned for his good taste. It took some time for George to put his heart back into the rivalry with Coats.

His fight with Auchincloss had continued, much to the consternation of the smaller thread companies, who were slowly being driven out of business by totally unsustainable price levels. They kept making overtures to the large Paisley firms to see what could be done and managed to engineer a meeting in September 1869 with James, Stewart, and George Clark and a Coats delegation consisting of Thomas, his newly recruited son James Jr. (Jimmie), James (USA), and another newcomer to the company, his younger brother Archibald, affectionately known as Archie. He had been a partner since 1864 and was being groomed to take the reins of the business, supported by his American based brother and his cousin. Both Thomas and Sir Peter had now reached sixty years of age and were turning their thoughts to philanthropy, allowing their offspring to assume responsibility for the day-to-day running of the business.

The meeting ended in deadlock.

To make matters worse, both cotton and yarn prices retreated further, so thread continued to reduce throughout the next eighteen months. Wholesalers became very fickle, willing to change suppliers for a tiny discount, so Coats reversed a policy of some thirty years and began to sell notable quantities direct to retail, something that Clark & Co. could not afford to do at the time. This gave Auchincloss important leverage with the domestic trade in the US, cementing their customer base. They also offered free shipments to anywhere east of Omaha (the geographical centre of the US), effectively neutralising the effect of an attractive Clark discount. They spent heavily on advertising, offering free display cabinets to retailers and wholesalers and making a big deal of their switch to true six cord, "in all lengths from No. 10 to 100". Although George Clark followed them with O.N.T., it took him a year to set this up, and they made significant sales gains over the period.

Whilst struggling with the switch to finer yarns, the ever devious George and one of the Clark Co. shareholders, Abraham Hooley, devised a scheme whereby Hooley, who was based in New York, imported Coats's finer count six cord from the UK and sold it to the US market. As Coats had not made the switch to genuine six cord in all sizes in Britain, it was then easy for anyone to point out that their advertising in the US was false, thus harming their reputation. Coats realised what was happening and changed the label colour in the UK from gold, which was almost indistinguishable from the US product, to green. They also brought legal action against Hooley's company (who had advertised the product), though more to frighten him than anything, as they were advised it would almost certainly fail.

Part of the reason for George's unorthodox behavior toward his competitor was his exasperation with his Paisley relatives. Whilst Coats was developing their new plant in Rhode Island, they got substantial quantities of thread from Ferguslie and built up large stocks in anticipation of the hefty tariff increase to be introduced at the beginning of 1871. They even built a warehouse to hold the excess.

George's supply from Clark & Co., on the other hand, was sporadic and insufficient, and no amount of cajoling seemed to make any difference. The members of the board of Clark Thread Co. were becoming infuriated by the seeming lack of concern shown by their colleagues in Scotland and suggested bypassing them and buying directly from Manchester or even fining them a shilling per pound for every unfulfilled order. As he explained to his brothers "Our President is very anxious to hold a fair stock in advance of the duty...and every day asks me if I am urging you. I say I am. He says show me the results. He is fully more disappointed than I am".

Despite all this and more, the flow of thread from across the Atlantic continued to be more of a trickle than a torrent. There were good reasons for this. The Paisley Clarks regarded O.N.T. as at least partial competition, and they understood that as the Conant mill came on stream, it would free up capacity in Ferguslie, which would then be used to attack them where they were relatively strong, in the UK and Europe. They were therefore very uneasy about aggravating Coats, which was George's greatest desire. So they were perfectly content to give George just enough thread to keep his shareholders happy and himself comfortably off, until their two businesses could be merged. New Year 1871 came and went, with a 20% duty increase in imported thread, but no more thread for George.

Shortly thereafter, Coats discovered who was behind the Hooley plot and wrote to George explaining that they had taken legal action against Abraham Hooley & Co., going on to accuse him directly, but offering him the "...opportunity to retrieve the injury done to us, by at once taking the necessary means to put an end to the business complained of."

George and his brothers immediately wrote deeply apologetic letters and received an affable reply from Thomas, suggesting that if the Hooley trade could be stopped completely, then business could resume as normal. Shortly afterwards, Sir Peter Coats was observed in deep discussion with John Clark in the centre of Paisley, which was felt by George to be further good news.

Within two weeks, hostilities ceased, much to the relief of the smaller companies who had been dragged along in the wake of this clash of titans. Coats and Auchincloss adopted a more flexible attitude to the antics of George Clark, and George himself became less aggressive as his business flourished. The lawsuit against Hooley was later dropped. Peace had descended on the sewing thread world.

George was so relieved as a result of this that he took off round Europe but in typical George fashion, his itinerary was anything but relaxing. He first visited London, Paris, and Cologne, sailing up the Rhine to Mainz, on to Hamburg, and then spending a few days in Zurich. He next scaled Rigi, a 5,900 foot peak in the centre of Switzerland, spending the night in the hotel that still exists at the top, followed by a day's sailing on Lake Lucerne. He finally took in Berne and Geneva, travelled over to Dijon, and made his way back to Liverpool via Paris, which he had enjoyed so much it merited a return visit. This took two months to complete, and he sailed back to New York on July 19 on the SS Russia.[1]

It turned out that this was to be George's last holiday. For the next eighteen months he was at peace with his competition, thread sales were buoyant, and his mill expanded. He bought more land on the east side of the Passaic and built a warehouse and counting house. Then, after breakfast on February 13, 1873, he complained of chest pains and summoned a physician, who stayed with him all morning but decided to leave at midday with the patient much improved.

1. On his final night in England, he apparently stayed in the Adelphi Hotel, and when he went to pay his bill the next morning he was a bit taken aback to be charged £6 for "Mrs. George Clarke, 2 children and nurse". After explaining his unmarried status and the spelling of his name, he sent for his bags, only to discover that these were missing. They had been sent with those of the mysterious "wife" when she had asked for hers to be brought down. After a "regular row" with the bell captain, he rushed to the docks, where he found the SS Russia, his bags, and the entire Clarke family (no relation), who were booked on the same ship.

Whilst this is a great anecdote, it is almost certainly apocryphal, as there is no sign of any of the mysterious other Clarke family in the ship's passenger list, though George was definitely on the boat. We can only assume that it was "embellished for effect".

Shortly afterwards, after drinking some water and feeling better, he collapsed and died before the doctor could return. In his last year, with the business finally going as he had envisioned, he had begun to talk of retiring to "auld Caledonia" to fish in Scottish streams and leave the pressures of work behind. After a funeral in Newark, he got his wish of returning to Scotland, his remains being sent there for burial. Little did he know that his death would finally allow his dream of a united Clark business to come true, but that was still in the future.

Many tributes poured in on both sides of the Atlantic. The board of Clark Thread in the US recorded the "loss of a true and noble man, whose ability and judgement made him conspicuous, whose modesty and gentleness combined with unflinching firmness gave him commanding influence".

George complained all his life of the lavish lifestyles and excessive generosity of the Coats and Clark families, and Peter Kerr was berated as improvident when he spent an admittedly staggering £20,000 on his mansion at Gallowhill. The Clark family in Paisley and, by extension, the Coatses, were all said to spend too much on the ostentatious trappings of wealth that had people murmuring, "You are well off, you are in the thread trade". He also viewed charitable munificence as an invitation for other competitors to enter an industry that was obviously a goldmine. It is therefore surprising, but at the same time gratifying, that his legacy included several generous gifts to Paisley, including the Town Hall (see page 297).

George's brother William was left in his place, and being less aggressive towards his competition, he dedicated himself to developing the business and expanding capacity in the US, rather than sparring with Coats. He effectively doubled the size of Newark within a year, adding George's greatest desire, a thread store, and acquiring a spool maker in Maine. He also bought up a second ten-acre site across the Passaic for future expansion, the Ballantine Brewery having taken all the land on the same side as the mill. This would turn out to be a shrewd investment for the 1880s.

With the main competitors at peace, others could prosper from the rapid increase in sewing machine ownership. John Clark Jr. of Mile End made steady progress on the eastern seaboard, particularly with his white thread, which was sold on black spools, making the product and the thread stand out.[2] They now decided to follow their rivals into local US production and established a finishing mill just south of William Clark's newly purchased site. It is not clear why they chose to be so close to the founder's second cousin,[3] but there may have been some collaboration between the two companies.

Meanwhile in Scotland, Ferguslie was modernising to keep up with ever increasing demand. Wages were rising, particularly for skilled jobs, and they had their first strike in 1870, amongst a group of night shift workers. Although this was dealt with swiftly and harshly (a lockout and thirty ringleaders dismissed), it was sufficient motivation for them to examine ways of improving productivity and reduce their dependence on labour-intensive processes. Invigorated by the success of new techniques in the US, Ferguslie set about replacing and increasing capacity throughout. They introduced ring twisting—the first textile company in the UK to do so. Spooling was updated with both Conant's new twin-headed invention and the even newer and improved ten spindle Weilds machine, which would become their standard for 100 years. They finally decided that they wanted control of their own colour application process, so

2. This so impressed Clark & Co. that they copied it, but John Clark Jr. and his partner Matthew sued George Clark as their agent, alleging trademark infringement (the spool end ticket was also similar to the Mile End version). They won, and the new article had to be withdrawn.

3. John Clark Jr., who died in 1866, was a second cousin of William, being the grandson of Allan Clark, eldest brother of the original James "tippence".

they bought up the Nethercraigs bleachworks and the George Street dye-house, where their thread was coloured.

They then turned their attention to facilities for employees, as they felt that a motivated workforce would be more productive. Besides buying more housing for them in the immediate area of the mill, they built a dining hall and a bowling green as the first stage in a policy of providing improved amenities. The mill was 2,700 strong in 1883, with production up 80% over the previous decade and productivity improved by 20%, largely thanks to automated spooling and, to a lesser extent, modern twisting. Even so, the Clarks had apparently done better.

During the 1870s, the expansion of the Clark complex was to eclipse the growth of Coats, to the point that they could arguably be called the number one thread manufacturer in Paisley (and, by implication, in Britain). The Paisley Daily Express in July 1878 pointed out that they were the largest consumers of gas and water in the town and that their wage bill was about £90,000, which was 50% greater than Ferguslie.

They got to this position by building two immense new mills, known as the Atlantic and Pacific, both five storeys high and located to the east of the other mills. They each housed about 70,000 twisting spindles, all belt-driven from central shafts, which ran the length of each floor. This system of power transmission had been championed by George Clark and met with the approval of his more conservative relatives in Scotland. The first was completed in 1872 and the second six years later.

The two new mills now sat beside the original Seedhill building, a four-storey hotchpotch which had been added to over the years and housed 12,000 twisting spindles and a large amount of finishing for export. Close by were Linside and Burnside, across the iron bridge on the other side of the Cart, but they abandoned the old Cumberland mill, which they acquired in 1854, as it was over a mile away and in poor repair. They consolidated production in the five remaining premises.

Anchor's total capacity had increased more than fourfold, and the workforce had doubled, reaching 3,000 in 1880. They had also taken the chance to modernise much of their twisting, with the new "ring" technology, just as Coats had done.

Interestingly, they still did none of their own bleaching and dyeing, as John Clark, the dominant force in the family, still believed it to be cheaper and more flexible to have it done on commission. Nor did they follow George Clark by starting their own spinning. Both would come in time.

By some measures, Clarks would appear to have taken the lead, with more spindles and a bigger workforce. They were also the first company in Paisley to introduce electric power, in September 1878.[4] But their profits were still well below those of Coats, hampered by the large thread range and consequent high cost base that was Anchor's burden, caused in part by amalgamating several different businesses, articles, and trademarks.

4. However, Coats got the drop on the Clarks when Archie became the first person in Scotland to have electric light installed in his house, Woodside, in 1882. Skeptics thought domestic subdivision and distribution of electric power impossible at the time. He had "200 lamps" driven by a 12½ HP motor, each giving off "16 candles of illuminating power", but he could only run 150 at a time. The bulbs were said to last 1000 hours, somewhat longer than they seem to nowadays!

Cotton sewing thread had one other connection with electric light. Edison experimented with it as a possible filament in his incandescent light bulb., some three years before. It was not a success.

Chapter 16

Management Changes

Every generation needs a new revolution.
Thomas Jefferson

Coats was being run to a large extent by Thomas, with Sir Peter working part-time and offering advice, but less interested in the day-to-day management. He had begun to spend far more time away from Paisley, either engaged in philanthropic pursuits or in Ayrshire, where he lived off and on until the death of his wife, Gloranna, in 1877. At that time he finally bought the house he had rented, Auchendrane, and moved there more permanently, splitting his time between Scotland and Algeria, where he wintered for health reasons.

With the withdrawal of Andrew from the US, Sir Peter's eldest son James (USA) had taken his place and had become an important junior partner in the Company. His younger brother Archie had remained in Scotland and, having trained as a multi-disciplined businessman, was being thought of as the one to take over from Thomas when he moved on. Thomas had three children who had become lesser partners, Jimmie, Thomas Glen Coats (who would eventually be knighted), and George, the future Lord Glentanar. Sir Peter's third son, also named Peter, rounded out the group.

In 1873, they had to rewrite the rules for dividing profits, as there were now eight family members involved. The split was typically cooperative, with Thomas and Peter each taking half. Thomas and his children then shared their part 62.5% for him and 12.5% for each of them, whilst Sir Peter took 40% of his half, with James and Archie getting 26.25% each, and his son Peter the rest, 7.5%. This was a ten-year agreement and would have lasted that long if Thomas hadn't died within months of the end.

As they progressed, the roles began to switch. Thomas was getting older and even took a year off in 1877 to sail around the Mediterranean with his wife and his brother Andrew. By the time he reached seventy, two years later, he was becoming frailer, losing his mobility, and taking more interest in his religion and hobbies (he was a keen astronomer) than the business. James (USA) had his hands full in the US, expanding Pawtucket and dealing with his Auchincloss relatives and the eccentric inventor Conant.

It was therefore natural that more responsibility should fall upon Archie, who was in his mid-thirties and had taken over his father's house at Woodside when Sir Peter moved to Auchendrane. Archie was punctilious, shrewd, energetic, dogged, and a master at grasping detail. He was quick to decide and act, but this sometimes made him impulsive and excitable. This was particularly alarming for those who went shooting with him, for he was quick on the draw and not terribly accurate, so they would always have one eye on their prey, but the other one firmly on Archie, just in case. He once shot his nephew, Alfred Coats, who eventually lost the sight in one eye as a result, but appears to have born no grudge, as he named his son Archibald.[1] Another time, John Clark returned early from a hunting trip with the Coatses and when asked why he was back so soon, he replied, "Archie Coats has shot every member of his family and now he has taken to shooting his guests, so I came home".

1. This Archibald never joined the company, as he was tragically killed at the very end of the First World War.

Archie was kindly and a good judge of character but could get loud and was almost too fond of practical jokes. He loved to fish both for salmon on the Tay and for cod and haddock from his brother Peter's boat, the Zara. But unlike most of his brothers and cousins, he suffered from seasickness, so although he often accompanied them, it was usually for day trips, always close to shore.

A Liberal Unionist, he had joined their new association founded in 1886 as one of the earliest members of the executive committee. He was asked to stand as a candidate in the next election, but surprisingly for a man who was to be constantly thrust into the limelight, he was of a retiring disposition and refused, preferring to work behind the scenes.

At work, Archie was skilled in selling and finance, but with no more than a passing knowledge of production. This had been "old" Thomas's original area of expertise, and he had been passing his knowledge to his son Thomas Glen.[2] Thomas Glen was artistic, well-read, and possessing the gift of empathy, a natural politician.[3] He also inherited his father's technical ability, so by 1879 he had moved into Ferguslie manufacturing, running the finishing department, but with a better general knowledge of production than the others of his generation. His brothers (including the young William Allan Coats, known as Willie, who at twenty-six was still not a partner) and Sir Peter's other two sons took on departmental management roles in the mill.

2. Thomas Glen-Coats was born Thomas Glen Coats. For reasons unknown, he changed his name to absorb his mother's maiden name in 1894, the same year he was knighted, becoming the redundantly titled Sir Thomas Glen Glen-Coats, reminiscent of Major Major Major from "Catch 22". His cousin, Matthew Arthur, made a similar change becoming Lord Glenarthur when raised to the peerage some years later.

3. He was the Liberal MP for West Renfrewshire from 1906 to 1910 and was active in the local party from his mid-thirties.

It is interesting, yet at the same time peculiar, that the two sets of four brothers neatly distributed and separated their roles within the business to such an extent that they knew almost nothing of each other's areas.[4] With Archie as Chairman and James in the US, Sir Peter's other two children looked after spinning (Daniel) and twisting (Peter). Both bachelors, they shared a rather modest house at 4 Garthland Place in Paisley and travelled to work together, never exchanging as much as a monosyllable. Such was their lack of knowledge of their fellow domains that they never discussed their respective departments and had never set foot in each other's territory. The same was true of their cousins.

Peter also had the important task of purchasing yarn. Ferguslie still bought about 70% of its yarn requirements, and he would contract a year's worth at a time (about 5 million pounds), which allowed him to command a very good price. He did not join the family company immediately, but first started a business in provisions in Liverpool. When this failed, he became manager of the Thorn Cotton Mill, where he learnt his trade in anticipation of working in Ferguslie later on.

He was a rather small man, immaculately dressed in a navy blue serge suit with a rose in his lapel during the brief Scottish summer. He sported a beautifully trimmed beard that became rather straggly and white in later life. Having had Scarlet Fever as a child, he was never in the best of health, and he had a perforated eardrum, so that despite trying a variety of hearing aids, he was always a bit deaf, which did not help his natural shyness. He never married; it never occurred to him. He enjoyed bridge, a good cigar, yachting, fishing, shooting, and archery.

4. The perverse pride they took in their ignorance of all things beyond the doors of their sections led to serious problems of coordination, and a plant general manager was taken on in due course to ensure a smooth flow of production.

Although generous,[5] he was also renowned for his extreme thrift, no bad attribute for a yarn buyer. After becoming a partner in J. & P. Coats at the late age of forty-eight, he bought Whitney Court on the Wye in Wales. To get there, he would go by train to Hereford, wait two hours for the connection to Hay-on-Wye, and would buy a separate ticket for each leg of the journey, because it was cheaper. On one occasion, he was being met at Hereford by a friend who was looking for a contribution to one of his daughter's pet charities. To seal the deal, he had bought Peter's ticket for the second train, costing 2/7½d., but Peter had a through ticket on this occasion and had no money on him, so could not contribute to the charity. However, he promised to send an appropriate amount in due course. When he returned to Whitney Court some weeks later, he was met by the daughter, to whom he handed a £5 note as a "small contribution for your charity" as well as 2/7½d, remarking "Please give this to your father. It has taken me some time and a good deal of correspondence to get it back from the railway company".

Peter's travelling companion to work, Daniel, was a man of unassuming appearance. He dressed so shabbily that the gateman at Ferguslie once refused him admission, as they "didn't allow tramps in"; the contrast with his impeccably dressed brother accentuated his scruffiness. He had a dry, pawky sense of humor, but was intensely shy. Despite all this, he was a proficient technician who understood the fundamentals of spinning.

He collected jewelry and coins, but as he grew older and more eccentric, he became obsessed with secrecy and would conceal his whole collection in various hiding places around the house. Someone once asked to see one of his rare Japanese coins and, after taking ten minutes to retrieve it, he remarked, "They will have a queer hunt to find this when I am gone".

5. He gave extensively to the Alexandra Infirmary and left his fortune in trust to charity.

He later bought Brockwood Park in Hampshire, where he enjoyed spending much of his time alone, even though it fed his strange paranoia. He had an extension and a water tower built by a Paisley architect, Balfour Abercrombie, into which a secret den was incorporated for his collection of knickknacks (and, it was said, bunches of £100 notes). The plans were kept secret and, as the architect died in the trenches fighting for the Black Watch in 1915, and the foreman in charge of the construction was also killed in the war, the whereabouts of the hiding place went to their graves with them.

Daniel died suddenly of a stroke, and the house was taken apart in an effort to find it, but to no avail. His will, which might have revealed its whereabouts, was never located: either he never made one or he hid it along with his valuables, so he died intestate, and his carefully hoarded collection was lost forever.

The remaining departments were covered by Thomas's children: Willie in dyeing, George in bleaching, Thomas Glen in finishing, with Jimmie overseeing the workshop and maintenance.

Willie was the last of Thomas Coats's sons to join the company, and he became relatively expert in dyeing, which was more of an art than a science in the late nineteenth century. He had spent a year in the coal pits before entering Ferguslie and retained an interest in collieries throughout his life, investing in and becoming a Director of Cardiff Steam Coal Collieries. He lived with his father until he married Agnes Muir in 1888, when they moved to Westfield House in Ayr. They had two sons, but she died at the age of twenty-seven after only six years of marriage. He had been a very quiet, private man and this tragic loss only reinforced that trait. His art collecting became his solace, and although he continued with his yachting and was a keen shot, he never remarried and his dedication to the company was never the same after her death.

George Coats ran bleaching. The polar opposite of Willie, he was a party animal who did extensive entertaining, and a keen sportsman with a passion for horse riding. His sporting instincts were not confined to his leisure time. He could sometimes be seen sneaking out of Ferguslie in disguise, bound for the stables, and when George was still quite young, a visitor to the mill was taken by surprise when he knocked on George's office door and, as it opened a crack, George's face appeared and exclaimed "Come in quick. I have a terrier in here...and some rats!"

He famously bought the Glentanar Estate, which is described elsewhere, and he was raised to the Peerage in 1916. As Chief Commissioner of the Scout Association of Scotland, he designed a special tartan for the use of scouts who had no tartan of their own. It was based on the Black Watch, but in three shades of grey, which made it exceptionally drab and therefore uniformly unpopular.

George was no technical wizard, but his natural exuberance, boundless self-confidence, practical nature, and infectious enthusiasm were great assets in the mill and later in the boardroom. He had an uncanny ability to separate the important from the trivial, and as would be expected of a man who had to run two estates and attend to business, he was a supreme delegator.

Thomas's eldest son Jimmie was shy to the point of being a virtual recluse when he was not sailing his yachts. He was a man of fine physique but was reputed to be a misogynist, so he never married. His love of sailing in all its forms was such that he had a house, Dunselma, built near Strone overlooking the Clyde estuary, so he could watch all the races. However, he hardly ever set foot in it, using it only on occasions for entertaining.

There is a story told of a man who appeared in the grounds of Dunselma one day and was informed by the gardener that visitors were not permitted. The stranger announced "I am Mr. Coats" to which the gardener replied with a look of amusement, "No", he said "there's mony a man comes here wi' a story like that, but when Mr. Coats turns up hisself, we'll ken owt". Thus dismissed, Jimmie turned around without pursuing the matter any further, unable to visit his own home. The gardener, who retired shortly thereafter, was given a handsome pension.

So Archie was supported by two brothers and four cousins in the mill. Any technical weakness that he had in this area was well covered, and the structure was a natural fit. The baton may not have been passed from one generation to the next, but the younger Coatses at least had a firm grasp of it.

On the other side of Paisley, the Clarks had put much of their infighting behind them, and the absorption of some of the different companies into the Anchor group had helped to simplify their commercial offering as well. This trend was set to continue.

The main event of the period for the family was the death of Alexander. He had been suffering from ill health and had put in only sporadic appearances in the business since he left Newark. His ailments got the better of him in 1877, and he passed away just before reaching the age of forty. This led to interesting discussions about the future structure of the Clark Thread Company in the US. George's shares had been taken up by various family members when he died, and if the same were done with Alexander's, and William agreed, the company could finally be absorbed into the Clark group, as had been George's original wish when he first set out for New York. This duly happened on January 1 of the following year.

James Clark of Camphill had been the senior partner for nearly twenty years and as such had tended to impose on his younger brothers and the others in the Clark organisation, much to George's annoyance in particular. James was getting older, and ill health was starting to affect him, so he took a back seat and allowed others to take over. This led to a more democratic and harmonious boardroom, with the role of leader falling naturally to his younger brother, John Clark of Gateside. He had been sympathetic toward George's expansionist inclinations in the US and was the most dynamic and open-minded of the family. His grip on the Clark business was to tighten over the period, and this helped accelerate their growth.

He was accompanied by his nephew Robert and two younger brothers. The oldest, Stewart, had a legal background, but was timid and shy, so he was completely overshadowed by his sibling. The second brother, William, spent his time and efforts on the business in Newark, and, as such, had little influence on the other regions. He eventually became an American citizen. Robert, son of James of Camphill, was a salesman, largely based in the UK covering London amongst other territories. From the late 1870s he would be destined to spread his net ever wider as competition extended beyond the shores of the UK and the USA. Constant travel to places all around Europe and Russia were to be too much for him, and he went to an early grave in 1885, aged only thirty-one.

Finally, the Clarks were still being supported by the Balderstons, with Robert managing Anchor mills for over forty years and John, his brother, another partner.

So the decade of the 1870s ends with both the Coats and Clark businesses well managed. They each have mills in the US capable of supplying that area largely independent of their Scottish factories, and the US plants have freed up capacity in the UK, which has also been modernised and increased. New markets are now required to fill it, so the new men in charge, John Clark and Archie Coats, will have to go farther afield to find new selling territories. The great war between the families continues, but the battleground is about to shift, and a new general is joining Coats.

Chapter 17

Otto Ernst Philippi

Everyone lives by selling something.
Robert Louis Stevenson

Choosing where to grow was not as simple as it would seem. The good news was that overall sales volume was rising, not only due to Singer, but also with increased population. The world had nearly 1.5 billion inhabitants in 1880, and Europe accounted for 320 million, over three times the size of the USA. The railways were making transport and communications easier, industrialisation brought income growth, and the unification of Germany and Italy gave these markets added attraction.

Price competition between thread companies was also limited. In particular, Coats, Clarks, Carlile, Kerr & Co., Ashworth, Brooks, and Chadwicks all dealt with trademark abuse, wages, working hours, excessive "gifts" as advertising, and underselling in similar ways, so a level playing field was the order of the day.

The less good news was that everyone was trying to expand into the same markets—Russia, Austro-Hungary, and Western Europe. With increased demand came increased competition. Clark & Co. and John Clark Jr. of Mile

End were much better established than Coats in the more attractive areas of Europe and Russia, and Jonas Brook had perfected their Goatshead polished article, which had become a market leader in many centres.

Europe was quite definitely different from the US, which was Coats's main area of expertise. Their European shipments went out through agents in Glasgow, Liverpool, Hull, and London, and selling was performed by four principal agents, Adolph Spitzer for Austro-Hungary, who had 40% of the volume, Morris Hart in London, managing Russia (20%), Nicolai Wulff in Hamburg for Germany and Scandinavia (12%), and Emile Goudchaux representing the notoriously tricky French market, as well as Belgium, Holland, Spain, Italy, and Switzerland.

Goudchaux was paid a commission on sales and had to coordinate agents, etc., in every country except France, where Coats had a warehouse and paid for a traveller. In all cases, the agencies were taken on unsystematically and acted independently, so territories overlapped. There was duplication of effort (and orders) in some areas, and complete neglect in others. For instance, Russian sales were concentrated in Moscow, St. Petersburg, and Odessa, but Coats thread was completely unknown elsewhere.

Coats had no effective control, beyond issuing general recommendations, which would be interpreted and passed on quite differently in each area and country. As they had done in the US with Auchincloss, stock was replenished monthly for the principal agents. Information supplied on sales and trends was unreliable and difficult to compare across markets, as it was filtered up from local agencies who were usually in the business to make a quick killing and for whom sewing thread was probably a minor distraction. Little forward planning existed, so there were excessive urgent orders. Bad debts were a real problem, reaching as much as 10% of sales in some markets.

Things were actually worse than this. Each market was seriously fragmented, so the Coats policy of making limited numbers of items in large quantities was ineffective, particularly in the areas where they were forced to sell against well-established competition, which dominated the large cities where volume items were more common. Purchasing power was lower, so six cord seemed expensive when compared to the local competition, who made two and three ply products in nearby factories working long hours and paying miserable wages. Brand loyalty was deep-rooted, so getting customers to switch was hard. All this added to their expenses, without even mentioning the misunderstandings that resulted from multiple languages, something they had not come across before. Exchange rate issues and political instability simply exacerbated the situation.

Archie Coats was well aware of all these shortcomings and was under pressure to do something about them, but his training had not prepared him for such complications, and he was unsure how to proceed. He then happened upon the solution, thanks indirectly to John Clark.

By 1878, Italy had raised their import duties, and other countries were threatening to do the same. Europe was in the grip of a downturn, and both the big Paisley thread companies found their capacity standing idle. Faced with this situation, John Clark started to make direct exports to South America, and Archie realised that he would have to get someone out there to take control before the Clarks got too firm a foothold.

Coats's sales to the region had been sporadic. They had made a few direct shipments and sales through UK customers, but lately the Hamburg agent, Nicolai Wulff, had been picking up some increased demand. It therefore seemed sensible to get someone from that agency out to the market to see what could be done. The company thought that the best person for the job was Wulff himself, but there was another contender who had come to Archie's attention in the Hamburg office. When offered the choice of travelling or staying, Nicolai was not keen to spend months in the heat and dirt of Brazil, Argentina, and Mexico, so he sent the other candidate.

This was Otto Ernst Philippi.

Mr. Philippi, which is how he was known and addressed by everyone in the company from quite early on, was born in 1847 in Solingen, Prussia. His father Martin was a teacher. His family was of Greek extraction and had settled as bankers in the Hamburg area. He was utterly brilliant at school, but contracted typhoid fever when still quite young, which robbed him of 80% of his eyesight and a large amount of his hair, and also weakened his heart. Despite these multiple setbacks, he emerged with a quick and organised mind, beautiful handwriting, a relatively short temper, and the ability to converse fluently in Spanish, English, French, and his native German. He also sported a thick pair of metal-rimmed spectacles, and a magnificent moustache, which gave him the aspect of an old-fashioned family physician.

After a short time as an apprentice to a Dusseldorf wholesaler, he renounced his Prussian nationality and moved to England, entering his uncle's cotton broking business in Liverpool. This was not to his liking either, so he took a steamer to New York in the same way as Andrew Coates had done, to seek his fortune. This obviously eluded him as he was soon back in Hamburg, but as a British citizen, working for none other than Nicolai Wulff.

This time it appears that he had found his vocation. He worked his way up to be put in charge of the Coats agency business in Scandinavia. This involved travelling to the region to visit customers, evaluating the competition, and suggesting strategies to confront them and improve sales. As part of his duties, he wrote letters to Ferguslie, and his elegant script and bright intelligence brought him to the attention of old Thomas Coats and, more particularly, Archie.

When the mission to South America was mooted, Philippi went to Ferguslie for briefing and was offered the job of Foreign Sales Manager at a salary of £500 a year, with an initial contract for two years. His task was to pursue trade directly in areas where Coats's products had not been sold, rather than simply consign the goods to a merchant and rely on them for promotion and sales.

However, his immediate assignment was to visit every main port on the east coast, all the way from Argentina in the south to Mexico. When you realise that it takes ten hours to fly from Buenos Aires to Mexico City today, you get an idea of the magnitude of the area he had to cover. South America was primitive at the time, so it would not have been very comfortable.

His brief was clear:

> ...we wish you, in places where our principal competitors have little or no hold, to sell at list prices. While endeavoring to get as many good houses as possible to take up the sale, we wish you, in every town or district, to get a first class firm to undertake to push the sale of our thread against all others, and for an inducement to do so, to offer such firms a commission of 2½% or in certain markets, should it be found necessary, a commission not exceeding 5% on all their sales and on all our manufactures sold in their towns and districts as far as we can trace them, this commission to continue for five years or if need be, for seven years. In addition to this commission, in places where Clark & Co. have a firm hold, you are at liberty, if you find it necessary, to arrange to supply 200 yard six cord and Extra Glacé, at a reduction from list prices, not exceeding one shilling per gross, and other lengths in proportion. The maximum discount on all occasions being 10%.[1]

1. From the Coats papers in the Glasgow University Archives. Also quoted by J.B.K. Hunter in his *History of J. & P. Coats to 1896* p. 85.

So he set out in June, 1878 and spent three months collecting complete market information, visiting agents, wholesalers, and retailers, and getting the lay of the land. When he returned in September, Archie was delighted to hear that he had secured the Lidgerwood Manufacturing Company as the main agent and stockholding point for Brazil, Buenos Aires, and Montevideo. They were heavily involved in the coffee trade but had their head office in London, a factory in Scotland, and excellent contacts in the area. They agreed to sell Coats thread exclusively and accepted a 2½% commission, but only if sales exceeded an agreed target.

He arranged for other smaller agencies to cover the areas farther north, but again he negotiated terms well within the guidelines he had been given. The Coats partners were so pleased with the results that he was offered an additional £100 a year on his salary and ¼% on the returns from all business done in countries where they had no agents, except for Australia. At the same time, his brief was widened:

> It is understood that while you are to devote special attention to pushing or increasing our foreign trade, you are to make yourself generally useful in our business, and we are at liberty, at any time, to send you, either alone or in the company of our partners, to visit our Continental agents and assist them in developing our business, without being entitled to any commission on such business—the addition of £100 to your salary having been made with special reference to this part of your duties. [2]

The scope of the job description is such that he was being recognised, even at this early stage, as their expert in all international sales, apart, notably, from the USA.

2. From the Coats papers in the Glasgow University Archives. Also quoted by David Keir in *The Coats Story Volume 1* p. 193.

In a way that is reminiscent of many US companies nowadays, the family was uncomfortable with the area of "abroad", which was not responding to their traditional methods as Coats The Threadmakers. Nevertheless, they had the intelligence and humility to accept that there might be someone else more able to handle it. They were not unanimous in their endorsement of Philippi. Jimmie thought that for the extra £100, he should cover all of Europe, independent of the agency arrangement in each country, and Peter did not want commission paid to him on returns from countries where Archie personally appointed the agent. Luckily, these protests were overruled by both Thomas and Archie, and the appointment was confirmed. It was, as John Clark later ruefully admitted, "cheap at the price".

He was now firmly established at Coats, with an excellent salary and the potential to make a fortune from the commissions. Almost immediately, he and Archie set out to tour Europe and assess the situation. They visited France, Belgium, Holland, Germany, Austria, Romania, and Italy, with Philippi doing a solo tour of Bordeaux, Spain, and Portugal a couple of months later. This initial survey confirmed Archie's fears. Coats had inconsistent and patchy market coverage, little control over the actions of the super-agents, no control over their subagents, and unacceptably high overheads.

Philippi turned the agency system on its head. He did away with the idea of the super-agent, leaving Goudchaux in charge of Paris only and taking Scandinavia away from Wulff. He then established a stockholding agent in every country, with regional offices in the larger countries.[3] Territorial boundaries were unambiguously defined, and every order in a particular territory was to be channeled through the agent, even if first it had been placed directly to Ferguslie. If the volume potential of the thread was

3. For instance, France had two agencies in addition to Paris, in Bordeaux and Marseilles.

insufficient to sustain a healthy business, they would sell non-thread items to supplement their income.

Within a very short time, Europe had been reorganised, with some agents confirmed and others replaced. New agency agreements were established in China, Hong Kong, Singapore, Batavia (now part of Jakarta), Philippines, Australia, South Africa, Turkey, Egypt, Beirut, and Algeria along with those already developed for South America as a result of Philippi's initial tour.

In less than two years, Philippi took rigid control of international sales. All decisions on pricing, terms, and selling policy were centralised through his office. Whereas previously the agents only detailed sales and stock positions annually, he now started detailed monthly and quarterly reporting, with information on important individual customers, including things like credit rating and product ranges used, as well as competition and market analysis. He would follow up relentlessly by letter or telegraph and made frequent visits to keep the agents on their toes. He called meetings in Paris or London or even Paisley, which was a long way for everyone except him, and he brought the brightest and best to Ferguslie for training and indoctrination.

A new floor was opened up in the mill for his expanding department. He had to take on new staff to sift and analyse the multiple reports pouring in from every market, and he included several clerks from overseas, particularly Germany, to deal with the linguistic and cultural differences involved. He ruled this group with an iron hand and was involved in all decision-making, however trifling.

The result was that each agency received exact instructions on what to sell and stock, which customers to woo, with pricing and terms, advice on borrowing, and even caveats on exchange rate fluctuations. The agents and salesmen got commission, which was reduced to 1% in 1881, when Coats absorbed the payment (and control) of additional expenses. The focus was on bonuses for increased sales, but there was little left to the salesman's discretion, and the emphasis was on pure, hard selling effort. He and his department controlled everything else.

He also encouraged the cultivation of individual retailers, offering attractive bonuses and heavy advertising using show cards, calendars, and free samples. He did not discount products with quality defects, but replaced them at full price. In the appropriate circumstance, he would even offer improved payment terms and breaks on transport costs.

All this and the rather onerous reporting requirements meant high selling costs, so there had to be benefits, and these came in spades.

He limited product ranges in each market, and each product offering was tailored to that particular area, so the range was much greater than the one being offered in America, but it was a great improvement over what he had encountered during his initial tour. This was particularly true of France, where there was a tradition of high style and variety, leading to a large assortment of products. Goudchaux had simply accepted this and sold everything to everyone.

The main products offered were Coats Six Cord and Extra Glacé, in standard lengths of 200 and 400 or 500 yards. Most sales were in black and white, but a growing range of colours was offered in shorter lengths. Some demand for 1,000 yards reels for factories was beginning to appear, but this was still miniscule. One hundred yard spools were sold in the poorer markets, but requests for fifty yards glacé were refused on the grounds that these would be all wood and would undermine customer confidence in the company, as they looked like a bit of a swindle. Some larger companies would ask for special products, but these requests were met with demands for minimum quantities and a higher price.[4] This reduced manufacturing variability and hence costs and made control of stock levels much easier. It allowed Coats to offer the formula that had given them such success in America: good quality products, with excellent availability at a fair price. This made them a highly desirable supplier, which in turn let Philippi solve two serious problems.

Bad debts had been a major cost factor, but with Coats products becoming so attractive, and with all the additional information flowing into the foreign sales department, they were able to be both proactive and assertive in confronting potential payment problems. Within two years, the losses from this problem area had reduced to only 1% of sales, a significant improvement.

The other area of concern was price speculation. It was common knowledge within the industry that thread prices moved with raw material costs, and as these changes were well publicised, it was not difficult for customers to order large quantities anticipating an increase, or delay orders awaiting a reduction. The agents would readily take orders in the former case and would offer price reductions ahead of the date in the latter, to control stocks. Under Philippi's command, they had no option but to follow his instructions, and he would only favour a specific customer in exceptional circumstances and under conditions laid down by him personally. He could get away with this through Coats's position as leader in quality and supply efficiency.

So Otto Ernst Philippi, this bald, rather benevolent looking Teutonic tyrant, with the strange eyeglasses and the quick temper, had made an enormous mark on Coats. There is no doubt that if Archie had chosen someone else for the job, some of the benefits would have accrued, as improved communications and transport had helped almost everyone,

4. A classic example was Bon Marché in France, who wanted samples of 1,000 yard Extra Glacé, but were told they could have them only if they ordered just over 7,000 spools.

but the requirements of the situation played notably to Philippi's strengths. He was disciplined, aggressive, and driven, with an ability to embrace overall strategy whilst grasping the minutest detail. He was prepared to stand up to the family, and with Archie as his champion, he largely got his way.

He was also the first high-level professional manager to be given an important role in the company, which signaled the beginning of the end of paternalism, at least in the selling end of the business. The tone of their dealings with agents changed once he arrived, partly because he understood the discipline of selling better than the family and could therefore communicate more confidently, and partly because he was more familiar with European culture. He had arrived at the right moment. Competition between the thread companies was about to intensify and a sure hand was going to be needed to guide Coats through troubled waters ahead. Philippi was the man for the job.

Chapter 18

Thread Wars 1880s

I have always believed that writing advertisements is the second most profitable form of writing. The first, of course, is ransom notes...
Philip Dusenberry, American advertising executive

For the next decade, the thread trade continued to thrive on the back of several unique factors. Sewing machine sales were still expanding, and the invention of the oscillating shuttle by Lebbeus B. Miller and Phillip Diehl (an ex-Singer employee) opened up the possibility of a gas- or steam-driven machine enabling greatly increased speeds when compared to the old foot treadle. Higher speeds meant more thread.

Populations were growing fast, thanks to medical advances and improvements in agriculture, with Europe up 30 million to 390 million, but the US grew even faster, from 50 to 63 million, partly for the same reasons, but mostly through immigration. Transport and communications had improved, and more clothing, particularly cotton, was being produced.

Making sewing thread was not difficult. Yarn or thread could be bought, sent for dyeing, and then wound up onto a suitable spool, tube, or bobbin relatively inexpensively, and the success of the Coats and Clark enterprises attracted a plethora of competitors, principally in Britain, but also in the US. The introduction of import tariffs in several European countries in the late 1870s encouraged others to have a shot, and a whole range of small local companies began to appear.

Dollfus Mieg & Cie. (DMC) in Mulhouse, France, had started in 1746, but concentrated on printed fabrics of various sophisticated designs until 1841, when they began to make sewing thread as a part of their efforts to diversify. Their main thrust was in embroidery and crochet products, so they were more annoying to Clarks than Coats, but their geographical spread was a concern. Ackermann (1855) and Göggingen (1863) in Germany were not only effective at home, but were making inroads into Russia and South America,[1] as were Fabra y Portabella in Spain in the 1880s. Salcher in Austria had moved into Central Europe somewhat earlier, and there were others in Switzerland, Belgium, and Italy.

However, the main battleground was still the UK, where there were about fifteen thread makers of consequence. Just as in mainland Europe, the principal tactic of the smaller producers here was to cut prices to wrest business away from the market leaders. The larger companies were forced to respond by reducing prices, and this had a destabilising and depressing effect on the overall market. The weaker companies found themselves exposed they began to fall by the wayside and were absorbed by the leaders. Acquisition was a new experience for Coats, as their growth had been organic up to this point.[2] Clarks had already absorbed several of their namesake companies, and this was to continue.

1. A major interest for Coats, as nobody produced locally and the population was expanding rapidly.

2. Apart from Conant, but this wasn't really a going concern when they signed their agreement.

The first was J. Clark & Co. in Paisley, which had the £ trademark and had been a (small) thorn in the side of Clarks for a dozen years. The cost was £14,000 and the year 1878.

Then came John Clark Jr. of Mile End, some five years later. This was a surprise, as they had both the volume and the expertise to compete effectively with the big two. Indeed, their success had been the main cause of a strike threatened at Clark's Newark plants just the year before. William Clark had introduced wage reductions, citing the keen competition from the Mile End factory, who were apparently importing labour from Scotland to cut their costs. With hindsight, this may have been their last desperate attempt to ward off insolvency, but their reputation was such that when Clarks took them over, they retained the Mile End trading name.

This amalgamation gave Clarks several advantages: they obtained a mill close to their Newark installation and another large mill in Paisley; they could use black spools for their white thread, which they had been prevented from doing many years before; they acquired a prominent position in several markets, notably Russia; and, most importantly, all the companies with the name Clark in their title had now come together, for the first time ever. This removed any last trademark confusion and created a united company on a par with Coats.

Despite this, all was not well with Clarks. They suffered a series of stoppages in Newark starting at the end of 1888, largely due to the actions of a superintendent, Herbert Walmesley. He had started a campaign to prevent the girls wearing bustles in the mill and then had a dispute with a popular foreman, who left as a result. Some of the girls stopped work in sympathy. A nine-day strike, the cause of which was unknown, followed the next summer, and even a half hour reduction in the working day, whilst apparently much appreciated, did little to alleviate the underlying atmosphere of discontent.

Things came to a head when Walmesley admonished a spinner for poor work in December 1890. The unfortunate worker decided to answer back in an aggressive manner and was summarily dismissed. A group of his fellow spinners immediately came out in sympathy, refusing to work until the superintendent was removed. They even burned his effigy out in Crane Street. As the dispute dragged on, other departments began to go idle for lack of materials. William Clark decided to play hardball and closed the mill down. He then hired on new spinners from as far afield as Canada to replace the strikers and reopened with these new men in place.

This infuriated the old spinners, so they gathered outside the mill on the evening of February 11, joined by a crowd of some 2,000 sympathisers, and attacked the new men as they left the mill, causing injury to several. The next evening, a plan to bring them out half an hour earlier with protection from bodyguards ended in violence, and although none of the new workers was hurt, several of their escorts succumbed to the missiles hurled by a mob which now numbered about 5,000.

The situation escalated, and ominously by Friday the 13th the mob had reached 15,000. The police were powerless, and so many windows had been broken in the mill that there were none left to break. However, this proved to be the worst of the protest, and although the spinners were not reinstated, the company offered to take them back as and when vacancies opened up. With no support from the remainder of the workforce, they were forced to accept, and a strained peace was reestablished, despite murmurings of discontent.[3]

3. Walmesley stayed on for ten more years, but did not get a salary increase in 1892.

Meanwhile, their rivals prospered. When Thomas died in 1883, Coats had formed a joint stock company with a capital of £2,000,000, split into 20,000 shares of £100. The two families took half each, but whereas Thomas's five sons divided them equally, Sir Peter's did not: Archie and James (in the USA) took 80% of their half, leaving Peter with 12½% and the other two sharing the remaining 7½%.

They got busy. Ross & Duncan, where James Coats Sr. had been a silent partner in the early 1820s, became available and was snapped up in the spring of 1882. This proved to be a very shrewd acquisition for a number of reasons. Philippi persuaded Clarks to share the cost and become joint owners, whilst he retained management control. He then used the Ross & Duncan trademarks to fight the price cutters, so he could discount heavily without involving the main Coats brands and, therefore, limit his losses. He ostensibly offered to do the same for Clarks (as well as Brook, who declined the offer), but in practice he had control and would always favour Coats; this ultimately proved to be the downfall of this scheme, which only lasted a few years.

Then the repeated price cutting finally became too much for the oldest thread company in Paisley. James Carlile, Sons & Co. had been operating since 1752, when they made linen and silk threads, and although they had never experienced the growth of their larger neighbours, they had kept a respectable business running at their Bankend Mill by the Cart on the north side of town. However, their liabilities were now only just covered by their assets and they could see no future in the climate of continual price wars, so they suspended payments at the depths of the recession of 1885. Coats bought their assets, trademarks, and a subsidiary, the Linen Thread Company, all for £2,000. Their operatives were absorbed into the larger mills within the year.

Others fared better. Strong competition from northern England included Manlove & Sons of Chesterfield, who were the pioneers of "industrial" thread (i.e., thread used in manufacturing), who introduced the original 1,000 yard reel. Ermen & Roby in Lancashire were small but successful, and their price cutting was highly disruptive. John Dewhurst of Skipton in Yorkshire was a spinner who had begun to make cotton sewing thread as late as 1869 and was fast becoming a serious player. Others were strong price competitors in specific geographical areas, especially R. F. & J. Alexander in Spain and South America.

But head and shoulders above all these manufacturers, there were three companies who represented the main competition for Coats. These were Clark & Co., Jonas Brook & Bros., and James Chadwick & Bro. The first of the three is very familiar, but not the other two.

Jonas Brook & Brothers (James and Joseph) came from a family of weavers. In 1774, their father William moved to a village in Yorkshire called Meltham.[4] The family set up a fulling mill to do wool scouring and thickening, which they combined with farming. William later abandoned the manufacturing and went into wool broking and banking. Jonas and his brothers branched out on their own as wool manufacturers, but they quickly diversified into linen and silk sewing thread, starting what became known as Meltham Mills. The Brooks' product was more inclined to lower twist embroidery than pure sewing,[5] and their sales were largely in hank form for others to finish, but they had a successful cotton thread by 1830 and were selling in the US when Andrew Coates arrived there ten years later.

4. The origins of Meltham are either Saxon—the name appeared in the Doomsday Book—or more likely Roman, being a shortened version of Melitton (a place where beehives stand) or a variation on Mel-tun, or Honey Hamlet. It appears that bees thrived in this area at the time of the Roman occupation, when beehives would have been made from the hollowed bark of trees, and people would bring them from far and wide at the time when the heather bloomed.

5. They claimed to have made a cotton sewing product in 1802, several years before James and Patrick Clark, but it was never sold and was probably too weak to be commercial.

They had a commercial arrangement with Carlile of Paisley, and in 1841 they opened a new silk mill. Within ten years they were also making cotton products from bale to spool, so they started spinning for themselves twenty years before the Clarks or Coatses in the US. They also started to develop their famous Goatshead glacé cotton, the trademark coming from the crest on the family coat of arms. They bought the Royd Edge Mill in 1882.

Even so, they were tiny compared to Coats and had never been a concern, though their polished article had been attracting attention, and they had a Machine Cotton which sold well. They had spread their net wide, with depots in Australia and east Asia, where they represented serious competition, as well as in Russia and the USA. They sold way below Coats prices everywhere.

James Chadwick and Bro. were located in Eagley Mills near Bolton, England. The plant had first been established around 1790 to card cotton for most of the neighbouring textile concerns. Chadwicks acquired it in 1820 and began to make cotton tapes, braided cords, and sewing thread. They were taken over ten years later by one of their larger tape weaving competitors, J. & N. Philips, but retained the Chadwick name and transferred the manufacturing of tapes to the Philips plants, concentrating on the thread business. Their new partners had a profound influence on them, and they started to build both workers' cottages and housing for their foremen near the mill, as well as a school and other facilities. They bought a spool turner in Staveley, Cumbria in 1850 and followed this with a bleachworks.

When they built a twisting mill in 1871, they became a serious threat to Coats, as they had perfected a very acceptable six cord and a competitive three ply, both sold on spools. They were really aggressive on price, refusing any form of agreement, and extensive advertising allowed them to make major inroads into several overseas markets. The most important of these was Russia, where they would undercut Coats by over 15% and offer longer credit, but they also appeared in places as far afield as Australia and Argentina. Their Eagley spool became the market leader in Scandinavia, Mr. Philippi's old stamping ground. They even set up a spooling operation in Canada and a small finishing department in Bridgeport, Connecticut, and although there is little doubt that they were losing money on a portion of their sales, their volume grew and they built a second, larger twisting mill at Eagley in 1881.

Chadwicks were not the only ones to use advertising to grow or protect their market. Previously, newspapers were the chief form of publicity, but this decade saw major developments in the use of other kinds of marketing for thread products.

The most common way of establishing a position with a particular retailer was to give him one or more thread cabinets. A simple form of inventory control was to keep the cabinets full, and, although they were expensive, and it was customary to give them away, they would normally go hand-in-hand with a large thread order, typically 10 gross (120 dozen spools) or more.

Most popular in America, but not restricted to that area, were a whole variety of other devices to entice the enthusiastic seamstress, for the customers were overwhelmingly female. Coats put a six-inch ruler on the side of their spool boxes, so they had a use beyond simply holding the thread. Everyone sold or gave away thimbles, fancy boxes, photographs, calendars, paper dolls, and even shaving mugs (though presumably not for their female clients!), but perhaps the most ingenious forms of promotion were the trade card and the jingle book.

The use of trade cards exploded in the 1880s. The postcard and advertising card had both made their first appearance in the previous decade, and their popularity grew rapidly. Most of the sewing cards depicted threads being used to perform feats of strength: holding Gulliver down in Lilliput, or as a dog's leash, but others were simply pretty pictures of young girls, kittens, or children at play.

Some were factual. J. & P. Coats produced one that showed a man, his wife, and his two children each holding signs. The man's sign says, "75 buttons off", the lady's, 81, the girl's, 96, and the little boy's, 180. The ad goes on to say:

> This family requires the average amount of button-sewing in a year, according to a recent Home Mending survey. If you think your family pops off too many buttons, listen to this: "The poorer the thread the more buttons come off", commented many a woman interviewed, "If you want to sew buttons on to stay, it pays to use J. & P. Coats Best Six Cord". [6]

Others would raise an eyebrow if produced today, referring to colour, often black, and usually with a black person involved. A typical example shows the sun blazing overhead and a coloured boy sitting on a black spool saying, "We never fade". Another depicts a young black girl out in the rain being invited into the house by a young white girl. The caption says it all: "Missy tells black girl to come in out of the rain who replies that she is 'like Coats Black Thread, the colour won't come off by wetting'". Hardly what you would call politically correct nowadays.

An even more insidious form of advertising was the jingle. The champion of these appears to have been Clark's O.N.T., which was featured in a series of modified nursery rhymes, the idea presumably being to brainwash children.

6. From the *Spokesman-Review* newspaper (Spokane, Washington), Oct. 31,1935.

The technique in a more modern form is still used today for all kinds of products. Here are two examples:

O where are you going, my pretty maiden fair,
With your red, rosy cheeks, and your coal-black hair.
" I'm going a-milking kind sir," says she;
" And then to the village store for a spool of O.N.T."

Pease-porridge hot, Pease-porridge cold.
Pease-porridge in the pot, Nine days old.
Spell me Cotton without a C,
Why that's not difficult O.N.T.

Some of the poetry was less infantile, but the message was the same:

Our wedding day came in September,
My dress was a picture to see:
Orange blossoms and white—and remember,
Every seam sewed with Clarks O.N.T. [7]

Testimonials were also used; we already saw one for the introduction of O.N.T. Most were highly subjective and therefore allowed for much unfounded praise. An endorsement of the Kerr & Co. product by Lily Langtry, the English theatre actress and by then ex-mistress of the Prince of Wales ("Bertie", the future King Edward VII), was typical. She wrote from her hotel in Coney Island in 1883, "I am so very pleased to find your cotton this side of the Atlantic. I have used it always on the other side; it is vastly superior to any I have found here, and I prefer the shape of the spool".[8] It is doubtful she ever did any sewing, and the remark about the spool boggles the mind.

7. The first two from *Jolly Millers Wife & Other Rhymes*, issued by the Clark Thread Co. in the US in 1880. The other from papers in the US offices of Coats & Clark.

8. From *The Coats Story, Volume 2* by David Keir, p.1.

But Philippi was not too concerned with publicity. His dissatisfaction with the competitive situation was growing as he tried to develop Coats's overseas trade. He believed that honest competition involved sales growth being achieved through having a high-quality product always available to the retailer and, hence, the ultimate customer. Advertising, frequent salesman's visits, and similar hard-selling tactics were totally acceptable. He was convinced that price undercutting with no basis in cost was disruptive, introducing uncertainty and undermining product quality that did not lead in the long run to company growth and success.

He also expressed a long-term objective for Coats to attain at least a 50% market share in every territory for their main six cord articles, unless a lower percentage cemented their position in a larger, more important area. To this end, he continued to work tirelessly to improve the performance of overseas agencies, replacing the inefficient, introducing more travellers where needed, and reinforcing his network of information. As a result, Coats's position in South America, Austria, and the Balkans improved, largely at the expense of Clark & Co.

The largest thread market in 1885 was Russia, but Coats's sales there had shown little signs of growth. Robust competition from Chadwicks and Ermen & Roby, who had opened a depot in Moscow, and lack of drive from the Coats agents, Hart in St. Petersburg and Ferdinand Ebner in Moscow, were seen to be the main problem, so Archie asked Philippi to visit. This not only confirmed his dim view of both agencies,[9] but he also discovered that any disputes between either agent and their creditors would likely fall back on Coats, as the principal. Given the poor performance of both and this new legal wrangle, he decided to open a Coats agency in Moscow, a "Russia House". Both relationships were severed, and he put a young Russian

9. In addition to poor performance, he found that Ebner had been embezzling funds.

named Mickwitz[10] in charge, with orders to develop a sales force and open depots countrywide. The Russia House was opened in the name of Archie Coats, for the splendidly Scottish reason that Russian law required the payment of £100 "guild" for each partner, so why have more than one?

The price wars continued. Any attempt to make agreements among the competing firms was futile for two main reasons. They would only be short-lived, as the leader in any market (usually Coats) would always be heavily favoured, and it was also very hard to have the same prices for all markets, given the myriad exchange rates, commissions, volume bonuses, and transport costs, not to mention different lengths and finishes.

Despite the discounting, the "big two" embarked on new buildings in 1885. Coats decided that spinning in Ferguslie was the way to go, after ten years of success in Pawtucket, so they built an 80,000-spindle mill (covering all their fine count six cord), a bleachworks, a chemical lab, and a joiners' shop extension.[11]

They had started on a finishing mill earlier in the year, as had Clarks, who erected a six-storey spooling mill, symbolically covering the ground where their original Seedhill mill had been established some seventy years before.[12] The two companies also considered and rejected starting joint manufacturing in Germany and Austria as a counter to increased local competition and rising import duties. The Coats board apparently even rejected an initial flirtation regarding a merger.

10. It is unclear if this is the same Mickwitz who was later senior director at the Nevsky Thread Mill (see page 310). It probably is.

11. The move to local Spinning was not because of supply problems, but rather for quality reasons, mostly linked to shade variation between different suppliers. They leant heavily on the US mill for technical support and training.

12. Still standing today, this iconic building now contains apartments.

A severe slump followed, and competition intensified. In June, both companies cut the price of their standard reels by 12½%, stating they would not hesitate to keep reducing prices. The effect on the industry could only be imagined.

Chadwicks countered with the highly creative "penny" reel. This was, in its way, the precursor to the Dollar General or thrift store item, where the price point is more important than the product, which in this case was a 200 yard spool. Coats countered with a 170 yard product at the same price and a 70 yard spool for ½d. The Ross & Duncan trademark was deployed to parry similar situations overseas. They also introduced a Mile reel, a penny crochet ball, and an extra strong machine thread for heavy-duty sewing.

The recession deepened. Both Paisley firms were on short time, and an unemployment relief fund was opened in the town. Despite a slow recovery that started the next year, price cutting continued, and Coats and Clarks became even more hostile to each other, mainly due to the way Philippi had been using the Ross & Duncan products. Clarks seemed to suffer most in the markets where the product was offered, and this was causing resentment. Brooks also complained. Their Goatshead sold better than any other glacé product in Scandinavia but was decimated by the introduction of a Ross & Duncan special to such an extent that two of their directors demanded to meet with Philippi in London to sort it out. Their meeting had a successful outcome, and they retired to have lunch at Scotts, where both Yorkshiremen produced oyster knives that they had secreted about their persons and ordered several platefuls of oysters, much to Philippi's amusement.

The Ross & Duncan arrangement eventually broke down completely. Coats sold the mill, rented back the part they needed, and agreed with the others that each could sell the goods separately as they saw fit. This agreement did not last, but Coats kept the brand and continued to use it. This infuriated Chadwicks, who disseminated a rumour that the reason Coats's prices were so high was that they did no manufacturing of their own, but sold thread made by others, including Chadwicks, so they could not possibly match the prices of the thread companies who produced for themselves. They then had a slanging match over Russia, where Chadwicks were forced to raise their extremely aggressive prices, but Coats would not follow.[13]

Relations between Coats and Clarks also deteriorated to the point where they were hardly speaking to each other. This must have given John Clark and Mr. Philippi some interesting moments, as they both lived in Largs, played billiards together, albeit not very well, and usually shared a ride to Paisley.

Philippi then accused Clarks of selling a cheap copy of Coats's Russian Blue Bear product, stating, "You must be aware of the fact that most of the Russian consumers cannot read at all, not to speak of the English lettering. To protect ourselves to some extent, we shall draw attention to the matter by circular and warn the public against your goods by advertisements in the newspapers".[14] At a chance meeting between Archie Coats and John Clark in the railway station, Archie asked that the article be withdrawn, and John Clark responded that the imitation was deliberate, that he was sure that the retailers could pass the spools off as if they were Coats's, and that they would not withdraw them unless they could reach a settlement.

Everyone desired a truce. Coats had suffered, but less than others. Brooks' Goatshead was no longer the market leader it had been in many countries, having ceded that position to Chain Glacé. Chadwicks had begun to get a taste of Coats's wrath in Russia and were working on slender margins, so they did not have the stomach or the resources

13. Chadwicks' Penny Reel had probably been selling at a loss as well, which added to their frustration.

14. From Coats' papers in the Glasgow University Archives.

for an extended battle. John Clark knew Philippi too well to doubt his ambitions for Coats or his ability to carry out his plans, which left Clarks feeling nervous. Everyone else in the industry was small and vulnerable.

It was against this background that Mr. Philippi conceived of his most brilliant idea.

Chapter 19

The Central Agency

Often the difference between a successful person and a failure is not one has better abilities or ideas, but the courage that one has to bet on one's ideas, to take a calculated risk–and to act.
Andre Malraux, twentieth century French novelist

The solution to all his problems came to Mr. Philippi when out for a gentle afternoon stroll with his wife. She had noticed that he was quieter than usual, which usually indicated that he was wrestling with some particularly perplexing predicament. They walked on in silence for some way when he suddenly stopped, and in a moment of Archimedean insight, exclaimed "I've got it!" What he had stumbled upon was a way of separating the marketing and selling issues he had from the effective part of the business, manufacturing.

He immediately wrote it down and hastened to explain it to the Coatses. The principle was simple. A joint selling agency would be set up to market and sell all the products made by Coats, Clarks, Brooks, and Chadwicks. One agent would represent all of them in every country, and the same travellers would sell for all of them. There would be no change in the way their mills were organised, so they could easily increase their profits by improving production efficiency; selling costs would be shared based on turnover.

This type of arrangement was unheard of at the time in Great Britain (where comparable schemes would come later), but was relatively common in Germany. Philippi was certainly influenced, through his education and work experience, by a similar system developing in Germany in a much stricter form, particularly in the paper, potash, and coal industries.

Unfortunately, it was not embraced with immediate enthusiasm by the three other potential participants. Brooks procrastinated and then decided against joining. Chadwicks felt that such a scheme would only work if the four companies were of similar size, but that with the present situation the smaller partners would end up losing. They countered with a proposal for an agreement in each country with a paid secretary as an independent mediator to monitor and report on any rules violations. Philippi rejected this immediately, as he believed that the Clark agents were so skilled at manipulation that they would be able to turn the deal to their advantage and no one could catch them, however expert.

Clarks themselves did not like the idea of Philippi being in charge and were beginning to foresee amalgamation as being the likely if not inescapable conclusion. They may even have aspired to some form of merger, although it is unlikely that John Clark would have supported this. In any case, they felt that if that was where they were heading, then they could cut a better deal for themselves outside an agency agreement rather than as a member. They declined to join, but suggested that a third-party arbiter be appointed to examine the alternatives. A mutually acceptable independent expert was found in July 1888.

Thomas Jackson, a respected Glasgow chartered accountant, was chosen and two months later had reported that something very similar to the Philippi scheme was really the only way to go. What Clarks and the other potential partners didn't know was that Coats had vetoed the other suggestions that Jackson had put forward, so the result was never really in doubt.

Clarks remained skeptical, but then mysteriously capitulated in November, so the Sewing Cotton Agency was born formally on July 1, 1889 with just two members. Faced with the joint selling agency between Coats and Clark, Brooks decided to join as well, but Chadwicks argued that it would be hard to unravel, so that once in, they would find it tough to withdraw. They still insisted that it benefited the smaller firms less, to which Philippi countered that the contrary was true, as they would find their selling costs reduced and their customer coverage improved.

The name was changed to The Central Agency (TCA) in October, and a separate office was set up, largely staffed by a nucleus of people from Philippi's overseas sales department in Paisley. It was represented by one person from each company, initially Archie Coats, John Clark, and Edward Brook, but was run by three delegates, Philippi (who for all practical purposes was in charge) and two others. The basic tenets were as originally conceived, with selling done on commission in all markets except the US, which was outside Philippi's jurisdiction.

As the agency arrangements in each market had to be changed, it was agreed that whoever had the largest share would have the final say on the agent to be chosen. Costs were split by turnover, roughly 45% Coats, 40% Clark, and 15% Brooks. The Agency also took on sales of Milwards needles and Lister & Co. silk thread; these both contributed to costs on the same basis.

The addition of a company from south of the border meant that the location of the office was not a foregone conclusion. Brooks did not want it in Paisley for obvious reasons, and Philippi, anticipating the prospect of a huge international organisation, plumped for London, but John Clark said that they would go anywhere outside Scotland over his dead body, so Glasgow was looked upon as a suitable compromise. The first office was near St. Enoch station, but within three years they moved to Wellington Street and eventually round to corner to Bothwell Street, becoming part of the labyrinthine office complex that extended through to 155 St. Vincent Street, where Coats would later established their head office.

One additional benefit of the new system was that it avoided double taxation for most sales made overseas. Governments were waking up to the idea of generating revenue by taxing profits made by international companies within their borders. Under the old regime, thread made in Ferguslie but sold in Germany could well be taxed on its full value in Germany and then again in the UK, once more on full value. With the Central Agency, their only margin in the country of sale was their relatively small commission, and the profit made by J. & P. Coats in the UK was a separate issue, not taxable overseas. Although this had not been foreseen as an advantage of his original scheme, it became an enormous secondary benefit.

It was far from plain sailing from the get-go. The learning curve for the new setup was long, and the representatives of the three companies and people at all levels were very suspicious of one another. Although the whole thing was based on Philippi's Ferguslie selling system, it was less disciplined and efficient than he had envisioned, and his ability to impose his will was limited, given the number of players involved.

Even so, it gradually established itself. Some of the controls instituted were extraordinary, considering the period. For instance, the travellers were monitored by inspectors who checked up on their routes; they were required to send postcards from each place they visited, so the office could keep track. They were also encouraged to help those customers who were interested in establishing and monitoring stock levels and were asked to send back information on competition activity. It wasn't perfect, but it did lay the groundwork for eventual full integration with the 1896 merger. A couple of hurdles remained before that could happen.

Chapter 20

The End of Auchincloss

A Salesman minus enthusiasm is just a clerk.
Harry F. Banks, Scottish (probably) soldier

Across the Atlantic, the same market forces were at work in the 1880s, and thread volumes continued to expand, even if price competition stopped values from keeping pace. Although the bulk of thread sold was still in six cord for the housewife with her sewing machine at home, industrial sales to factories were beginning to make their mark, helped by increased sewing machine speeds and the availability of band knives capable of cutting stacks of cloth, so multiple inexpensive copies of identical garments became a real possibility. Most of the factories were small, often consisting of groups of immigrant tailors in a tenement who would cut, sew, and press cheap clothing for the poorer sector of the population, who wanted affordable clothes for everyday use. Sewing operations could easily be contracted out for a pittance, which kept costs and overheads down. Department stores were beginning to appear with the growth of urbanisation, as were the phenomena of chain stores and mass advertising, so demand was building up quickly, and price competition was keen.

The market for industrial thread was in cheap four, three,

or even two ply glacé with longer lengths than the traditional 200 yard spool. Improvements in sewing machines meant that the thread could be made from these simpler constructions and ring spun, which was much more economical than mule spinning. There was prohibitive duty on imported threads, which impacted the cheapest articles most, so new and expanded local competition for sewing thread meant that there were some fifty producers by the early 1880s, mostly concentrated on these products.

This was the high growth sector, but it did not mean that the best-quality six cord trade was stagnant. On the contrary, it continued to expand, but at a slower rate and still dominated by three companies, Coats (Conant), Clark Thread Co., and Willimantic. This sector of the market was far less competitive, with the import tariffs that had forced the Coats and Clarks to set up local manufacturing now affording them the same protection as the other local manufacturers.

Ironically, they were accused of hiding behind the protection of these (now prohibitive) import duties. When asked to testify to the commission set up to establish the Tariff Act of 1883, the group argued that their level of protection was fair, as they were major employers in their areas and could not compete with the much lower UK wages without import duty. They even suggested a tariff of 15¢ per dozen for 200 yard six cord. The final decision and the tariff imposed in 1883 was 7¢ per 100 yards—effectively 14¢ for their main article.

The fact was that they did have a hold on the market for that particular product, but there were still nearly fifty competitors. In their testimony, Coats raised several other points. Prices were no higher than before the War, but wages had increased, as had the cost of cotton. The stresses that the faster sewing machines placed on threads had meant the introduction of more sophisticated and therefore more expensive products, and modern machinery was more costly to buy and maintain. They argued that recommended pricing was necessary to avoid inferior quality, short lengths, and the inability to service some of the more remote locations effectively. Perhaps most telling, they pointed out that thread is a very small proportion of the total cost of the garment, and any quality failures have expensive consequences.

What they failed to mention was that productivity had improved with modern machinery, and economies of scale had reduced costs. The thread companies had all weathered recessions and were relatively prosperous, particularly compared to other cotton textile concerns. Their healthy profits certainly indicated that they were not passing on all their cost savings to their loyal customers.

The upshot of all this was that it drew attention to the sewing thread market and created more competitors. Various local American companies became active and successful, amongst them the Merrick Thread Co., in Holyoke, Massachusetts, run by Timothy Merrick, whom we already came across at Willimantic. Overseas manufacturers were also drawn to the US, with Chadwicks opening a plant in Bridgeport, Connecticut in 1883 and Kerr & Co. starting to spool a $ trademark in Newark in 1882. They followed this up by forming the Kerr Thread Company USA in 1888, with manufacturing starting in 1890.

In the end, the protection from import duties and other measures could not change one characteristic peculiar to thread customers:

> The average woman will not be severed from her opinion that there is no sewing cotton so good as the one she uses, and which her mother used before her. Willing enough to try a new kind of needle or gloves, she sticks with peculiar tenacity to the thread of her mother. Consequently, the established threadmakers have in her an ally which permits them to bid defiance to new makers that may come to the front. It is the kind of protection that the Government cannot give them and that legislators cannot

> remove...the people themselves establish a monopoly, unwittingly no doubt, but as certain a monopoly as any that exists in America. [1]

It would seem that all the advertising aimed at children was having an effect, but this certainly explains why there was no need for a Central Agency stateside—they were already well provided for.

By late 1888, increased competition, lower cotton prices, and a further recession caused Merrick to reduce their price for 200 yards to 50¢. This precipitated a whole series of reductions till prices settled at 45¢, with reduced discounts. Chadwicks and others soon hit 40¢, but they merely reestablished their original bonuses and discounts and left it at that. As a result, sales recovered by late 1890, but at a much lower level than previously.

This lower pricing introduced some friction with Hezekiah Conant, who had been pocketing a decent salary and 8½% of the profits, and although we don't know how much these were, it is not unrealistic to think that he could make $75,000 in a good year. As far back as 1882, Coats had wanted to set aside 3¼% as a deprecation allowance, whereas Conant thought his twelfth share should be on gross profit. Coats won this battle, as well as a dispute over the way they paid Conant as the manufacturer. They then moved him to a fixed salary of $41,000, which was generous given the reduced pricing at the end of the decade, but which would mean a distinct drop in his income if the market recovered. His complaints fell on deaf ears.

More troublesome was the Coats-Auchincloss partnership. Philippi had not been involved up to this point, but had started to take an interest as his stature within the company grew and the success of his reorganisation of selling bore fruit. What he saw distressed him, as instead of detailed information on sales, competition, and other

1. New York Times, June 5, 1882

commercial data flowing back to the centre, there was literally no information at all about anything. Their control was absolute, and they made changes to terms and even prices without informing, much less consulting, Paisley. They decided on where they would have stocks, offices, and travellers, largely financed by Ferguslie, and they kept (or were assumed to keep) customer accounts to themselves, allowing Coats no access. They also financed cotton purchasing as required, which gave them additional leverage.

The association had really developed by neglect. When Andrew was still in the US, his vigorous style had kept Auchincloss on their toes, but the rest of the family were largely interested in manufacturing and had allowed Auchincloss to act for them unobstructed. Their initial prosperity helped to reinforce this behavior, and when Andrew left and James (USA) took over, they assumed that things would continue as before. But James's marriage to Sarah Auchincloss had inevitably changed his relationship with the agency, making him soft on them. Nor was he as sharp as his uncle, so things were allowed to slide, with Auchincloss progressively becoming a law unto themselves. They had grown rich on the back of the thread business and had become complacent, particularly when compared to the new and dynamic organisation Philippi was establishing in Europe.

As early as 1870, Coats had wanted them to develop the western US by putting in more depots and increasing the sales force as the region expanded. Auchincloss had dragged their feet, citing high costs as the main reason for inaction. By the mid-1880s, sales growth was considered unsatisfactory and the amount of market information being relayed to Scotland woefully inadequate. Despite this, when they restructured as Auchincloss Brothers in 1885, Coats increased their commission to 5½%, and a year later W. S. Auchincloss was appointed agent for Philadelphia when Bates & Auchincloss (formerly Bates & Coates) wrapped up.

Faced with declining sales at the end of the decade, they asked Coats to pay for more travellers as well as increased commissions. James (USA) agreed to pay Auchincloss higher allowances going forward, but he did this without asking Paisley. The family was furious when they found out. A new Arrow long length three ply article was launched in late 1890, and Coats let them take on a wool agency in an attempt to boost volume, but this only postponed the inevitable.

In 1891, Willimantic suddenly lowered their prices. Auchincloss raised their packing charges to Coats, who were forced to pay up against their will, as James (USA) had again authorised the increase. This may have been the straw that broke the camel's back, as an edict was issued shortly thereafter, completely restructuring the agency agreement for the USA, broadly similar to that established by Philippi elsewhere. After an acrimonious exchange, Auchincloss refused to comply and stated that they would no longer act as agents after the year-end. Their resignation was duly accepted, and Archie and Philippi sailed to the US to set up their own selling organisation, the Coats Thread Company. They rented offices in New York and arranged for this new joint stock company to begin operating from the new year. Stuart Coats, James (USA)'s son, was to be the office chief and Theodore Frelinghuysen, James's son-in-law, the treasurer. The Secretary was C. H. Probst, who came from TCA. They were to handle all the sales, advertising, and collections for the Pawtucket mills, which were leased by Coats under a new company, J. & P. Coats Ltd., Pawtucket Branch. The rent was set to allow the Conant Company to continue paying a 15% dividend, and the arrangement appears to have been an attempt to keep Hezekiah happy, whilst linking the Coats name more directly with manufacturing.

The W. S. Auchincloss agency in Philadelphia carried on, ostensibly under the new rules, but no trading information was forthcoming, sales continued to decline, and a general impression of indifference prevailed. Coats sent a letter giving notice till the end of the year, and although there was a brief flurry of activity, all ties with the Auchinclosses were finally severed two years later. Their association had lasted over fifty years and had made both families wealthy.

The TCA selling system was steadily introduced into the US after this. Depots were opened in Chicago, St. Louis, New Orleans, Atlanta, and Milwaukee. The Boston and San Francisco locations, which already existed, were taken over and improved. Detailed centralised planning of all activities, improved reporting, and strict control of costs, especially entertainment, were introduced. Incentives were based on effort and results rather than length of service, and attention was focussed on opportunities for promotion. Stock reduction became a major goal, and inventories went from 30% of sales in 1890 to about 25% six years later, largely through improved information on what products were required and where. Sales costs increased as they had in Europe, but volumes compensated.

The market was becoming more sophisticated. Rising incomes fueled greater demand, but for more variety in styles and shades, finer fabrics, and faster colours. The gap between domestic thread for household consumers and industrial thread for factories was beginning to widen though most clothing still came from artisan producers rather than the assembly line. The growth of department stores continued to have an influence and drove the move towards mass production of inexpensive fashion items in larger quantities.

Manufacturing was changing too. H. A. Lowe had found a way of improving the mercerising process by tensioning the thread, and it became a commercial proposition around 1895. This introduced another cotton thread finish to add to the two already available, soft and polished (or glacé). Mercerised thread was as pliable as soft, but had the improved strength and sewability of glacé without the stiffness. It also had improved lustre, so could be an acceptable substitute for silk. It became the darling of the handicraft producers but was an important addition to the gamut of sewing threads as well.

The thread world faced an ever-increasing need for higher quality, a proliferation of thicknesses and finishes, more (and faster) colours, and more varied packaging. On top of all this, 1893 saw the start of probably the worst depression of the century, a consequent collapse of prices, and a protracted recovery.

Coats was lucky again. They had been expanding fast into the West and Midwest of the USA, chasing the population as it spread out from the East Coast. These were the areas least impacted by the downturn, and the six cord domestic spool was also less affected than longer length industrial products. Local competition was increasing. Clarks had built another 60,000-spindle mill in Newark, which started production in 1890, and a five-storey finishing mill in 1893. In the same year, Chadwicks followed their plant in Connecticut with a much larger one in Jersey City, and Merrick had been joined by other strong US producers. Price agreements did not hold once the recession bit. Competition sharpened.

Unlike Coats, Clarks were very hard hit. Their sales territory in the US was in the East and their range of products was more vulnerable. Their old nemesis, the "other" Clark company, had reared its ugly head again. William Clark (no relation), who had been George Clark's mill superintendent, had left them and started his own company with a mill in Rhode Island in 1891.[2] He was selling a 200 yard six cord as Clark's N.E.W., which was hitting their O.N.T. sales. It was removed from the market five years later, as it was deemed to infringe trademark law, but they were stuck with it for the duration of the downturn.

2. He resigned from Clark Thread, along with both his sons, during the Newark spinners strike in February 1891. Those were dark days for his namesake, who ran the company at the time

Clarks cut the price of their Mile End six cord and stepped up production of three-ply long length products. Coats hit back by starting manufacture of crochet and darning threads at Pawtucket for the first time. Hostilities intensified, but as cotton prices were also falling at the same time, they both managed to survive the slowdown relatively unscathed. This was not true of many of their smaller competitors, most of whom paid reduced or no dividends. Several went under.

Chapter 21

Publicly Quoted Multinational

If a business does well, the stock eventually follows.
Warren Buffett, American business magnate

In Russia, Coats was faced with a similar situation to the one they had confronted in the USA twenty years earlier, and they made the same decision to start manufacturing there in 1887, though they didn't implement it for another two years. Duties on imported cotton thread had risen five times between 1877 and 1885, and a further increase was introduced the following year as a result of pressure from a local producer named Zhukov. When reports started to circulate that Chadwicks were considering local manufacture and that another tariff hike of 75% was likely, the board resolved to act.

They did not do so with great determination. They wanted to start out with a small mill, mainly as an experiment. Finding a suitable candidate took time, but in May 1889 they acquired the Naryshkin Mills and some five acres of ground near St. Petersburg. They then persuaded their Central Agency partners, Clarks and Brooks, who both faced similar problems in a potentially large market, to join them in financing the erection of a new larger mill.

By a stroke of fate, a potential local competitor, Nevsky Thread, was also in the throes of building a mill just down the road from the Coats venture. When they heard about their new competition, they lost their enthusiasm, took fright, and made overtures to Paisley to see if they could come to some sort of accommodation.

The origins of this company dated back to the beginning of the century, when a wealthy Jewish financier from Hanover, Ludwig Von Stieglitz, established a banking business in St. Petersburg and accumulated a large mansion, extensive property in the south of Russia, and a summer residence on Kamenny, which is an island in the Neva estuary where his next door neighbour was a Russian imperial palace. He also picked up a number of industrial concerns along the way, amongst which was the Nevsky cotton mill, which he started in 1833. He hired a Lancashireman called Beck as mill manager and brought a number of technicians over from England to fill the key positions in the plant, so it was renowned for the quality of its products.

When he died in 1843, his son Alexander inherited his father's title, property, wealth, businesses, and some of his financial acumen. However, his marriage was childless until the year after his father's death, when a baby arrived, literally, on his doorstep. A servant had answered the doorbell and found nobody there, except for a small basket with an infant in it and a note saying that the child, whose name was Nadezhda (meaning Hope), had been born on December 10, 1843, and her father's name was Michael. The little girl was wrapped in exceptionally fine linen and had a gold cross round her neck.

His wife was naturally eager to adopt the child, but he was hesitant. They were still discussing it the next day when an emissary arrived from the Czar and summoned Alexander to the Summer Palace. The Czar was short and to the point: he knew about the baby and who the father was, and he wanted the Stieglitzes to raise the child and ensure that she was properly educated.

Stieglitz returned home and, to his wife's joy, informed her that the child was to be theirs. So they raised and cared for Nadezhda Mikhaylovna Yunina, who grew to be a multilingual beauty, well versed in the arts, literature, and music, and heir to the Stieglitz fortune—a real catch for any young suitor. She was also notoriously profligate.

Her son swore that her father must have been the Grand Duke Michael, the Czar's brother, and this was an open secret in Russian society. He reasoned that her mother was probably a foreigner of some importance, perhaps English, for if she had been a servant, then she and the child would have been spirited away to Siberia, never to be heard of again. Others said she was indeed a servant, identified by the single letter *K*.

In 1861 Nadezhda married Alexander Polovtsov, eleven years her senior, and he immediately gained both a dowry of a million rubles as well as the goodwill of the Emperor, who was watching over his niece. When Stieglitz eventually passed away in 1884, Polovtsov got at least partial control of the rest of the family fortune, which included the Nevsky Thread plant.

In the intervening years, Robert Hammerschmidt (who was also Brooks' Russian agent) had become Managing Director, and the technical management of the plant had passed from the original Beck to his nephew James, who became the real dynamo of the business. He persuaded Polovtsov in 1888 that there was a great future for the cotton cloth and thread trades in Russia, so they should build an additional spinning mill for the former and new twisting and finishing mills for the latter. They had started on this with great gusto when Coats suddenly appeared just up the road and they decided to negotiate.

They did this initially on paper and largely with Philippi.

However, the prospects of a deal looked so promising that a delegation consisting of Archie, Philippi, Kenneth Mackenzie Clark, C. L. Brook, and T. J. Hirst (representing Chadwicks) descended on St. Petersburg in October 1890, and a deal was done. Two companies were formed and registered in Russia. The first was the Nevsky Thread Manufacturing Company (NTM), which owned the Naryshkin mill, the new Polovtsov thread mill, and all the TCA stocks in Russia. It also became the agency for all TCA thread sold nationally and any made by these mills. The ownership was split 50% to Nadezhda Yunina (now Mme. Polovtsova), 30% Coats, and the remainder divided between Clarks and Brooks. The other business (the Nevsky Cotton Company) remained with the Polovtsovs and consisted of all their spinning and weaving. They supplied yarn to NTM.

Although Coats had only a minority interest in NTM, they were aware of the free-spending reputation of the majority owner, and it was therefore no surprise when she borrowed £200,000 from them against security of a block of her shares, equivalent to 13% of the company's total capital. This effectively handed them complete control.

Whilst they were completing this deal in Russia, a subject which had been discussed sporadically for some time came up again. This was the question of the company structure. Several of the Coatses felt that the whole business was getting too big to continue as a family concern. They now employed about 6,500 people and the two "mega-plants" at Pawtucket and Ferguslie covered the better part of fifty Hectares. They had moved into Canada[1] and now Russia,

1. A finishing department was established in Montreal, Canada in 1873, named for their agent, Rankin Beattie, but 75% owned by Coats. The production was all black or white six cord thread wound on thirty-two spooling machines, and the spools were made from Canadian silver birch in a mill they also acquired in Three Rivers. Three years later, they incorporated the Canada Thread Co., which bought the two mills, increased the spooling capacity, and was set to develop twisting as well, but this was shelved. Ownership was split 50/50 Coats/Rankin Beattie.

and the likelihood was that they would have to start investing in other overseas factories, as tariff barriers and local competition became tougher. The last two mill buildings at Ferguslie had cost £200,000 each, Russia was going to need a lot of money, and so would any further expansion abroad. Philippi's new sales strategy was proving to be immensely successful, but with high up-front costs.

In short, the calls on new capital were becoming greater, and although these had always been financed by borrowing from the shareholder directors, the new generation appeared less willing to put large sums into the business the way their fathers had, partly because the amounts were greater, and partly because they were probably less passionate about the company than their forebears. Another source of finance was required.

Sir Peter's death in March 1890 precipitated action rather than discussion. The buoyancy of the stock market at the time no doubt helped the family decide to investigate floating J. & P. Coats as a Limited Liability Company (LLC). This form of enterprise had already been around for some thirty years, and despite initial misgivings and a few dramatic and transitory flops, it was becoming all the rage. Barings had promoted Guinness Ltd. in 1886 and this had paved the way for many more, but almost without exception they were small, and the issues were usually in Debentures or Preference shares. Large numbers of ordinary shares in manufacturing companies were as rare as ice cubes in Hell.

Philippi was dead against the idea. He feared a loss of control from the introduction of shareholders with no company responsibility. The family ignored him and plowed ahead, looking to sell the company for £6.25 million, though finally settling for somewhat less. The stock market, although still bullish, was beginning to show signs of a "bubble", and such august publications as *The Economist* were talking of stagnation, which did not bode well for a flotation of the size they were contemplating. In any case, an offer on this scale was almost unheard of, so the risks involved were huge, particularly as the company was not well known.

There were several reasons for their relative obscurity: they were less flamboyant than most of their competitors; their location in Scotland left them physically isolated from the rest of the textile industry; they made a unique niche product; and they were notoriously secretive about everything they did. Commentaries in the press, which surfaced along with rumours about their plans, were uncomplimentary and demonstrated ignorance and some prejudice against them.[2]

Caution prevailed, and the company was listed at £5.75 million, £2 million each in 4½% debentures and 6% cumulative preference shares, and 175,000 ordinary shares of £10. The listing opened on August 12 simultaneously in Glasgow, Edinburgh, London, Manchester, Liverpool, New York, and Montreal, and after a whirlwind of activity 14,000 potential investors made applications for £15,000,000 worth of stock. The floatation had been a dazzling success, with the ordinary shares proving particularly popular, trading at a premium of £2 10s. after the dust had settled. The massive launch was a milestone in the history of the stock market, and J. & P. Coats Ltd., as it was now named, went on to become the top Blue Chip company for the next quarter century.

2. One article that appeared in the *Stock Exchange Times* on August 3 showed jaw-dropping disregard for truth, affirming that Coats "had been for some time on the down grade and, in consequence of the push and energy infused into the business of several competitors, the canny Scot, Sir Peter Coats, had lent himself for the time being to the blandishments of the wily promoter and is now endeavoring to raise a very large sum of money for his White Elephant". It continued in similarly inaccurate vein and concluded by warning any potential investors not to put any money into "a concern which is little more than nothing at all". The (extremely defunct) Sir Peter must have been spinning in his grave, with apologies for the pun.

"Going public" meant big changes. For the first time since James Coats Sr. had started out in Ferguslie sixty-four years before, there were non-family members directing the company. Archie was still chairman, with his brothers James (USA), Peter, and Daniel beside him, as well as cousins Jimmie, Thomas Glen, Willie, and George. Mr. Philippi, who had become such a driving force within the company, was given just reward by being promoted to board level, and three outside directors joined him: Sir James Whitehead was an industrialist and city of London alderman; Sir James King had been Provost of Glasgow and was deputy chairman of the Caledonian Railway Company.

However, it was the third "outsider" who was the most interesting. Sir William Arrol had the greatest claim to a seat on the board, for his father had been a manager at Ferguslie and had likely got him his first job at eleven years of age in the turning shop. He had then gone on to find fame as the builder of both the new Tay Railway Bridge and the Forth Rail Bridge, which was opened just before the formation of J. & P. Coats Ltd.

The success of the stock market launch cemented the company's position as number one in the thread industry and strengthened their hand for amalgamation, at the very least with Clarks. This was looking increasingly likely, for despite their mistrust of one another, they were collaborating ever more, through TCA and ventures like Nevsky.

The exposure that surrounds the requirements to publish accounts and other company information helped get the attention of potential investors, but it also raised their profile and attracted criticism from all sides. Their investors wanted all the profits (and more of them) distributed as dividends, whilst the company felt the need to be conservative and build up reserve funds. In direct contrast, the growing influence of the Labour Party and socialism meant that others found their profits excessive, with accusations of exploitation and meagre wages.

The money raised allowed them to finance two new ventures in Europe. The first of these was in Spain, which, although not very important to Coats as such, had commercial ties to Latin America in particular. Coats thread was often sold on to that part of the world by way of the Iberian Peninsula. When Philippi first visited Spain in the 1870s, Brooks had already established their Goatshead three ply polished thread as the market leader to the point that the brand had become the generic word for sewing thread. Several years of his selling prowess had then helped dislodge them from their exalted position, and Chain Three Cord Extra Glacé became the best-selling spool in the market by 1890, but not before he had to buy out a trader who had previously registered the trademark.

In the meantime, a local Spanish company, Fabra y Portabella (FyP) had started in 1884, combining three factories from earlier enterprises: Manresa made cotton sewing thread, San Andrés produced linen thread, and San Martín made fishing nets. By 1890, they were becoming a serious competitor, using low sewing thread prices to win market share and subsidising these through their profitable plant in San Martín. Their main trademark was charmingly and, to Philippi's way of thinking, appropriately named Serpiente (Snake), for they turned out to be slippery customers when it came to striking a deal. A proposal involving joint selling based on relative volumes was turned down flat.

Two years later they were outselling Coats in volume when a further blow fell. Spanish import duties were raised to 40%, and Coats could see that the only way forward was with local production. The initial idea of a small dyeing and finishing unit costing £15,000 was abandoned almost immediately, as the duty on grey thread[3] made this a nonstarter, so a twelve-acre site in the minute village of San

3. Grey thread is the name given to the raw form of sewing thread before it has had any treatment in the dye-house.

Vicente de Torelló, some fifty miles north of Barcelona, was chosen.

FyP reacted immediately, suggesting combining the two mills and splitting everything down the middle. This was rejected, the final nail in the coffin of this proposal coming when Clarks agreed to help build the mill, but to let Coats manage it. They took a share equivalent to their volume in Spain, which was about 20% of Coats, and the plans were adapted to take account of this. It was September 1893, and the budget for the mill was £63,000, a number so breathtakingly inadequate, it is hard to believe.

With hindsight it is easy to see where they went wrong. The population of Torelló in 1877 was 646. A construction project on this scale was never going to find sufficient labour in such a small agricultural village, so workers had to be brought in from other parts of Spain. This took time, was expensive, and created conflicts with the locals. The lack of social amenities worsened this situation. The cost of getting everything to such an isolated site was far greater than they had allowed for, and it also took longer. Language problems, which they had avoided in Russia by hiring local management, were a source of constant misunderstandings and mistakes. Attitudes to timekeeping and discipline were quite different from those experienced in Paisley, and the managers and foremen sent out to supervise the project became frustrated by this and their inability to communicate effectively. The first general manager and his assistant had to be replaced; this helped, but the project still took too long.

The plant was finally up and running by spring of 1896. It was a fully integrated three-storey mill with 6,640 ring spinning spindles and 7,000 for twisting. It was set up principally to produce Coats's best seller in Spain, a 500 yard three ply Chain Extra Glacé, and it had water and auxiliary steam power plants and electric light. As there was little infrastructure around the plant, they also had to add forty workers' houses as well as homes for managers and supervisors, separate schools for boys and girls, a hospital, a workers' club, a theater, village shops, a café, a garden with vegetable plots, and an abattoir. The Roman Catholic church, known as the Chapel of Our Lady of Borgoñá, was inaugurated in April 1898. The story goes that it was built after the female workers refused to enter the factory alongside the non-Catholic foremen and teachers sent out from Paisley. The company put the church in a position overlooking the mill to "bless" the working environment, and with this guarantee the problem was solved.

The final price tag for the mill was just over £161,000, more than two-and-a-half times their original estimate. However, there were two important lessons learned, and they formed part of the framework that has carried Coats forward ever since. It was resolved that any important future capital expenditure projects would be subject to main board approval and that if the actual amount to be spent was to exceed the budget by more than 10%, then further approval had to be obtained at board level before continuing. This is still the system in Coats today. The other discipline that was introduced was the requirement for management to learn the local language before taking up an international position. This remained a prerequisite for as long as expatriates were being sent to manage businesses in other countries, but their numbers were drastically reduced in the 1990s, as business priorities changed, so this is no longer an issue.

The second overseas acquisition was in Austria, where a local manufacturer based in Harland, forty miles west of Vienna, had been competing successfully with the Paisley firms for a number of years. Mathias Salcher, a farmer's son from Maria Luggau, had started this business in 1828. In similar fashion to the Clarks and Coatses when they first arrived in Paisley, he had become a weaver's apprentice with his uncle in Passau and had then found his way to Vienna, where he married a blacksmith's daughter and founded a company making braids and tapes. He also sold buttons and is supposed to have carried his merchandise around to local villages in a cart pulled by dogs, graduating to horses as his business grew. In 1845 he diversified into silk button manufacturing on an imported machine which he modified, obtaining a patent for his improvements. He moved this business to Wagstadt (now Bílovec in the Czech Republic) in 1864, where he also started a weaving department and extended his button range to include other materials such as metal.

By this time his four sons had joined him, and in 1859 he founded Mathias Salcher & Sons, based in Vienna. Having extra help allowed him to diversify further, so that year he also started a plant near Harland on the Traissen River, the first in Austria to wind Eisengarn (iron thread)[4] on cards. With his eldest son helping him in Vienna, he left the thread part of his empire to his second boy, Josef. This son had expansionist ambitions, so he took the Harland mill and grew it into a complete thread manufacturing complex along the banks of the river, which he needed as a power source.

Coats had become increasingly aware of Salcher, who had developed a very respectable six cord spool that sold well in central Europe, and their prices were embarrassingly low. The prospect of import duty increases made production in Austria a serious consideration in 1885, when Coats and Clark again discussed the possibility of a local joint venture. Clarks were less keen than Coats, who decided they would go ahead alone if need be, but the tariff increase failed to appear, and the plan was shelved.

Then Clarks' Austrian agent made a stupid mistake. He forgot that the Anchor trademark had to be reregistered by law, and Salcher got wind of this. Their representative nipped down to the office, registered the trademark for them, and within a short time they were selling spools with

4. This was not, as the name implies, a metallic thread, but rather a polished cotton sewing thread, whose name derives from its durability and strength. It contained no iron.

the Anker name and symbol, perfectly legally. On the back of this triumph, they redoubled their sales efforts, extended their range to include crochet thread, added further capacity in Harland, and bought out their only major local competitor, in Hochstadt, Bohemia (now the Czech Republic). This not only gave Salcher an extra mill, but also a depot in Vienna and some useful trademarks.

Mathias died in 1879, and his four sons all followed him between 1885 and 1889, so Josef's son, Josef Jr., who had been technically trained in Manchester, took over, helped by his brother Carl. He proved to be as resourceful as his forefathers and set about building a new spinning mill, which was finished in 1892. The total Salcher workforce had now reached 1,500.

Philippi's initial approach to Salcher was for some form of selling agreement in the typical TCA style but this was rejected, so he decided to attack on three fronts. He lowered prices to the Austrian's levels and kept matching them. He started to sell buttons, Salcher's most profitable line, at rock bottom prices through TCA. Then the following year Coats bought a small factory in Wilhelmsburg and equipped it to finish Chain thread imported from Ferguslie, which was then used to undercut Salcher. Georg Richter, the TCA inspector in Vienna, was put in charge.

Josef realised too late that he was in deep trouble. The price war he had entered into with Coats and the Anchor-less and understandably furious Clarks was draining his company of much-needed cash for day-to-day operations. The death in rapid succession of his father and three uncles had added a further financial burden, as several of their heirs pocketed their inheritance, and the others all had different ideas on how to run the company and deal with Coats, so internal squabbles added to his woes.

Having already borrowed 500,000 Gulden (£50,000) from the banks, he and Carl went to Glasgow in May 1893 to try and strike a deal, but left empty handed. Within six months Josef had returned "almost on his knees asking for an arrangement", this time needing £200,000 to cover his debts, with none of the banks willing to extend more credit. Philippi managed to skillfully engineer things to get what he wanted[5] without beating the Salchers into the ground. After all, they would be an important part of the future business in Austria,[6] and there was no point in alienating them before they had even started.

Josef Salcher broke down and cried before signing the agreement and had to be given a glass of water by John Clark, who was also present during negotiations (to sort out the Anchor trademark dispute). This was more likely from relief at reaching an acceptable deal rather than despair at having been humiliated, and indeed he proved to be an enormous asset to the business going forward. The mill was also modern and well run, so it needed little done to it to conform to Coats's rigorous standards.

Back at home, they had fared well in the period after going public. They took more market share from competitors and continued to expand Ferguslie, which was still their main production unit. They added Mill No. 8,[7] which held 150,000 spindles of Ferguslie ring twisters.[8]

5. This was a half share of the thread business and some form of control over the buttons, which he got by lending them £20,000 against a mortgage on the button factory.

6. Josef became the Salcher director and was retained to run thread selling and administration.

7. A highly modern building where, amongst other design innovations, the mill windowsills were ingeniously set at a 45° angle, so cups and other items could not be left there.

8. These were based on an in-house modification of their American machines. Ferguslie had started to design, modify, and build their own production machines, and many of these were sent overseas, especially to Russia.

A new dyeworks was built to replace George Street, which suffered from ancient plant and equipment.[9] Electric light was tried in the spooling section in Mill No. 7 and was such a success that Mill No. 8 was electric from the start. The remainder of the site was later weaned off gas and onto the new, brighter and safer lighting system.

Strikes by the railways in 1891, cotton spinners in the next two years, and coalminers in 1894 had impacted Ferguslie, and despite having their own colliery at Nitshill, getting the coal to the mill had proved very difficult. Then a labour shortage delayed the start-up of No. 8 mill, and they needed to recruit from as far afield as Greenock, which took time. Improved labour productivity therefore became a major goal, so a costing department was set up under the watchful eye of Mr. Philippi, giving the company much more accurate product costs, based on the concept of replacement value, which was almost unheard of at the time, but which would become absolutely vital as they ventured into high inflation areas like Brazil. An attempt was also made to allocate overheads, still relatively easy for Coats with their limited product range. They therefore understood their product margins much better than their competition and could set prices more exactly. It was also the progenitor of the costing systems they would use worldwide throughout the twentieth century. However, there was one more important bridge to cross before reaching that point.

9. They gave up this site and paid £3,000 to put up a technical college there.

Chapter 22

Merger

Life has taught us that love does not consist in gazing at each other, but in looking outward together in the same direction.
Antoine de Saint-Exupéry, French aristocrat, writer, aviator

Size Does Matter.
Anon

The possibility of amalgamation had been on the minds of the two biggest thread companies for some time. Others were also interested. Coats had rejected an overture from Clarks as early as 1885, and Chadwicks had suggested the idea before they declined an invitation to join TCA three years later. It must have occurred to the smaller companies who felt battered by repeated price wars. The formation of TCA suggested that it was just a question of time before the different enterprises became more formally linked.

Then in 1890 a New York merchant made a bid for the US businesses of Coats, Clark, and Willimantic. This was not immediately dismissed. Competition had become intense, and the number of thread companies had mushroomed. The selling agreement binding the three together was tough to maintain, and the rumblings of US antitrust sentiment made its long-term outlook uncertain, so Coats was considering a more formal union with Clarks and possibly others stateside. The fact that someone else had a similar idea (and cash) presented an opportunity to finance expansion in Paisley and more units overseas. Turning this into reality hinged on their ability to get good value for their businesses.

James (USA)[1] suggested that they should accept eight times earnings as a good price, but they decided that twelve was a better multiple, plus the value of stocks. After lengthy negotiations, a final offer of eight was rejected, so the deal fell through, and Coats was left with their problem, the question of consolidation still very much to the fore.

There were ructions within TCA as well. Although superficially the introduction of single agencies in each country or region had gone well, in practice there was unavoidable favouritism, based on historic loyalty. Mistrust persisted, particularly after Coats became an LLC. Disagreements continued, and arguments about allocation of expenses nearly caused a collapse. Philippi was so concerned with the situation in March 1893 that he wrote to the board: "It would be injudicious to let outsiders know the position in which The Central Agency finds itself".

Better sales in 1894 helped to right the ship, but Clarks could see their relative position weakening, particularly during the various strikes, which hit Anchor far harder than Ferguslie. John Clark passed away that year, and his death probably removed one of the last obstacles to an alliance with Coats. The next generation saw the future with less optimism than their parents and were therefore more willing to throw in their lot with their neighbours in Paisley. The prospect of a potential windfall helped to sweeten the pot. At the same time Philippi was frustrated with TCA and viewed a more permanent arrangement as a neat solution. The charge was laid and all that was needed was someone to light the fuse. In stepped Chadwicks.

1. Now Sir James as he had inherited the title upon the death of his father, Sir Peter. He will continue to be called James (USA) for clarity.

They had become a public limited company in 1891. They now had a decent-sized complex at Eagley, offices in the UK and Germany, a small finishing unit in Montreal, their plant in Connecticut, and 40% of the Riga Company in Russia. Their intention was to use the £750,000 from the floatation for a new spinning mill at Eagley, a larger plant in the US, and the other 60% of their Russian operation.

That year they were again invited to join TCA. They declined, and after suggesting a modified agreement along similar lines, their CEO, Arthur Greg, intimated that they should merge, but when he mentioned their proposed general terms, talks broke down. Chadwicks decided to attack the market with almost destructive pricing; TCA sales suffered.

Then an incident blew up over ticketing. Chadwicks had introduced a Lion brand, which looked so similar to a Coats product that an illiterate person could easily mistake them. When challenged, Chadwicks said that this was a retaliatory measure for Coats's use of the Carlile ticket, which in its turn looked remarkably like one of Chadwicks' spools. This, Philippi pointed out, was because Chadwicks had copied the Carlile motif back in the 1880s. Legal action was threatened all around, but then the 1893 recession hit, and Chadwicks found themselves with more pressing problems, like having to borrow to pay their preference shareholders. The next March, they agreed to withdraw Lion, and Coats modified the Carlile design.

The following year saw something of a recovery, but Chadwicks passed their dividend again.[2] They had a number of disadvantages over their larger competitors, which put them under intolerable pressure. Their mill efficiency suffered from having to make too many products. They made a lot to order, so with a larger range and smaller overall volume, their production runs were small and

2. They could not pay an ordinary dividend the year before either.

expensive. Added to this, they still had too much hand-operated machinery in finishing, with inevitably higher costs. Their pricing strategy kept their margins tight and even at the best of times they struggled to make a profit.

Answering to shareholders meant an additional burden, so it was no surprise when they found themselves back in Glasgow to discuss a merger. This time Philippi asked for a specific proposal, but the resulting valuation was again too high, with excessive guarantees being sought. The talks came to nothing.

A war of words ensued in *The Drapers' Record*, with Coats accused of coercion and Chadwicks of deception, but in the end, this was all just jockeying for position, and the three members of TCA and Chadwicks probably realised that their future would be better together. The only thing left to do would be for each to engineer the best deal possible. Further manoeuvres followed.

Coats bought Kerr & Co., who had assets in the US and Canada. Their three founders had died, and they were then hit very hard by the recession, so they could no longer continue independently. Their Underwood mill was modernised by Coats, and their N.M.T. six cord and polished threads continued to sell, but through TCA.

Then, in March 1896, Clarks informed Philippi of their intention to go the same way as Coats and Chadwicks as an LLC. Although the main reason for this move was to get the merger talks on a more urgent footing, they also wanted to build a new finishing mill at Anchor, on a grander scale than anything yet undertaken by Coats in Ferguslie, and this needed financing. It was designed partly as expansion, but also to allow them to relocate all the production from John Clark's Mile End Mill, which had been partly destroyed by fire in 1891. Cotton thread manufacture had already been moved to Paisley, with the processing of wool continuing in Glasgow, and this building would allow them to complete the transfer and close the Glasgow facility completely.

Things moved fast, so fast that it is likely that Coats, or more specifically Philippi, had been preparing the groundwork for some time. Highly confidential talks took place between the Coatses and Mr. Philippi on one side and Kenneth and Stewart Clark on the other, and agreement was reached in principal within a month, based on ten times the Clarks' profits for recent years, plus stocks and accounts receivable. Payment would be one-third in debentures, preference, and ordinary shares, with the remaining two-thirds in cash. Final agreement had to await the arrival of William Clark from Newark and he would not travel over until his daughter Elizabeth, had married a Mr. Thomas Laidlaw of Glasgow. Their son would go on to be chairman of the company, and their grandson later became CEO in the USA, so, unbeknownst to them, the wedding was an extremely important one for the company's future. It took place on April 15, and William left for Scotland forthwith.

Although these discussions were supposedly hush-hush, speculation had already started when the two families sat down together, and the value of Coats's shares started to climb. Towards the end of April, the arrival in Ferguslie of an accountant from London took on huge significance, and the rumour mill started working overtime. A week later, Coats's shares rose an amazing 18/9d within less than a day on the Glasgow Stock Exchange. Coats was forced to inform the Exchange that negotiations were all but complete and that the merger would be effective from July 1, 1896. As it turned out, it took another ten months to draft the fine print on the contract, and the final valuation was based on 9.3 years' profits with Coats having to find a total of £2,535,905.

Clark & Co. became an LLC, wholly owned by J. & P. Coats Ltd. and represented by three members on the Coats board—Stewart, Kenneth, and William Clark. Their manufacturing was to remain largely as it was, with the autonomy of Anchor and Newark preserved. Production levels were maintained at "the existing proportion of their combined output", which seems (and was) very vague and proved to be a point of dispute later on. Purchasing was merged, giving the newly formed company some serious buying power, with massive leverage in contracting both cotton and yarn in particular. Selling was all centralised and tightly controlled by Philippi.

Faced with this fusion, Brooks followed swiftly, disinclined to face up to the mammoth combine on their own. The deal they struck was broadly similar to the Clark agreement, with the price based on ten times earnings, Meltham Mills left as is (though Peter Coats dissented) and producing proportionately. They became an LLC with two board directors (T. J. Hirst and Sir E. Hildred Carlile) when they also joined J. & P. Coats on July 1. The price was just under £700,000.

In the meantime, Arthur Greg and Walter Mather, a fellow director of Chadwicks, were back at the negotiating table with Philippi. Greg had been persuaded to try again by a yarn merchant called McNicol, who had helped to broker the Coats-Clark deal. He contended that it was now or never if Chadwicks wanted to join the conglomerate, and he thought that Coats would accept the continuation of production at Eagley, as they had at Anchor and Meltham.

It transpired that Coats was more than happy to leave Eagley in place, but that they would do away with any useless agencies and, most importantly, would have absolutely the last word on group pricing. They also refused to pay any compensation to Eagley managers, as suggested by Chadwicks.

The final hurdle was the actual price. Chadwicks wanted one Coats share (at £40) for every two of their own, but Coats countered with one Coats share and £5 cash for every five shares, so there was a wide difference between £20 per share requested and £13 offered. There was some to-ing and froing, but Chadwicks realised that they were in a weak position, given the deals already struck with the others. By the end of May, they had agreed on four Coats Preference shares for five Chadwicks and one Coats Ordinary for three Chadwicks: £16 for the Preference and £15.3 for the Ordinary at current prices. They merged at the same time as the others, with one board director, Arthur Greg.[3]

When the merger finally happened, Coats had raised £4 million to pay for the deal,[4] and the shares already stood at £65. They had come a long way from the little factory by the Candren burn with its 12 HP motor. The thirty workers had become 21,000 in seventy years, with just over half of them employed in Britain. Their largest competitor had 3,000. The Group had 16 production units in 7 countries, 60 regional offices, 150 sales depots, 30,000 customers in Britain, and over 100,000 worldwide. They sold in 30 currencies at 7,000 different prices and made most of their profits overseas.

They had also achieved one of Mr. Philippi's goals. With the notable exceptions of France and Germany, they had taken over 50% of the local market in nearly every country where they sold. They produced 80% of the cotton sewing thread made for consumers in the UK and about 65% in the US. Alas, with this dominance came something that Coats had previously managed to avoid, variety. The acquisition of Clarks, Brooks, and Chadwicks had brought with it crochet,

3. Mather, who had conducted the final sessions with Philippi, was exhausted and took three days off afterwards, as "I feel a couple of days on my bicycle will do me good as my nerves are a bit upset with the last fortnight's excitement".

4. This was done by issuing 125,000 Ordinary £10 shares, 41,611 to be used as payment to the three companies being sold, as well as all of 50,000 Preference shares of £10 each. The remaining Ordinaries were offered at £50, considered a realistic figure based on the projected profits of £930,000 for the four companies together. Clarks and Brooks decided to take up 31,339 of these in lieu of cash, with a proviso that they were not to be sold before July 1888. They had wanted more, but this was their final allocation, with the remaining 52,500 offered first to existing shareholders—three for ten—and then to the public.

knitting, darning, embroidery, and linen threads,[5] as well as wool mendings and a whole variety of longer length industrial sewing threads, an area in which Coats had only dabbled until now.

Their size was impressive, not only in itself, but relative to others. The Group was now not only the largest cotton thread manufacturer in the world, but also the largest company in both British textiles and manufacturing. The combination of their technical supremacy, which was quickly rolled out from Ferguslie to all their production facilities, their selling organisation, their dominant market position, their financial acumen, their solid capital structure, and their experience in setting up local units when tariff walls were thrown up, made them a force to be reckoned with.

Yet they were not alone in the industry and had some serious competition. This came from as many as twenty companies in Britain, over forty more in Europe (protected by some very effective import tariffs), and at least two major rivals in the US, along with numerous smaller ones. The merger did not go unnoticed by many of them.

5. A hangover from Carlile.

Chapter 23

Competition Reaction and a New Century

The wise learn many things from their enemies.
Aristophanes

There is little doubt that the companies that made up the new J. & P. Coats Ltd. were the cream of the crop. Several of the remaining UK sewing thread firms had offered to join the Coats group, but had been turned down on the basis that they would weaken the newly formed conglomerate. They had suffered from the various price wars and were just as fed up as Coats was with their arbitrary nature and the resulting losses. Most of them had formed an Association in 1887, but it had been largely ineffective and had lapsed after a number of years.

In the face of the new Coats alliance, the need for a more permanent amalgamation was recognised, and in December 1897, fourteen companies got together to form the English Sewing Cotton Co. (ESC). This was a real hodgepodge. Only eleven of them made or sold sewing thread and several specialised in linen or silk. They all retained their individual identity (i.e., they continued to operate largely as before) but were reconstituted as limited liability companies, all owned by ESC, who had a board of seventeen directors representing all but one of the companies. They subsequently absorbed R.

F. & J. Alexander from Paisley and Alderns of Stockport, effectively converting the British Sewing Thread market into a two-horse race.

Things did not go well for ESC. There were conflicts with Coats,[1] mainly in Cuba and Spain, where Alexander's had a business. Their costing methods were inefficient, and they did not adopt the Coats system (whereby "every last cent could be traced"), even though it was offered to them. This was only one manifestation of their incompetent management, who struggled with old-fashioned machinery and ideas, and a stubborn belief in their own way of doing things. Excess capacity was identified but was not always idled, and even when it was, as with three plants in 1903, the cost was not written off the books.

Coats had already sold 100,000 of their shares when ESC first asked for help in 1899. Their profits had never been anything to write home about, but fell from £173,000 in 1898 to a loss of £127,000 three years later. The shares fell from £2/7/6d (£2.37½) to 9/6d. (£0.47½) over the period. Mr. Lawton, one of the directors, talked of "the gross over-capitalisation, the questionable finance, the extravagant and inefficient management, the bad buying, bad manufacturing, and bad selling".[2] Not a formula for success.

The shareholders now demanded a committee to reorganise the business and none other than Mr. Philippi was put in charge of this. As a result, Algernon Dewhurst stepped down as chairman, the board was reduced to seven, with only two of them coming from the original vendors, and a more economical salary structure was introduced, with performance incentives incorporated. Coats, through Philippi, had effectively taken English Sewing under their

1. Despite this, they were not completely hostile to the Coats group, who had been invited to take up shares and spent £200,000 for about 10% of the capital.

2. *Financial Times,* March 27, 1902.

wing and at least partially under their thumb and, although this didn't solve all their problems overnight, it did allow them back into profit by 1905-6, when they made £286,582, allowing them to pay a dividend of 8% and to put £70,000 into the reserves. They were on the mend.

On the other side of the Atlantic, a similar reaction to the Coats merger led to the creation of the American Thread Company, which was incorporated on March 10, 1898 and was made up of thirteen firms from the New England area, the largest being Willimantic. The capital was $12 million, $6 million in common stock, and $6 million in preferred shares. However, this company was far from being independent of the new thread group in the UK. The common shares were almost all bought up by ESC, which meant they had control, as the preferred stock carried no voting rights. Three ESC Directors were on the board of American Thread, and a year later, American Thread bought 125,000 shares in ESC.

Coats also had a small chunk of the business, having bought $500,000 worth of preferred stock, and they had another connection with them, through one of the thirteen companies in the group, the Kerr Thread Company of Fall River, Mass. Coats had bought their parent company in Scotland back in 1895. James Kerr was a director of American Thread, so Coats did not require their ESC connection to keep abreast of events in the US.

Lyman R. Hopkins of the Merrick Thread Company was the first president and under his leadership, American Thread was far more successful than ESC. They formed a Thread Agency, loosely reminiscent of TCA, to handle their marketing. They closed and wrote off the less efficient mills, reorganised the remaining plants with a rationalised product range and greater specialisation, and amalgamated the separate companies into one entity in 1903.

The success of the Coats conglomerate soon spawned yet other fusions within the textile world. The Linen Thread

Company was formed in 1898-9 by the union of six producers, and although their structure was more like ESC and they were relatively small, they resembled Coats in that there was one dominant company (William Barbour of Kilburn), and they operated in various countries, including the US. Coats had some interest in this new group, as some of the family had bought shares, and Sir Thomas Glen-Coats was on the board. Barbour would eventually become part of Coats about a century later.

May 1898 saw the creation of the Fine Cotton Spinners and Doublers Association (FCSA), made up of thirty-one companies spinning and/or doubling Sea Island and Egyptian cotton. Initial capital was £4,000,000, and Coats, for whom they were by far the largest source of externally purchased yarn, took 100,000 £1 shares. This group copied some of the more successful Coats strategies: centralised purchasing and selling, mill specialisation, and further acquisitions, so that within seven years they had over fifty companies (including a colliery) and some 3,000,000 spindles, and their capital had nearly doubled. Coats continued to buy about 70% of their yarn requirements for their UK mills from FCSA, so they were one of their most important customers.

Other mergers followed in quick succession. The Bradford Dyers, Yorkshire Woolcombers, Calico Printers, British Cotton & Wool Dyers, and the Bleachers Associations were all formed within two years. They had mixed fortunes, being mostly based on the ESC structure rather than Coats, and indeed the Bradford Dyers, where Coats had invested £50,000, collapsed within six years, whilst the Calico Printers had to be reorganised, a task which fell to Mr. Philippi in 1902.

None of them attained the level of prosperity of Coats, whose profits for the next year had reached £2,684,531—about five times the level recorded just before the merger. There had been few changes in the constituent members of the board in the interim, but there were several to come in the first five years of the new century as well as a change of leadership in the US and the death of the last surviving member of the first generation.

After his spectacularly successful sojourn in the USA, building the selling foundation of the family company, Andrew Coates had lived out the last forty years of his life in Scotland, first in Glasgow, but mostly just outside Perth. He had had little to do with the company, apart from the income paid by them for his part in Bates & Coates, but in 1878 the brothers bought his share of that company for £30,000 and then advanced him another £10,000 to help him start up a dye-house in Perth, named Coates, Pullar & Co., and £7,000 to buy Pitcullen House outside Perth in 1881. He took to hillwalking and would cover five or six miles every day, these distances slowly diminishing as he grew older. He remained active in many philanthropic ventures and helped to found the Perthshire Natural History Museum, the Perth Swimming Baths, and the Kinnoull Recreation Grounds, amongst others. His other loves were billiards and whist, though he never gambled.

He died on February 10, 1900, aged 85. His longevity was attributed to his extreme abstemiousness. As his son expressed in a biographical sketch produced for his funeral "He was so sparing in his diet that many of his friends wondered how he sustained life". If his photographs are anything to go by, he was extremely thin, bordering on emaciated, but he had a spark in his eyes and exuded vitality. All the Coats family with ties to the business attended his funeral, paying their last respects to the man who, probably more than any other, made the whole thing possible.

A year later, James (USA) returned to Scotland. He continued to serve on the board until his death in 1913, but he handed the management of Pawtucket and the American business over to his eldest son, Stuart. This transition was short-lived, as Stuart, a converted Catholic, decided to abandon thread, first for politics and then for the church. His political fortunes were mixed, as he unsuccessfully contested Morpeth in 1906 and Deptford twice, in all cases as the Unionist candidate. He then won the Wimbledon seat as a Conservative in 1916 and East Surrey two years later, and served in the House of Commons for four more years; hunting around for a safe seat had finally paid off. He had a rather longer tenure as Private Chamberlain of Sword and Cape (an honorary title given to Catholic laymen) to four successive Popes, and was suitably decorated by the Vatican.

He took no further part in the thread business after 1904, when his younger brother Alfred took over.[3] Alfred was a natural choice. He had been in the States since the age of one and was US educated, ending up at Yale. He had become a US citizen, married an American girl from Flushing, New York, and had settled permanently in the country. He went on to become actively involved in every aspect of life in Rhode Island.

Just as James (USA) left the US, Hezekiah Conant also retired.[4] He had been a valuable member of the company due to his technical skill, but at seventy-four had slowed down to the point where he attended sporadically and with little enthusiasm. Most descriptions of the man indicate that he was dour, straightforward, and rather private. His management style was not adapted to teamwork, which was becoming vital as his tiny mill grew into the monster complex it turned out to be.

A pension was arranged to allow him to retire gracefully, and he left without remorse, regret, or indeed any emotion. Coats had probably saved him from bankruptcy and made him a rich man. He had given them a foothold in the US at a

3. The same Alfred Coats who was shot by Archie and lost an eye.

4. He sadly did not get long to enjoy his retirement, as he died the following year.

critical time, and no end of ingenious devices for processing thread, but this interdependence never translated into any real rapport. His relationship with James (USA) had been courteous, and there was great mutual respect, but strange as it may seem, in the thirty-two years they worked together in the same office, they never visited each other's houses and never met or knew any of each other's families,[5] unless fleetingly through the obligation of a company function.

Back in the UK, the first major board changes of the period took place just after the merger, when Sir James Whitehead resigned, and his place was taken by Peter Mackenzie Coats, one of Archie's twin boys. Little is known of him, except that he worked in the Glasgow office and was therefore involved with sales, and that he was keen on cricket and fishing and encouraged these two pastimes within the company. He was to die of pneumonia within sixteen years.

William Hodge Coats, his twin brother, joined the board shortly after this. He had inherited a shrewd business sense from his father and, unlike many of his relatives, he was naturally gregarious, getting on well with people from all backgrounds. He also had a superb memory for names, so knew almost everyone he met and could address them appropriately, which was only one of the reasons he was liked by all. His main claim to fame was that he was fastidiously punctual. The citizens of Paisley were reputed to have set their watches by the time he left his house to get to Ferguslie in the morning. He would then equally punctiliously take the train to Glasgow to visit TCA and had only ever missed a train once, due to a flock of sheep on the road; he brought his schedule even further forward as a result.

5. Conant was married three times, his first two wives being sisters and both dying very young. He had two children, a son and daughter, by his second wife, but neither inherited his inventive flair.

At the same time, Daniel Coats stood down from the board and was replaced both there and in the mill by Peter Herbert Coats, whose father George was Sir Peter's fifth son. George had never worked for the company, having become a moderately successful grain merchant. Peter Herbert had been educated in both England and Germany and was the first true technician to run the spinning department, which by now was taking on far greater significance as Coats looked to increase the amount of yarn they made for themselves. He was a stickler for maintaining the quality of the Coats product and frequently visited Pawtucket where he served as president for a short time. He even sent his son Seton to do two years' training in preparation for taking over the management in the US, but Seton decided against it, resigned, and returned to Scotland.

Willie Coats left the board in 1901, though he appears to have continued with the dye-house, at least part-time. His seat was filled by Peter Herbert's younger brother Ernest, who also gradually took over Archie's son Peter's duties[6] in twisting and yarn buying. He had been educated at the University of Geneva, Switzerland, so as he gained experience, his international outlook made him a natural choice to represent the firm on the boards of Coats companies around Europe. He became one of its most travelled members, particularly as Mr. Philippi began to slow down. He was gregarious and loved the business but was said to be quick-tempered and inclined to "blow off steam".

The last change in the Coats family board membership was the retirement of Jimmie in 1904.

The Clarks were also witnessing a changeover. William Clark had recently returned from the US and settled in Curling Hall in Largs. Although he attended most board

6. Peter's appearances at work were becoming more sporadic. To add to the confusion with names, he was now known as "old" Peter.

meetings, he was but a shadow of his former self. He died on board his yacht Cherokee in July 1902.

Stewart and Kenneth Clark were so seldom at these meetings that the family interests were not being fairly represented. Their newfound wealth seemed to rob them both of any motivation. Kenneth Clark's son, the famous broadcaster and art historian who shared the same name, quipped that his parents were "members of a section of society known as 'the idle rich', and although, in that golden age, many people were richer, there can have been few who were idler".[7] He also said of his father "He thought to himself, if business interferes with your pleasure, give up business".

So John William Clark (William's oldest son) was invited over from the US as a board member and as managing director of the sorely neglected Anchor Mills, for at least twelve months. This turned out to be a highly successful two-year stint, after which he returned to Newark.

In his absence, William Campbell Clark (Kenneth's brother) took over the running of their US business. He had been in the US since the age of sixteen and had attended Rutgers College for two years, after which he started his career at the Newark mills. He subsequently took up US citizenship, married an American, and became a director of the American Insurance Company and the Essex County National Bank. He was, according to the family, more American than the Americans.

When John William Clark returned to the USA, his vacant position on the board was taken by James Oscar Max (known affectionately as J.O.M.) Clark. He was the son of another of Kenneth's brothers, Robert, and although still very young at 28, he had already had extensive thread experience with Clarks and had been instrumental in

7. From *Another Part of the Wood* by Sir Kenneth Clark, 1975, Harper & Row, London, page 1.

keeping the peace between his family and the Coatses in the aftermath of the merger. His slight frame belied his strength of will and determination, and although he was a man of few words, he commanded tremendous respect amongst his elders and peers, showing clarity of thought and an unflappable nature. He was also incredibly fit, as he would often walk from Anchor Mills to Troon, a distance of some thirty miles, and was such a keen tennis player that he co-authored a book called *A History of Tennis* in 1924.

He would go on to take an active interest in the growth of their US business and particularly the development and success of handicraft threads, such as the Anchor embroidery floss and Pearl cotton.[8] The advent of practical forms of mercerising helped him to develop a lucrative market which is still thriving today.

The merger caused other changes in the business. For one thing, the pace of expansion overseas accelerated with the dawn of the new century.

8. Coats had had little involvement in this area.

Chapter 24

Expansion Overseas

It has been said that arguing against globalization is like arguing against the laws of gravity.
Kofi Annan, UN Secretary-General 1997-2006

The new conglomerate's first overseas acquisition was quite close to home, in Belgium, where the thread industry had started around the same time as it did in Scotland, but based on linen rather than cotton. The first two mills had been built in Ninove, and it was a native of this town, J. B. Jelie, who opened the most important of three further companies in nearby Alost in 1822.

The arrival of the sewing machine in Belgium around 1870 spelt the end of linen thread and strengthened the position of those who, like Jelie, had moved into cotton production. He amalgamated with two competitors and changed the name of the company to Filature & Filateries Jelie. Louis van Langenhove, whose father had married Jelie's daughter in 1847, represented the family on the board. They became F&FR (Filature & Filateries Réunies), expanded rapidly both domestically and abroad, and absorbed Cumont-Leclercq, one of the three original Alost companies. This brought them to the attention of Coats, who started discussions regarding joining forces. Progress was slow.

Labour costs in Belgium were extremely low, so F&FR could beat Coats's prices and still make a decent profit, but continued price-cutting was shaving even their margins. Their product was of inferior quality, and they had a polished six cord article called Cats which had an awfully familiar look to it, with just a letter "o" missing. Negotiations dragged on, but when Coats threatened to build a local mill, Philippi had the lever he needed to seal the deal, and Coats gained a 67% share of the business for £230,000, equivalent to eighteen years' projected earnings. The spinning operation was not included; it became a standalone business.

The deal was not an immediate success. The wording of the final agreement caused some friction, as it implied that Belgian volume would be maintained, but was interpreted differently by the Belgians and the Scots. This became a bone of contention, as F&FR found itself withdrawing from many of its export markets as the Coats expansion rolled out, and although there was some local growth, it did not compensate.

It was, however, the last deal done by Coats in the nineteenth Century, and was only the first in a series of countries where they would set up local production.

They next took over the Lodz Thread Manufacturing Company in the town of the same name, in Poland. This had been set up in 1895 by two local spinners called Heinzel and Kunitzer, with complete modern manufacturing and some good-quality products under the Troika trademark, with the hope that local supply would give them a competitive advantage over Nevsky. Unfortunately, Coats proved too strong, so in 1900 the owners threw in the towel and sold 75% of their shares to them.

The next two years involved industrial turmoil in the area, and the operation was closed after Kunitzer (who had a spinning mill nearby) was murdered, and unrest in the plant became unsustainable. Production resumed within the year, and under a new, more robust agreement the mill worked satisfactorily despite multiple stoppages in neighbouring factories. Production resumed for both local use and for Nevsky, and the company progressed.

In the meantime, Coats had bought the Alexander mill in St. Petersburg, principally for access to the very popular Shuk (Beetle) trademark. The mill turned out to be totally unsuitable for quality thread production, so they scrapped the machinery and sold the building in 1898, transferring production to Nevsky. Despite this, the acquisition was a success, as sales of Shuk soon rose to 220,000 gross per annum, some 20% more than their popular but more expensive Blue Bear.

They next tried for the James Beck Spinning Company, which was situated next door to the Nevsky mill, and only failed to make a purchase because the owner collapsed and died on his way from the Central Hotel in Glasgow to the final negotiations with the Coats Directors, a few hundred yards away. His son subsequently sold the company to their competitor, Morosoff (for a better price), but Coats were allowed to continue buying yarn from Becks, despite this.

They picked up the Koenig Spinning Mill, which had stood idle for years and was also located in St. Petersburg. This was re-equipped to add capacity, and the production of the Chadwick mill at Riga was absorbed. They erected a five-storey mill at Nevka, also in St. Petersburg. This was achieved in a remarkably short three months by operating round the clock with three building crews working in shifts. By the time the machinery was installed and the workforce trained by Paisley specialists, only a year had passed, and the mill was operating as a specialised three ply production facility. With Koenig making the high-quality six cord threads, all the remaining articles were concentrated in Nevsky and the rationalisation was complete.

Coats had by now reached a market share in Russia of a remarkable 90%, but this truly magnificent position would not last too much longer, as the Russian Revolution was just round the corner. More of that later.

In the meantime expanding sales in Austria were met by modernisation in Harland and the construction of a new mill in Pressburg, now Bratislava. The mill at Ochsenburg was extended, and a new electrically driven plant was built on the Wilhelmsburg site in 1905. A tram was also installed to convey goods and people between Harland and St. Polten, and schools, a coop, and a sausage factory (apparently an Austrian priority) were added.

Germany had been largely off limits to Coats as the competition was fierce, the prices low, and tariff protection recently reduced, so local manufacturing had not been a priority. Then Coats was offered a small mill in Saxony which had burnt down and been rebuilt and modernised. The company was bankrupt, but as they had been guilty of copying trademarks in the past, it was felt that this was a good enough reason to buy, quite apart from the benefit of having a presence in Germany and a chance to get at the two main competitors. So they took over the Witzschdorf company in 1904, leaving the existing manager there but transferring a trainee of Philippi's, James Henderson, ostensibly to push the export trade, but really as his watchdog.

Henderson had joined TCA as a fifteen-year-old apprentice in 1897 and Philippi had immediately been impressed by his command of languages, his enthusiasm, and his intelligence. He had sent him to the TCA office in Hamburg in 1902 and then on to Frankfurt and saw this as a golden opportunity to let this budding talent blossom. Henderson did not disappoint. Within months, he was running the selling and administration, and became general manager in 1906. Two more years of improved manufacturing and more focussed selling, particularly on glacé products, saw the company completely turned around. With everything running smoothly, Mr. Philippi looked around for something else to occupy his protégé. He did not have to look far.

In Italy in the late 1800s, Tuscany became the main area for sewing thread producers, and the first to start up there was Carlo Niemack, who opened a unit for polishing heavy linen threads in Acquacalda di Lucca, a mile northeast of the ancient walled city of Lucca. Although this is an area of great natural beauty and extensive history, the main attraction was an endless supply of girls who would work for 4d. a day, and it also had a great source of water, both for economical power and dyeing. He made a cheap product and a respectable living.

His main competitors were two cotton mills, Pegli, near Genoa, and Cantoni, near Milan, which was owned by Baron Costanzo Cantoni, chairman of the Italian Cotton Association. The former company had a well-established trademark, Ariete (Ram),[1] which was renowned for its exceptional shine. The latter was the most important piece goods producer in the country, who made sewing thread as a sideline. In 1890, Cantoni closed this department and sold the machinery to Niemack, who moved it all to Lucca. His company was renamed Fabbriche Italiane di Filati Cucirini (FIFC), and he and Cantoni became partners (as chairman and vice-chairman, respectively). They struggled from the start.

Competition from Pegli turned out to be more vigorous than they had anticipated, and Niemack decided to leave. Then they were hit by a new product that they could not reproduce without considerable expense, mercerised cotton. This was sold on Spagnolette (200 yard tubes) at less than half the price of their more traditional polished article. The

1. Brooks sued, claiming it was a copy of their top article, Goatshead. The Italians prevailed, as it was established that they had registered their name first.

effect on their trade was immediate and catastrophic, so they approached Coats, who bought 75% of FIFC, renamed it Cucirini Cantoni Coats (CCC) and quadrupled the capital to 3.2 million lire. Peter Mackenzie Coats and Mr. Philippi joined the board.

The usual reorganisation of selling followed, but the company also absorbed Pegli and nine other smaller firms in rapid succession. It seems that once the others saw that Coats was established, they realised the writing was on the wall and decided to get a decent price for their business while it was still prosperous. Coats now had about 85% of the market and the wherewithal to make almost any product demanded, but such diversity needed to be better organised. They set about consolidating and modernising the Acquacalda site and put Baron Cantoni in charge, which turned out to be a big mistake.

Cantoni was an intelligent, well-trained engineer who was enthusiastic, quick-witted, and charming. He was also a stereotypical Italian: he talked "in a loud and explosive manner", gesticulating constantly, and was subject to extreme changes of temperament, which were difficult to deal with. He spent much of his time travelling between his various interests, rushing from board meetings to the next train, and although he walked fast (his gait was reminiscent of John Wayne, with his knees wide apart), he was seldom in Lucca, so he was compelled to delegate. This did not work well, as his force of personality was such that no one would do anything important without his blessing. With no hands-on coordinating force between projects and departments, the expansion program quickly fell behind.

Production control was nonexistent and the still-independent mills would quite often continue to make thread that was unsaleable. Cantoni was even prone to on-the-spot orders, which he would then forget about, leaving effectively dormant goods. None of the improvements or centralised control that Coats had suggested were implemented. Unable to tolerate the situation, Mr. Philippi called on James Henderson, who transferred over from Germany.

Henderson quickly got to grips with the problems in Lucca, where he spent his first five months. He discovered that the Baron did not like having unproductive people in the mill, as he felt they added unnecessary expense, but he would accept the incorrect production quantities and other errors that resulted from lack of planning. He was also prepared to save money on cotton quality, which led to all sorts of problems of variability within the mill and jeopardised the market leadership of the Coats brand. Lastly, Henderson was appalled by the wage levels within the mill and persuaded Paisley that they needed to be increased. The Baron was not happy, but as he was seldom there, Henderson effectively took over the mill, and the building and machinery program got back on track. Minimum wage levels within the mill rose 67% from 60 centesimi to 1 lira, which drove up overall wages, incurring the wrath of the other producers in the area, who were forced to follow suit or lose their workforce. However, this was not the only measure that annoyed the competition. In a move unprecedented in Italy, the weekly mill hours were reduced from sixty to fifty-five, which gave people Saturday afternoon off for the first time.

Henderson next turned his attention to the Milan office. On his first day there, the only person (besides himself) who had turned up by the appointed start time of 9:00 a.m. was the doorman. Henderson immediately sent out a memorandum on the "disadvantages of unpunctuality", and although he had no official position or title within the company, he signed it for CCC. The next morning, everyone was at his or her desk on time. He also scheduled regular meetings for the company managing directors and took over as secretary. Sales were brought under CCC, production coordination was introduced, and financial controls were improved.

Unfortunately for the Baron, the result of all this was that a red flag was raised over a private account in the ledgers in his name, through which he had withdrawn over 800,000 lire. A director from TCA went to Italy to investigate and quickly discovered that he had done the same with all the companies in which he held shares. He resigned, and the company bought him out at a generous price, whilst the loss was absorbed by two of the Italian directors and the three British directors—Ernest Coats, Peter Mackenzie Coats, and Ernst Philippi (Mr. Philippi's son). The other Italian directors refused to help and were dismissed.

James Henderson became one of the managing directors of CCC and, under the watchful eye of Mr. Philippi, virtually assumed control. By the beginning of the war he had rationalised the product range, closed the smaller mills, and liquidated most of the useless stocks.

In Spain, Alexanders had a mill in San Andrés, Barcelona, but had agreed to export all their output to Cuba, as part of the agreement with Coats when ESC was formed. In exchange, Coats withdrew from the Caribbean Island. However, when Spain ceased to have authority in Cuba at the start of 1899 as a result of the Spanish-American war, preference for Spanish products also ended and the effect on exports was immediate and devastating. Alexanders reverted to selling in Spain, which led to protests from Coats, but FyP also suffered, so they decided to make an approach to Coats to see if they could sort this situation between them.

As a result, Coats acquired 60% of a new company, Hilaturas Fabra y Coats, with FyP taking 33% and ESC 7%. Fernando Fabra remained as chairman, and Ernest and Peter Herbert Coats joined the board.

This company owned a multitude of depots and five mills: three from FyP, the Alexander mill in Barcelona from ESC, and the Coats Torelló plant. The depots were quickly rationalised and brought under the Philippi sales control system, with new ones opening in Madrid and Seville. Two of the three FyP mills were disposed of and the Barcelona plant dismantled, the workforce being transferred to the Alexander mill. This became a dyeing and finishing plant, with the Torelló mill becoming a spinning and twisting unit only. Coats steadily adopted this production model in several parts of the world, but this was the first time this particular split was made.

In neighbouring Portugal, Coats was forced into local production under a set of unique circumstances caused by the country's quirky legislation. In 1903, a rich and well-connected cotton and wool manufacturer, Delphin Pereira da Costa, applied for a monopoly for the manufacture and sale of cotton sewing thread in Portugal. Under the law, if he could establish that he was starting a completely new industry for the country, then he could get ten years of exclusive production rights and tariff protection - a complete monopoly. Thankfully, the TCA representative in Oporto, Sr. Emilio Biel, got wind of this and came to Coats's rescue.

Karl Emil Biel (he changed his name later to become more "Portuguese") had come to Portugal at the age of nineteen from Saxony in 1857 as an employee of a German company, but after three years in Lisbon, he moved to Oporto. Apart from being a pioneering photographer and butterfly collector, he was a gifted businessman, responsible for importing many innovative products for the first time. The list is impressive: the gramophone, the hydraulic turbine, the movie projector, and the first automobile, a Benz. He also drove the first tram through the city streets and brought in the first installation of electric light.

Amongst his multiple commercial interests, he became the sales representative for Clarks thread sometime in the early 1880s. When TCA was set up in Portugal, A. R. de Macedo handled Coats thread, but Biel stayed on with Clarks, and after the merger he took over the agency in Oporto. When John Clark first considered making thread in

Portugal two years before his death, he turned to Biel for advice, and the project had progressed to the point where he visited Oporto to view building plans and site options. However, the old man fell ill and as Biel put it "the whole affair was left hanging".

When the da Costa threat emerged, Biel cabled Glasgow that they should send out two hand-spooling machines without delay. He set these up in his garden saloon, which he converted into a sort of factory, producing as much thread as he could, using the black and the white hanks sent with them. It did the trick and the government denied the claim.[2]

This little scare was sufficient to galvanise Coats into action. They tried to set up a joint venture with Grahams, a Glasgow firm who, apart from producing Port wine, also owned two spinning mills in Oporto, but the deal fell through. So they decided to build a mill on their own.

The Companhia de Linha Coats & Clark (CLCC) was formed in 1905 and a sixty-seven-acre estate acquired on a hill in Vila Nova da Gaia, on the south side of the Douro River, near where the Port wine makers keep their warehouses. There were two flat areas within the site for a mill, and the tram came close to the gates, so transport would be easy for the employees. Local labour was abundant, inexpensive, and surprisingly intelligent. A small mill for the production of black thread and white thread soon took shape and finally went into production in 1908. Transport problems caused some delays, as imports arrived at the docks on the Douro, but then had to be brought a couple of miles up the hill on indifferent roads. One of the larger boilers was dragged up by fifty pairs of oxen over several days until it reached the installation site.

2. Da Costa did not take his defeat easily and started to manufacture six cord at very low prices, but his quality suffered—the public would try it but then revert to the products they already knew. Philippi eventually reached an agreement with him.

Even more serious was the water situation. They had to dig wells, but sources were hard to find. The problem was eventually resolved by an illiterate local farmer, who identified a spot where he said they would find a spring between twenty and thirty feet down. This proved to be the case, and two wells were constructed, feeding four storage tanks. CLCC thrived, and although they continued to import their coloured threads and handicrafts, the mill was extended in 1912 and employed some 400 workers by the start of the First World War.

Coats also bought a small twisting and spooling mill in Stroppel, Switzerland, which seemed obsolete and rather isolated for their taste, but the price was right.[3] They modernised it, added amenities, increased wages, and reduced working hours to help retain the labour force, but this all annoyed the Swiss Textile Employers' Association so much that no local firms would supply them with yarn. As spinning had never been contemplated, they continued to import from Ferguslie or Lancashire.

Production focussed on higher-quality three ply glacé threads for export, 75% going to ten neighbouring countries. By then, all the thread in Switzerland, apart from the bargain basement trade with department stores and certain army contracts, was sold by them or F&FR Belgium.

Coats's first venture into Latin America took them back to familiar territory for Mr. Philippi—Brazil. Since his visit there in the 1870s much had happened. The monarchy had ended and the country had become a republic in 1889. Slavery had been abolished at about the same time, and after a terrible period of rampant inflation the government wanted to stimulate local industry. Exports were heavily dependent on coffee, and São Paulo was the centre for this growing trade, which did help to improve infrastructure and attract immigrants. But the country needed other products to create

3. It included the family farm, but excluded their favourite horse!

wealth. Import duties were introduced to see if this would stimulate the country's manufacturers.

Coats had expanded their sales through a series of agents working under TCA, but around the turn of the century there was talk that the government would start to tax the parent company in Scotland as well as the subsidiary in Brazil, so they hurriedly formed Machine Cottons Ltd., a completely separate enterprise. This firm continued to import and sell as before, and with the coastal region developing rapidly, sales rose steadily.

By 1906, economic prosperity had precipitated a further tariff increase to the point where Coats, with their annual volume now over 400,000 gross, would be paying £130,000 in duties and although this still allowed them to make a decent profit, they worried that another company might open a local factory and effectively clean up. So they started to look for sites for a mill themselves.

They chose Ipiranga, now a suburb of São Paulo, where there was an appropriate flat site available (from the Dante family) beside the Tamanduatei River, providing water for the dye-house. The area already had some industry, largely pottery, and a plentiful supply of labour. In June 1907 they formed the Brazilian Sewing Thread Company (or CBLC in Portuguese) and the mill, which became known as the "factory of the English" was ready by 1910.[4] It included worker housing, for which a nominal rent was charged, and eleven houses for the managers. A dining area was built with

4. Specified by Coats in Glasgow to be "of the plainest and cheapest description possible...taking into account what materials and work can be obtained at moderate expense in the country and local conditions generally". This is rather droll, for although the buildings were made from plain exposed brick, which is economical, the bricks themselves came from Scotland!

a wood-burning stove (often fueled by defective spools) to cook soup, which was served with bread and bananas, and there were sports facilities and the predictable soccer pitch.[5] Within three years, additional machinery was added, and the workforce reached 400.

Further north, Coats had sold thread in Mexico as far back as the 1870s—Mr. Philippi had visited when he first joined the company. Now in charge of TCA, he set up Diego S. Dunbar as a stock holding agency to penetrate the market, which till then had been totally disorganised. An experienced Coats traveller, James Dunbar, was put in charge and quickly discovered that his main competitors in the spool market were the Chadwick agent, Robert Kevan [6,7], and, to a lesser extent, a local firm called El Salvador—a hosiery, cotton underwear, and balled sewing thread manufacturer in Mexico City. They were in trouble and arranged to borrow money from Dunbar, but when the Mexican revolution started in 1910, that was the final straw. After three years of unequal struggle, they were overjoyed

5. This is where Archie McLean, who could justifiably be called the father of Brazilian football, played. He had worked as a mechanic in Ferguslie and was still playing for St. Johnstone when he was transferred to São Paulo for three months in 1912. He stayed for forty years.

He started a factory team called the Scottish Wanderers, who played in the São Paulo State League, but ended up with Sport Club Americano, who represented Brazil against Argentina in 1913. He became known as Veadinho (Little Deer) and was a classic outside forward, but was most famous for introducing the short, sharp passing game that came to make Brazilian soccer so exciting. It caught on quickly, first known as "Scottish" but now called "tabelinha" (best translated as rhythm).

6. The agencies remained separate until 1904, when they moved into one building where Robert was said by a visitor to have "the smallest office I have ever seen".

7. Robert was enormous. He was the scourge of the local donkey and horse population, the main mode of transport—apart from very scarce railways—and his size was such that he not so much rode as engulfed his chosen mount. Frequent changes of steed were required for all but the shortest journeys.

when Coats agreed to buy them out for 600,000 pesos, a little less than £29,000 net. This was Coats's last acquisition before the First World War.[8]

They started selling through Dunbar using imported cotton, but bandit activity restricted travellers to an area in and around Mexico City and interrupted the flow of many supplies, particularly cotton. Financial systems broke down; a series of banknotes came and went, issued by successive rebel generals in different parts of the country. Corruption was rife and conventional business almost impossible. Despite all this, the company showed a small profit in its first year of operation and weathered the revolution.

8. They also started the La Plata Reel Cotton Co. in Argentina in 1900, but this was only a selling organisation.

Chapter 25

Unrest in Paisley

Technology...is a queer thing. It brings you great gifts with one hand, and it stabs you in the back with the other.
C. P. Snow, English chemist and novelist

Despite all this overseas activity, the mills in the UK were still the biggest manufacturing facilities that Coats possessed, and Ferguslie was used as the benchmark against which others were measured. Whilst the board were making their strategic acquisitions worldwide, the UK factories were reorganising and taking advantage of a series of technical advances which were not of themselves earth-shattering, but, taken together, allowed major improvements in production, productivity, and, therefore, cost.

Capacity in the UK continued to be tight, even though they now had over 500,000 spindles and 10,000 employees. Employment was much sought-after, and it was said that you needed "a line from the Holy Ghost" to get a job in the Paisley mills. The Anchor complex had grown with the addition of the six-storey Mile End mill, which had been planned before the merger and was completed two years later. This was built to take in the last of the production from the John Clark Jr. mill in Glasgow, but also allowed them to close and absorb Kerr's Underwood mill and Burnside.

Ring spinning began to supplant mule spinning for all but the finest counts. Bobbin sizes got larger, and speeds were raised by nearly 100%. Modern combers increased output, electric light improved visibility for the workforce, and the company began to dabble in individual electric motors, which spelt the beginning of the end for the shafts that ran the length of each building with drive belts running each machine off them. These were unwieldy at the best of times, but could be downright dangerous. Mechanical dyeing[1] and automated spooling, balling, and ticketing were also added.

The modernisation of Ferguslie and the attempts to bring the other mills up to the same technical standard led to frequent modifications to working conditions within each plant. Further changes were caused by the beginnings of some specialisation within the UK mills, with Anchor and Meltham starting to make handicraft articles and Ferguslie and Eagley moving towards spinning and twisting. All this coincided with the birth of the Labour Party in Britain and the rise of the trade union movement. Paisley had always been a hotbed of protest, and the socialist movement saw Coats as a typical capitalist employer with large profits and therefore a likely target for criticism, even though they were fundamentally good employers with a loyal workforce.

Against this background, disputes arose from time to time. Ferguslie suffered less than Anchor, as it was still run by individual Coats family members in each department, so there was a continuity of policy and management. Anchor's stoppages were more serious and lengthy. The Clark directors were less hands-on than their partners, and their long-serving plant manager Robert Balderston had died in 1897. His son and successor was definitely not a chip off the old block, so the Meltham mill manager was transferred in

1. Dyeing had been done by dipping the hanks into the dye liquor and moving them by hand. The new Sellers machine had rollers that automatically turned the hanks through the dyebath for a fixed amount of time in either direction.

in 1903, to see if he could improve things. Unfortunately, being a Sassenach,[2] he was always viewed as an outsider and was never accepted or trusted. The superintendents under his charge did not help the situation either, so an atmosphere of tense unease permeated the whole complex.

In both plants it is fair to assume that many of the conflicts that arose were due to misunderstandings. Changes were almost certainly imposed without being explained properly and when earnings appeared to be affected, the knee-jerk reaction—doubtless encouraged by trade union activists—was to down tools.

Two minor incidents in Ferguslie presaged more serious action in Anchor. The first was a two-day stoppage by the spooling department in 1897, where a change in the distribution method for spools was alleged to have affected earnings by interrupting production. The workers were persuaded back after a further day's lockout. The second problem blew up some three years later when a new testing procedure in cop winding appeared to reduce take-home pay by as much as 25%. This strike lasted several weeks and although it was limited to the one department, it eventually affected other parts of the mill, leaving assorted sections idle. It also gave the burgeoning trade union movement some useful propaganda, though they hardly needed it. The company was accused of moving production abroad to avoid paying higher wages in Scotland—an unfounded claim at the time. Even more outrageous was the suggestion that wage levels in the mills were so poor that many of the girls needed to supplement their income through prostitution. This provoked one of their number to write, "There is no girl gets a wage so low she needs to resort to the streets to make money. I think it is only because we would not join the Union that this unjust and untruthful statement has been

2. An English person, from the Gaelic for Saxon. Usually used disparagingly by the Scots.

made".[3] Archie Coats's reaction was more direct "No lie is too palpable, no slander too foul!"

All this helped fuel the tension in Anchor, and it finally boiled over into a strike in May 1904. Hankwinders (who unwind dyed skeins in preparation for finishing) stopped work, and by the fifth day had persuaded all the winders, ballers, spoolers, and the boys who supplied the spools to join them, a total of over 1,000 people. The company's first offer at compromise was rejected, so they attempted to break the strike by locking the workers out until 10:00 a.m., after which any who still wanted their jobs were to enter. The strikers threatened the few who did, so that soon failed, but a better offer in the afternoon was accepted. The plant reopened.

The following year the same group persuaded over double this number to come out in sympathy with their grievance. This was eventually resolved, but the company was losing patience.

Both strikes followed a similar pattern. The strikers would parade through the streets, some on carts as if it were a carnival, the lads from the corn-mill would offer them peasemeal to use as ammunition, and workers from other factories would come out to watch the fun. Managers and foremen would be jostled, and stabbings with hatpins were not uncommon.

A study on wage rates was instigated by J.O.M. Clark, but agitation for increased wages continued, fueled by outside union officials. The next year started out with a very full order book, but production could not keep up due to absenteeism and sickness. Stocks were depleted. Wage increases were granted in early spring, but soon afterwards the company announced that any plans for further buildings and machinery in Ferguslie had been abandoned as the conditions were too uncertain with all the industrial unrest.

3. *The Glasgow Herald*, April 12,1906.

Coats had decided to switch the increased capacity to Lancashire, and to this end they bought the Ashworth mills at Egerton, near Bolton, from ESC, who were happy to sell.

This purchase made sense, quite apart from the question of labour relations. Although the buildings were very run down, once modernised they neatly complimented Chadwicks' Eagley mill, which lay nearby, and there was ample labour available, an important factor with 1,000 operatives needed. The additional capacity was quickly brought on stream, which helped alleviate the overall shortage of spools in the market, and it continued to operate as overflow capacity until 1912, when it was closed.

A rumour propagated that J. & P. Coats, weary of labour problems, were going to abandon Paisley completely in favour of Canada, much to the consternation of all who depended on the company for their living. It turned out that this was caused by a classic case of mistaken identity. A carpet maker from nearby Potterhill had published the following when they suffered a stoppage: "Owing to the interference of the Socialist element during the strike of carpet weavers at Colinslie, Messrs Coates Bros. intend building new works in Canada, and gradually closing down those in Paisley".

Although greatly relieved to discover that it was another Coat(e)s that was leaving Paisley, the town council were still very concerned about the freeze on further expansion in Ferguslie, and they begged the company to reconsider. This was politely but firmly refused. Coats also indicated that whilst they in no way actively opposed the workers "forming themselves into a Union for the protection and promotion of their own interests", they would never deal with outsiders who claimed to represent their workers and would only negotiate with deputations from their own workforce in cases of dispute. This did little to enhance their reputation and brought further criticism.

This took the form of an attack on their position as a monopoly. Coats had acquired Wardle & Davenport in Leek before buying Ashworth. This came hot on the heels of vigorous press criticism of the Lever Brothers Soap Trust. When Coats announced their 1906 profit at nearly £3 million, the anti-monopoly pressure group were infuriated. Their principal mouthpiece was the ironically named Liberal MP, Mr. (later Sir) Leo Chiozza Money, champion of sweatshop labour and scourge of powerful conglomerates.

He complained to the president of the Board of Trade, David Lloyd-George, that J. & P. Coats had a virtual monopoly on the sewing cotton market of the UK and asked for legislation to control "a trade which affects every working woman in the country". He also wrote in the press: "The buyers of sewing cotton are numbered by millions. But there is only one shop. It is the shop of Messrs. J. & P. Coats".

Lloyd-George responded that there were over twenty sizable independent thread makers in the UK, so "there is no monopoly of the sewing cotton trade". However, that did little to satisfy the MP, who continued to accuse Coats in a series of exchanges throughout the year. Others joined in until the chairman's statement in November, where Archie defended the company position, pointing out that it had taken a century to build the business to where it was and that others could not make the same level of profits, as they were less efficient and had poorer quality. He also asked why Coats should be seen as a species of malefactor, having to apologise for the profitability of the business. He responded to accusations of exploitation of Paisley workers by pointing out that over half the profit came from overseas and noted that the majority of these profits went back into the business to provide for such things as pension funds.

He also remarked, to rapturous applause and laughter, that: "the attempt to make our workers dissatisfied has so far met with little success, although it must not be overlooked that among so many there is bound to be a certain number who think they have cause to complain and those are almost invariably the worst workers, who would not be able to make good wages under almost any conditions".

Despite these assertions, the situation in Anchor was still far from settled, the problems stemming as much from these "worst workers" as from unsympathetic management. Pressure for the girls to join a union (the National Federation of Women Workers was a favourite) had grown to the point where even the fiery founder and secretary of the NFWW, Mary McArthur herself, held forth at gatherings by the mill gates. Both mills continued to suffer with minor disputes and, although Ferguslie handled these quickly and efficiently, an anxious calm settled over Anchor. It was clear that there was a storm brewing.

This finally broke on September 24, 1907, when the boys from the turning shop struck over the introduction of a Ferguslie system that they claimed would lower their earnings. The offer of a time rate as they got used to the system was rejected, and the next day the hankwinders and polishers came out in sympathy. Other departments were affected, and on the morning of October 1, a demonstration by a crowd of workers turned ugly, and they began smashing windows. The police were called and turned out in force. They were pelted with flour and then attacked with hatpins when trying to make arrests. There was no alternative but to close the plant.

At this point the girls turned their attentions elsewhere and "...three or four thousand of them marched along the High Street to the West End shouting and cheering...",[4] on their way to Ferguslie to see if they could persuade their colleagues to support the strike. In this they were unsuccessful, so they attempted to storm the gates of the mill, and in the process injured several Ferguslie workers, despite the best efforts of the police to control the mob.

4. *The Scotsman,* October 2, 1907.

Coats closed the mill, fearing further violence.[5] Police reinforcements were drafted from outlying districts in an attempt to keep the peace. A delegation from Anchor met with the company in Glasgow, and the strikers went back to work on October 4, "in high good humour" according to the *Glasgow Evening Times*. Negotiations resumed in Anchor, and although the turners struck again "without reason" (and without support) a few weeks later, things calmed down.

Concessions were made on both sides. The workforce accepted a period of two weeks' notice of strike action, and the company agreed to change the management. J.O.M. Clark began to take a more direct role in Anchor, and both sides took the opportunity to make a fresh start. This coincided with some of the company's overseas investments coming on stream, so production pressure eased, and the mood inside the mill improved.

Things got even better at the end of the year when wage rates were increased by the equivalent of between one and two shillings a week, and in January 1908 working hours were cut from fifty-six to forty-nine. This almost unique period of labour unrest was over, and although it may have seemed serious, relations within the Paisley Thread mills remained harmonious until the 1970s. There were good reasons for this.

5. They continued to pay full wages to the workforce.

Chapter 26

Pay and Perks

Man becomes great exactly in the degree in which he works for the welfare of his fellow-men.
Mahatma Gandhi

Although we would not view the Coats & Clark mills of the late nineteenth century as comfortable places to work, they were a far cry from Blake's "dark satanic mills" and were considered exemplary in their day. They were spacious, clean, well-lit, and had regulated heating insofar as it was possible prior to refrigeration and other modern conveniences. Both Anchor and Ferguslie were highly praised in an 1893 report by the Royal Commission on Labour, where Margaret Irwin, the Lady Assistant Commissioner who wrote the section on the Textile Industries in Scotland, described the former as the "finest in the kingdom" and praised the latter as the best she had seen for "sanitation and general internal appointments", noting particularly the efforts to control temperature and supply other amenities. The rates of pay were competitive with the industry as a whole and with other regional employers.

The criticism is often leveled at the thread "barons" that they exploited the workers and grew rich as a result. The evidence to support this accusation is less clear than the emotive reaction that comes from today's society where the government supplies free education, unemployment benefits, and other support that was not available in the late 1800s. At the turn of the century, the welfare state was still in its infancy. The Labour Party, which had around thirty candidates in the 1895 general election, was just emerging, and the trade union movement was growing along with it.

Against this background, Coats and Clarks wage levels—particularly for females—were rather better than those offered by other available employment opportunities. A shop worker in the 1890s would have worked an eighty-hour week and earned 25% less than a mill winder, whose week lasted fifty-six hours and would soon be further reduced. Dressmakers did marginally better than the women in retail, and nurses were the worst paid of the lot, a situation that hasn't changed to this day.

It is true that the women made much less than the men in the mills, but that was no different from the rest of Scotland, where the average male's wage was nearly 2.4 times that of their female counterparts. Women in Britain were still second-class citizens; their right to vote on the same terms as men would not be granted till 1928, and even today total wage equality between the sexes does not exist across all industries at all hierarchical levels.

It is when you look beyond the simple question of wages that Coats was innovative and original. The UK state pension first appeared in 1909, but Coats had anticipated this when they introduced a formal pension scheme for salaried employees in the early 1900s. This was the successor to an informal, voluntary, noncontributory system from even earlier, where they frequently granted pensions or ex gratia payments to long-term personnel. The exact details of this are unclear, but the minimum service they considered for such loyalty payments appears to have been twenty years, and the fund stood at £200,000 by 1905. They extended similar help to those injured or who became too ill to work and would often pay for funeral expenses. They had established a Friendly Benevolent Society as insurance for workers in cases of sickness or death in 1884, and finally formalised pensions for females in 1920 with the creation of the Women's Thread Workers Benefit Fund.

Jimmie Coats took it upon himself to finance and arrange outings to Largs for older Ferguslie workers. Although these were much appreciated, they were discontinued after he retired as it was felt they discriminated against employees of all the other plants in the enlarged group.

Existing workers were offered other forms of support. Loans were made available in cases of dire need, and although the company would charge interest, it (and sometimes some of the principal) was not always collected. Another example of a different type of help was given to a young spooler who was injured at work. She not only had her wages paid whilst recovering, but also had £100 invested for her, to be received upon reaching an appropriate age or when she married. This was not common practice in the nineteenth century.

The company distributed coal in the early days, particularly to those affected by recession, and later they gave out scrap wood from spool turning. Free thread was provided for all employees, but this had to be restricted to 100 spools and 100 crochet balls a day, due to excess demand.

Both companies were also singled out for praise for their outstanding attention to health and safety in the Irwin report of 1893 and although by then all the male employees were being given first aid training, this was before much of the real progress was made. The first ambulance service at Ferguslie began two years later, and in 1911 the Voluntary Aid Department, affiliated with the Red Cross, was established at Anchor Mills. Coats followed during World War I. This department not only handled first aid within the mills, but also distributed gifts to sick employees and pensioners, who were also called on by "lady visitors" hired by the company for this specific purpose in 1921. The medical facilities in both mills were completely rebuilt and updated that year, and a full-time dentist was installed three years later.

The Coats and Clark families were active in improving the hospitals and healthcare facilities in the town of Paisley. Oddly enough, it was Andrew Coates in Perth who may have started this philanthropic trend. He and his friend Laurence Pullar had set up a business together and went on to create Homes for Incurables in Edinburgh and Kirkintilloch. Archie's wife Elizabeth went to visit Andrew and returned in high spirits, persuading her husband to fund a similar venture in Paisley, the Gleniffer Home for Incurables.

The Clarks also contributed. Stewart's wife Annie started a fund for Incurables, and he had the Victoria Eye Hospital opened in Gauze Street. This was subsequently enlarged and moved to Mansionhouse Road, where it had seventeen beds.

George and "old" Peter Coats were heavily involved in the modernisation of the Alexandra Infirmary, the principal hospital for Paisley. After obtaining land for a brand-new facility, and with the usual struggle to find funds, it was eventually built in 1894, creating a clinic with 142 beds at a cost of £55,000. Peter also pledged £50,000 to the building of a nurses' home for the hospital and this was not only completed in 1896, but he paid for an extension and tennis courts some five years later, buying up all the surrounding derelict buildings just to knock them down and improve the view.

A sanatorium, or "fresh air home", on Gleniffer Braes was opened in 1911, courtesy of a gift from J. & P. Coats Ltd. This was called the Peesweep and was specifically for sufferers from tuberculosis who were sent there to be cured.

It required continual financial support, which the family provided for years; it was eventually made over to the county council.

After their owners' deaths, a number of the Coats mansions became homes for the elderly or infirm. Woodside (Sir Peter's and then Archie's house) became a home for mothers and children, and Glencoats house in Ferguslie Park (the Glen-Coats residence) and its grounds became the Glencoats Auxiliary Hospital with twenty-five beds.

The companies also recognised the need for adequate nutrition. As early as 1850, they provided a separate area where the mill workers could sit and eat their piece (a Scottish sandwich), rather than have to rush home and back in often inclement weather. They then started to supply tea and coffee as well, and by 1880 had developed a dining hall with ovens where meals could be heated. This became so large that it could take 500 at a sitting and soon began to supply a hearty meal of fish and potatoes for 2d.(£0.0083).[1] Anchor started their canteen shortly afterwards along similar lines, and in 1901 bought Stewart Clark's house, which stood in the grounds of Anchor, as a canteen and recreation centre.

Both families' commitment to education, which had started in earnest with old Thomas Coats, continued both within the town and at the mills. As far back as the 1830s the younger girls in the mill had been allowed off work an hour early to attend evening classes. The George Street Dyeworks became a Technical College, thanks to Coats, and in January 1887 Peter Mackenzie Coats opened the Half Timers' School, which had been built on the site at Ferguslie.

Apart from being an architectural gem, this building fulfilled a need that the company had long recognised—improved education for their younger mill workers. These were known as "half-timers", as they worked half a day in

1. The cost for the half-timers was only 1d., which was also what the company charged for a good Scots breakfast of porridge.

the mill and then spent the rest of the day at school, a common enough practice all over Scotland and England at the time. It was an unfortunate fact of life that parents were keen to get their offspring out to work and earning,[2] even if it interfered with and sometimes ruined a good education. Truancy was common with this system, and the children lost a great deal of time in transit between home, work, and school. Coats wanted to see if it could be improved.

The school at Ferguslie was groundbreaking for a number of reasons. The girls there would work alternate days at the mill and the school, which was felt to be more conducive to learning than the traditional "split" days. The six classrooms in the school were well lit, with nearby cloakrooms and toilets all on the ground floor, whilst in the basement there were kitchens where nutritious meals were prepared. Lessons were confined mainly to the three Rs,[3] and the academic level attained was as good as any in the area or, indeed, the country. Up to 400 girls could be accommodated, and there was also a gallery which overlooked the ground floor, where concerts, plays, or recitals could be performed. After the introduction of compulsory full-time education for children and the raising of the school-leaving age to fourteen in 1904, its administration was taken over by the Paisley education board and it eventually became a canteen. There followed a spell as a social club and then a nightclub, but it was subsequently vandalised and is now unhappily derelict.

Technical education was also a priority. John Clark left £5,000 in his will for a new dining room, pool, and gym for the industrial school on Albion Street. Coats paid the fees for their young men (discrimination was a fact of life back then) to attend colleges such as the Paisley Artizan's Institution, established back in 1847, and people took night classes in subjects as diverse as languages, chemistry, engineering, and

2. To the point where they would falsify birth certificates to get their children working at an earlier age.

3. Reading, wRiting and aRithmetic.

accounting. After 1900, they started to create internal promotions by taking the brightest of the bunch and giving them interdepartmental training to assess their potential.

Not all of these evening classes were vocational. The girls were also sponsored to take further education, but the subjects had a different orientation: domestic science, dance, dressmaking, health, millinery, and several academic subjects were the typical choices. Jimmie Coats personally financed sewing and cookery lessons until he retired. Many of these classes were held by the company at the Girls Home, opened in 1901. This was a hostel with accommodation for girls who were homeless or lived a long way from the mills. It had a library, several common rooms for recreation, and a hall, as well as dances and concerts. Its stated aim was "to promote self knowledge and self development", but it proved unpopular and closed within five years.

Nursery education for the children of single mothers, either widowed or never married, was offered post-1880, and both crèche and nursery amenities were provided to ease the burden of working mothers with multiple offspring.

All work and no play makes Jack a dull boy, so sports and recreation were also seen as important, especially as most of the employees had neither the wherewithal to join a club nor the space in their own cramped living quarters for leisure activities. Probably the first mill "club" was the Ferguslie Brass Band, formed in 1856 and limited to thirty people initially, at a time when the mill was still relatively small. They practiced twice a week and were very regimented.

The opening of the Ferguslie sports ground and pavilion in 1883 was the start of more extensive activities, including lawn tennis, quoits, lawn bowls, football, and cricket, for which a full-time professional was retained by the company to train the players and do the groundskeeping. The club's first match was against Kelburne CC, who viewed their opponent with such disdain that they allowed them to field seventeen men, instead of the usual eleven. The result was to be expected—rain stopped play—one of the reasons why to this day cricket has never caught on as a sport in Scotland (though Kelburne CC still exists).

Anchor had more limited sporting facilities until 1923 when their recreation club was opened. To celebrate, they held three-legged and sack races for the mill girls, and a film of the proceedings was subsequently shown at the Palace Cinema on the High Street, much to the delight of the participants who got a chance to see themselves for the first time on the silver screen.

The Clark employees enjoyed a similar range of activities as their colleagues across town. They opened their Bowling Green in June 1896, and this became the first major centre for inter-mill fixtures. J.O.M. Clark donated a cup for which all the local clubs competed and which both companies won on several occasions. They also had an annual private challenge, when they played each other for the aptly named Loving Cup, an event not unlike an Old Firm (Celtic v. Rangers) football match or golf's Ryder Cup, given the strength of feeling and partisan nature of the spectators.

Both mills also had indoor activities available, including smoking rooms, billiard tables, board games, and newspapers. Other clubs, societies, and musical activities were encouraged and sponsored over the years, including the Wellington Golf Club, which is still active after 110 years. Through it, the company sponsored international tournaments between all the Coats units for many years.

One of the mostly keenly anticipated events of the year in Paisley was the annual outing, which Clarks initiated in 1869 and Coats a year later. No record of these first excursions has survived, but in 1873 Clarks went to Rothesay and 1,200 Coats employees spent the day in Ardrossan. By 1889, when Coats visited Girvan, there were 4,000 attendees. The destination was usually on the west coast of Scotland, the participants visiting the likes of Ayr or Gourock, but they sometimes went farther afield, to Edinburgh or later on, when buses could be used, to faraway Braemar.[4] The day was usually Sma' Shots day, a famous local holiday held at the beginning of July in Paisley, and one of the oldest workers' celebrations in the world.

The Sma' Shot was a strong fine weft thread used to hold the materials together in the famous Paisley shawls. It was not intended to be seen as part of the pattern, but was essential to make the fabric perfect. The weavers bought their own yarn and thread and sold the finished shawls to greedy buyers known as "Corks", who refused to pay for the Sma' Shot as it could not be seen in the end product. After a long dispute, during which the Charleston drum was beaten to call the weavers out on protest marches, the buyers relented and from then on paid for the hidden thread.

From 1856, the first Saturday in July, which was a traditional holiday for the weavers, was renamed Sma' Shots Day to celebrate this victory, and the same drum was beaten at the head of the procession leading the weavers on their annual outing, usually to a seaside town such as Ayr. At some point in the proceedings, an effigy of the "Cork" was burnt in a symbolic act of defiance. The thread factories picked up on this tradition (apart from incinerating the dummy), but on a much grander scale.

These days out were a mammoth undertaking. The employees would put small amounts aside weekly during the year into the Holiday Book, usually held by some trustworthy soul within their department. This gave them some spending money for the big day and although they were expected to pay a small amount for the trip, the company heavily subsidised the whole thing. Everyone

4. After the First World War, a special excursion was arranged for ex-servicemen and their wives, on the SS Iona, which sailed down the Clyde from Paisley Harbour.

would then meet at the mill at dawn and march to the station behind the brass band—as many as 10,000 in its heyday. They would then catch one of several trains especially reserved for the occasion and upon arrival would be escorted to an appropriate area (with tents in case of bad weather) where there would be prayers and a meal followed by music, dancing, sports, and games. These could be anything from running races, egg and spoon, or tug o' war, usually with departmental teams competing and were followed by prize giving. The return would be late in the evening, and quite often large crowds would appear to watch the procession wend its weary way back to their place of work. The last one took place in 1949.

The other important annual social event arranged by the company was the Soirée, where smaller groups of employees would get together, usually for a meal, and would listen to a talk from one of the company directors, a loyal employee, or even a religious leader. The family was aware that they were becoming more remote from their workforce as the company grew, and this gave them a chance to talk with their employees directly. These evenings, which started in 1871, involved much speechmaking and mutual backslapping, and the theme was more often than not the company's success, their mutual interest in its continuation, and the dangers of poor workmanship. They would also impress upon those present the virtues of godliness, sobriety, and thrift.

The practice of putting money aside for the future, which James Coats Sr. had seen as being so important and which pervaded every business practice of the company and the subsequent generations, was encouraged in all who worked for them. From as early as when they were half-timers, employees were encouraged to save five shillings a month in an account with a local savings bank, and this amount was then matched by the company.[5] This would

5. Anticipating, by about a century, what some American firms do nowadays with 401k accounts.

yield about £20 after three years and promoted the principals of self-help that the Coats family fervently believed in. It then made their subsequent job much easier when persuading their employees that putting larger amounts into the same (Paisley) Savings Bank was prudent. They were obviously successful in that the bank's assets grew by over 50% between 1854 and 1871.

These types of benefits were also introduced in the mills that Coats opened overseas. Ferguslie became as much a welfare as a technical model to be emulated by the other plants in the group. There is little doubt that this concern for employee well-being helped enormously in fostering good labour relations around the world.

Chapter 27

USA

Quality is never an accident. It is always the result of intelligent effort.

John Ruskin, Art critic of the Victorian era

Welfare played a leading role in the success of the company's units in the USA. The formation of large conglomerates such as Standard Oil had created a reaction from organised labour, who were also marshalling their forces into larger combinations. The American Federation of Labor had been formed in 1886 and had over two million members by the turn of the century. Labour unrest was as common as in the UK, and there were thousands of strikes every year.

The company plants largely escaped all this. As in Paisley, they had a policy of paying slightly above the average rate for the area, and they all offered attractive working conditions. Fringe benefits at the Coats plant in Pawtucket were recognised to be outstanding. Apart from all the more usual provisions, they set up a fund to help needy workers with food, fuel, and medical expenses, and they helped with cases of tuberculosis. The Clark mill in Newark was the only one in the area where they had reduced Saturday to a half day, and instead of making their employees queue in all sorts of weather to collect their pay, this was delivered to everyone at their workplace. They also had a pension scheme and in 1910 introduced a savings plan. The Clark Building & Loan Association was run by a group elected from the workforce and designed to help with and promote home ownership. Their sporting facilities were outstanding, and they were one of the first to introduce soccer to the US, forming the Clarks O.N.T. team on November 15, 1883 and winning the inaugural American Cup in 1885, as well as the next two. Several of their players were picked for the national team, which played international fixtures against Canada on the Clark ground. They also had a successful baseball squad, but their cricket team fared less well.

The introduction of the same technical changes as those initiated in Scotland paralleled the program in Paisley. Similar productivity improvements were made and disputes arose, but there was remarkably little disruption. The trade unions had even less influence over the US thread mills than in Scotland, and the only conflicts occurred in 1906 and 1909, when wage claims that had been okayed by the Pawtucket management and blessed by Paisley were vetoed by Alfred Coats, the GM. He resented the absentee directors breathing down his neck and resisted the tight control imposed from Glasgow. He also spread himself rather thinly, taking on multiple directorships of other companies and local associations. In the end his independence became too much for the company, and in 1910 he was forced to resign.

The American market was very much self-contained with little of the mills' production being exported. Volume was not growing as rapidly as it had in the aftermath of the invention of the sewing machine, and with the productivity and production rate improvements resulting from modernisation of machinery, overcapacity began to build up. A price increase for 200 yard spool thread from 5¢ to 6¢ (after over fifteen years) created a backlash from both the customers and the anti-monopolists in the US, and although it was justified on cost grounds,[1] it was still soundly rejected by their customers and resulted in significant lost sales. After less than a year, the increase was reversed, but the damage had been done and further capacity fell idle.

The company had restructured their selling systems soon after the merger, bringing together George A. Clark & Bro. and the Coats Thread Co.[2] to trade as The Spool Cotton Co. They moved into offices at 80-82 White St. in 1902 with Theodore Frelinghuysen from Coats in charge, and the Philippi selling methods were applied, much to the consternation of the Clarks salesmen, who were unaccustomed to such close supervision. One of their number, Deane Pratt, composed a poem entitled "A Drummer's Dream" in which he included the verse:

Always we dressed in the latest style,
Could smoke Perfectos fine,
For all went on expenses,
But now they draw the line.
We dare not use a postage stamp,
Or on a street car ride,
Unless permissions cabled first
From o'er the other side.

Purchasing was also amalgamated, but manufacturing consolidation had hardly been examined, with Pawtucket and Newark making all their own products from bale to bobbin.[3] This was partly due to the different structures and styles of the two companies, with Pawtucket being directed by Ferguslie, whereas Newark was owned by Clark & Co.

1. These were up by about 35% in the corresponding period, with cotton up 134%, wages 24%, spools 41%, and general supplies 119%. This makes a 20% price increase appear modest, but the 5¢ price point was important and departing from it was viewed by the consumers as unacceptable.

2. Their offices were both on Broadway, a few doors from each other.

3. Unlike Paisley, they bought in almost no yarn.

in the US and more loosely overseen by Anchor. An American committee was set up in Scotland in 1903, and with the creation of central testing and production efficiency departments in 1908 to promote the comparison and standardisation of products, followed by Alfred Coats's exit in 1910, some integration could finally begin.

The excess capacity also allowed the companies to introduce new products, and with both J.O.M. Clark and, to a lesser extent, William Campbell Clark being fervent promoters of handicraft threads, a number of these were introduced.[4] Some embroidery cotton had previously been sold in the US, but with little success, as the established market leaders, the French firm DMC, dominated the market with four cord Coton-a-Broder and six cord Mouliné. The timing of the launch of these new products was fortuitous, as the First World War would severely restrict the supply lines for the French and allow Coats to get a foot well in the door. The war also helped to stimulate demand for these items, presumably as many women were stuck at home, worrying about their loved ones, so they took to crochet as a form of distraction. The company resuscitated the publication of pattern books and advertised heavily in women's magazines. Volume grew rapidly throughout the war and for several years afterwards.

With the introduction of more handicraft articles, some specialisation could take place and Pawtucket began to take on the Ferguslie role, making grey thread for the others, whilst Newark emulated Anchor, becoming something of a handicraft specialist. The other smaller mills filled in the gaps.

Now that Coats was doing a much greater proportion of their own yarn spinning, they had developed close relationships with brokers Henry W. Frost in Charleston and John Malloch in Savannah. In late 1870 they set up their own

4. Clark's Pearl Cotton and Coats Mercer Crochet are two examples.

warehouse in Florida for storing cotton bought and financed through Auchincloss, but it wasn't until 1889 that they started to buy major quantities from the Florida Manufacturing Co., who bought seed cotton from the planters, and ginned and baled it for onward sale; they also dealt in seed and seed oil. After financing much of this operation through loans, J. & P. Coats took up 60% of the ordinary share capital of the company when it was reincorporated in New Jersey in 1900, the other 40% being bought by the FCSA in Manchester. Sadly, the company was destined to fail, finally being dissolved on June 10, 1918.

This was largely the fault of an extremely destructive pest called the boll weevil. This beetle crossed the Rio Grande and first entered the USA from Mexico near Brownsville, Texas in 1892. It then spread about sixty miles a year, the infestation reaching all cotton-growing regions by about 1920.

The insect lies dormant during the winter. When it emerges, it starts to devour immature cotton bolls. The female will lay 200 eggs, one in each small boll, in a two-week period. With a life cycle of three weeks from egg to adult, there can be up to ten generations in a season and all the mature adults feed on and destroy the cotton bolls. Late-maturing cotton varieties such as those used for sewing thread are therefore the most vulnerable, as they remain in the boll state for longer.

The planters were caught in a bind. They normally worked with credit from the bank, using a loan to buy all the seeds, fertilizers, and pesticides they required, planting and harvesting the crop, which was then sold by the banker who recovered the value of the loan plus interest and expenses, and returned whatever was left to the farmer. With the arrival of the weevil, they could no longer get the loans, so they abandoned the long staple cotton varieties in favour of shorter ones that would mature before the beetle could inflict any serious damage.

Coats feared that much of their traditional supply would dry up. As well as increasing their purchases from Egypt, in 1904 they persuaded some farmers in Puerto Rico to switch away from their traditional crops of tobacco and sugar to cotton, by offering to finance them. They then got Florida Manufacturing to send them seed, and, when the crop was a success, dispatched a number of gins to process it. Three years later Coats bought 438 acres in Barbados, mostly suitable for cotton, and the next year they spent £10,000 on further land for cotton cultivation in Florida and Georgia, with the intention of developing alternative strains to replace the Sea Island variety, where both quality and quantity were deteriorating. Nothing much ever came of all this, as the advances they had made in processing allowed them to replace it with Egyptian cotton, which proved perfectly suitable for sewing thread and became their group standard.

They also made a move to control their sales of cotton waste in partnership with ESC and FCSA and absorbed both Stowell and MacGregor,[5] their spool wood suppliers in Maine after the First World War.

All these arrangements and investments had an ulterior motive. It allowed the company to have command of supply and therefore of quality. High-grade raw materials, processed on the best machinery in a standardised manner throughout the group, with a well-trained and motivated workforce allowed them to make a uniform, very high-quality product that would be so good that anyone attempting to compete would find it extremely difficult. This could then be distributed efficiently and effectively using statistical data garnered from the TCA salesmen and agents. Centralised control was paramount in achieving this, but was becoming much harder with the group's increasing size.

5. MacGregor himself had been a spool turner in Ferguslie, but emigrated to the US and became the spool-turning supervisor for Clarks in Newark. In 1876 he moved to Maine and established an independent spool-turning factory, where he developed economies that allowed him to supply them at an improved price, which he had done ever since.

Chapter 28

As Good as It Gets

When you're on top the only way is down, and more importantly, vice versa.
Unknown

The First World War marked a major turning point in the history of the company. It was not, in itself, a cause of the change, but a series of events at the time led to the emergence of a different organisation in the 1920s from the one that we leave in 1914.

First, the company had reached a size that was becoming increasingly difficult to manage from the centre, despite the major advances that had been made in communications. Independent spirits who sought autonomy were appearing—James Henderson and Alfred Coats were just two, but there were others. Resentment over the sheer weight of reporting (and paper) needed and the requirement that every last price change be approved centrally was growing. The systems introduced by Mr. Philippi so effectively when the group was small began to look unwieldy as the number of countries and products multiplied almost exponentially. Coats now owned some sixty companies and manufactured in sixteen countries worldwide. The product portfolio was already too large to count accurately. An army of administrators was required to sift through the data collected and, with the possible exception of Mr. Philippi himself, no one had the time or the inclination to analyse it all. A move to devolution of power was inevitable.

A major change of personnel in the boardroom was also taking place. This was largely, though not exclusively, due to the deaths of various members of the Coats family. As we have seen, four each of Sir Peter and Thomas Coats's sons had been involved in the business at the board level, and two of the second group had already retired, Willie to collect art and Jimmie to dedicate himself to yachting and supplying Scotland with some 4,000 libraries. He passed away in 1912, but was predeceased by Archie, who was replaced as chairman by Sir Thomas Glen-Coats. The next year saw the demise of both Sir James (USA) who had returned from the US and was living at Auchendrane, and "old" Peter, who had been in charge of Ferguslie twisting and was the yarn buyer for the group. Tragically, Peter Mackenzie, one of Archie's twin sons, contracted pneumonia and died less than a year after his father.

Within days of the end of the First World War, George, who had become Lord Glentanar in 1916, died peacefully at his home at Aboyne, and when both Daniel and Sir Thomas Glen-Coats passed away in 1922, the whole of that generation of Coatses had gone from the company. Although more of the family took their places, there is no doubt that something intangible was lost.

Another sad loss was that of Mr. Philippi. He had been persuaded by his doctor to leave Scotland in 1901 and go to live at Crawley Court, near Winchester in England. He had tendered his resignation at the time, but this had not been accepted, and the board reorganized things in such a way that he could continue to operate as managing director from the South, by remote control, as it were. It is a testament to him and to the strength of the group that this arrangement worked, particularly as he apparently hated the telephone, refusing to have one in the house.[1] He sent missives and instructions by cable or letter, expecting immediate action and replies, even on weekends. He would travel to Glasgow once a month for board meetings, but he also handled negotiation of international acquisitions and his various obligations with ESC, Calico Printers, etc. from his home.

He was, however, getting older and he travelled less, leaving much of that to Ernest Coats. His son, Ernst Alex, became a board member in 1906, doing some of his other donkeywork and functioning as his go-between where necessary or expedient. His isolation down south reinforced his autocratic and dictatorial style, and this did nothing to help quell the desire for more autonomy amongst the management who had to deal with him, often as a result of a peremptory summons to his house on a Saturday. Once he had lost the support of his great champion Archie, it was only a question of time before he would resign; this he did in 1916.

He and Coats had been highly successful. When it was suggested to him that he had "done pretty well out of Paisley", he rightly replied that, "for every penny I have taken out of Paisley, I have brought several pounds into it". He had become wealthy with Coats, largely due to his ½% commission, for his salary had remained quite modest. Before the company went public in 1890, he managed to earn about £8,000 a year, of which only £600 was salary. Although this was a very respectable amount, it was dwarfed by what came afterwards, which allowed him to rebuild both his own house and much of Crawley Village, including a bowling green and roller skating rink. Of course he could not leave it at that, setting up a village shop selling goods at subsidised prices and renting cottages to the locals at rates based on their particular circumstances, as determined by him. He

1. There was an apartment owned or rented by Otto Ernst Philippi in central London from 1905, and it had a phone, so he may have weakened and cheated in the end.

even knocked down one of the pubs and refurbished the other one to help create his model village, where he became a sort of benevolent potentate.

The war treated him badly, as he was caught up in a wave of anti-German sentiment, even though he was fiercely British, with two sons who fought for the allies, one winning a Military Cross for gallantry. Even after setting up a medical centre for wounded British soldiers, his loyalty was still questioned, and he was eventually obliged to issue a statement condemning Germany as responsible for the war, calling their methods "inhuman and wicked" and reaffirming his Britishness.[2]

His wife's death at the start of 1917 proved to be too heartbreaking for him, and within three weeks he quietly slipped away in his sleep. James Henderson, his great protégé, summed him up perfectly in a little anecdote about learning German. "Anyone else sending me to Hamburg to learn the German language and the ramifications of the German business would have chosen a period of 12 months or 18 or even 15. Not Mr. Philippi. A master of the language himself, he chose 14 months as the exact mathematical time required for me to master it too".

The company he left behind now employed some 39,000 people, was consistently turning a profit of £3 million annually, with a nominal share capital of over £10 million and a net worth of £70 million. It was the largest company in Britain, by a margin so great that it was very nearly as big as the next three combined (Rio Tinto, Imperial Tobacco, and Guinness). It had become the third-largest industrial company by market capitalisation in the world. Only US Steel and Standard Oil were bigger, and as if to prove that it is better to make the "software" than the machinery it runs on, Singer were eighth on the same list. With production

2 *Hampshire Chronicle*, May 22, 1915.

units in sixteen countries, Coats had become the "pioneer manufacturing multinational".[3]

It had been 100 years since the Clarks first thought about setting up at Seedhill, and it had been a century of almost continual growth and prosperity for the company. Their conservative stance regarding profit distribution, though often criticised by greedy investors, had allowed their shareholders to grow rich and had made the company both strong and resilient. They had met inflation in places like Brazil before the rest of the world knew what it was, and their accounting systems could deal with multiple currencies, laws, and conventions. Their reputation for quality was unrivaled in the thread industry and their production methods were modern and efficient.

On a personal level, things were also pretty good. Several of the Coats family had been knighted and one had been raised to the peerage.[4] Fame and fortune had smiled upon them. In short, they had reached their zenith and were well prepared for their second century, which would bring us to where we are today. This was to be a far more problematic period.

3. As described by Mira Wilkins in "Mapping Multinationals" from *The Global History Reader,* edited by Bruce Mazlish and Akira Iriye, 2005, page 88.

4. Paradoxically, the Coats crest had an anchor (the Clark trademark) in the top centre. This seems incredible, considering the animosity between the two families. Even as late as the mid-1970s, a Miss Clark, then the sole remaining family member in Paisley, refused to allow her gardener, who was one of the supervisors in Anchor Mills to even mention the name Coats in her presence. Nowadays, the enmity is a thing of the past.

Emblazoned proudly below the crest was the curiously ambiguous family motto, "Be Firm".

Chapter 29

The Trappings of Wealth

I've been rich and I've been poor. It's better to be rich.
Gertrude Stein, American writer

It's no what we hae but what we do wi' what we hae that makes us happy or miserable.
Johnnie Holms, textile manufacturer, stockbroker, art collector and contemporary of the Coats "First Eleven"

With so much wealth comes much responsibility but also the opportunity to spend, spend, spend. The different generations and families approached this in different ways, but none of them was wildly extravagant, and all of them were generous to others.

Sir Peter had chosen to give much of his money away, although he did splash out on Auchendrane. Thomas had a fine collection of early Scottish coins, which was donated to the Hunterian Museum in Glasgow in 1924. He bought his house in 1845 and lived there right by the mill until his death. His only real indulgence was his yacht Hebe, though he once bought a velocipede through the Coats agent in Paris, for 345 Francs (about £13). We will never know if he ever rode it.

His estate was assessed at £1.4 million. This is probably a conservative valuation as about 60% of it was his stake in Coats,[1] which was understated if compared with the equivalent landowners at the time. At his death, his income was the fifth highest in the UK; he would certainly have been on the *Sunday Times* Rich List had it existed. Andrew never had great riches, though he was no pauper.

It was the next generation who were the really prosperous Coatses, taking full advantage of the substantial sums that came to them when the company went public. They were all philanthropic, Jimmie in particular, and each left over £1 million when they died, several to charity, but they still found ways to enjoy their newly acquired affluence. The main areas they chose were mansions, art, and yachting.

Not everyone built himself a castle.[2] James lived quite modestly in the US. Archie upgraded his father's house, Woodside, but remained there all his life, though he bought Battleby later on for the sporting opportunities it afforded. Daniel and "old" Peter both bought large houses in England.

Thomas's children were more lavish. Jimmie built Dunselma Castle, though he never lived there. Sir Thomas Glen-Coats erected the pretentiously named Glencoats House in Ferguslie Park, which later became a hospital, and Willie bought Dalskairth House in Dumfries after living at Skelmorlie Castle till 1913. He also had a house at 30 Buckingham Terrace in Edinburgh. Andrew was an explorer but bought Castle Toward for when he was in Scotland, and George (Lord Glentanar) was the most ostentatious,

1. He also invested in steamship lines, coalmines, tea, telegraph companies, newspapers, gas, and two hydrotherapy institutions. He even had a share in a ship which bore his name, the *SS Thomas Coats*.

2. When Bill Coats (who would be the last family chairman) retired in 1986, he lived in a house called "The Cottage". In discussing possibly writing a book not unlike this one, he wanted to title it "From the Cottage to the Castle to The Cottage" to reflect the ebb & flow of the generations and as a homage to Andrew Coates's book.

buying the vast (forty square miles) Glentanar estate, even although he already owned Belleisle in Ayr and a luxurious townhouse at 11 Hill St., just off Berkeley Square in London.

The Glentanar estate had been leased by a millionaire Manchester banker and MP, Sir William Cunliffe Brooks, in 1871 from his son-in-law, the Marquis of Huntley, who had an unfortunate gambling habit. He eventually bought it twenty years later for the rather modest sum of £120,000, but that was the mere start of his investment. He spent huge amounts on general improvements, including houses and bridges. He put in new kennels, with heating and electric lighting for fifty dogs, creating a level of canine comfort that was probably not afforded to the estate workers' quarters. He then topped it off by building a granite mansion on the ruins of the old farmhouse, with thirty-eight bedrooms (fifteen for servants) and a Victorian ballroom that could hold 170 people. This let him share his passion for hunting, shooting, and fishing with an endless stream of houseguests.

The property's proximity to Balmoral meant that two of his more frequent visitors were the Prince of Wales and his mistress, Lily Langtry, whom we have already come across advertising thread for Kerr & Co. It was quite common for her to stay there on her own, when the Prince was busy with royal duties, and she used to entertain herself by tobogganing down the main staircase on the household's best silver trays. The servants were forced to hide them away to discourage her.

When Brooks died in 1901, George Coats leased the estate for four years and then bought it outright for £155,000. He took up the challenge of continuing the tradition of lavish entertainment and counted Harry Lauder, a passionate deerstalker, amongst his friends. George died in 1918, just days after the armistice was declared, and his son Tom had to hasten back from the trenches to assume the title and the running of the estate. It continues to be administered by his descendants to this day.

If you own a mansion or castle, you need to decorate it, so works of art become important. Archie was a keen collector, as were his three cousins, George, Thomas Glen, and Willie, who was the most enthusiastic of all of them. He amassed a collection of 341 paintings,[3] so he was constantly looking for appropriate places to hang them. His taste was for nineteenth century French and Dutch art, but he also had a number of British paintings, including several works by Gainsborough and Constable. His most famous acquisition was Vermeer's *Christ in the House of Mary and Martha*, which now hangs in the National Gallery of Scotland in Edinburgh, and he also owned several Rembrandts. He was highly thought of as a serious collector, some saying that his taste influenced William Burrell, a contemporary of his. Most of the collection was sold after he died intestate, presumably to pay death duties, which would have been substantial, as Churchill had just raised the rates for large estates, and he left over £4 million.

In the days before airplanes and at the dawn of the era of the combustion engine, executive jets and the gold-plated Rolls Royce were still not an option for the most affluent members of society. Instead, one of the most popular ways to enjoy one's wealth was on the sea, in a sailing or steam yacht, and this was especially true of the rich industrialists in the southwest of Scotland. The Clyde estuary with its offshore breezes was the ideal setting for both recreational boating as well as the more serious business of racing. The reputation of the boats from this area was enhanced by the existence of excellent shipbuilders as far west as the Ailsa shipyard in Troon, supported by several of the top designers, including the famous naval architect George Lennox Watson.

He was responsible for designing four yachts to challenge for the America's Cup and, although he never won, his boats were amongst the fastest afloat. He also

3. His catalogue of these paintings was an elaborate leather-bound tome with a reproduction and description of each. It weighed 15 lbs.

supplied several vessels to the Coatses and Clarks. Both families were enthusiastic yachtsmen, and their love of sailing allowed them to indulge their urge to compete with each other, away from the world of sewing thread.

The first Coats to own a boat was old Thomas, who bought a yacht named Hebe back in 1877. This was 300 tons, had ten staterooms, a large saloon, and a crew of fifteen, and he used it to sail around the Mediterranean that same year, when he took time off due to ill health. He would often be away for months at a time, once he could leave the business to the next generation, and he sometimes travelled with his brother, Peter. Yet it would appear that the Coatses were once again beaten by the Clarks, as James of Camphill had purchased a more modest sixty-ton boat named Snowflake from Lord Middleton some eight years earlier.

The tradition of floating palaces continued for years, and a certain rivalry can be detected in the endeavors of each family to outdo the other in size and sumptuousness. One of the most celebrated of these was the Zara, built in 1891 by Fleming & Ferguson of Paisley for "old" Peter Coats. At 271 tons and 136 feet, this was a quite modest craft. He would sail with his brothers, James (when he was over from the US) and Archie, who loved sport fishing from the deck for haddock, cod, or pollack. Daniel would also join them on occasions, and their cousin George, from the "Ham" side of the family, was a frequent guest. These were never long cruises; out for the day or for a weekend.

Jimmie Coats was a fanatical sailor,[4] coming alive when out to sea despite being a near recluse once ashore. His first large craft was a houseboat, which was built in 1878 and was a replica of a steamer, funnel and all. It had all the comforts of home, including a large games room, but had to be towed around, so he eventually had it cut in two, lengthened, and turned into a proper steam yacht, named Siren.

4. Even when he gave up sailing completely, he kept on two yachts, as he could not bear to put the seventy people he employed out of work.

Some twenty years later, Watson designed a new boat for him. It was called Triton and became his pride and joy. Built in 1902 at the Ailsa shipyard in Troon, it was one of the only ones made with a plumb bow (rising vertically from the sea). Unlike Peter, he didn't like to entertain and was often at sea alone (apart from the crew), visiting the far-flung corners of Scotland, particularly the lighthouses.

When he died, it was sold to Sir George Bullough, a keen yachtsman and the owner of the island of Rhum in the Scottish Hebrides. Since then, it has been lengthened and had a second deck of cabins added, has changed names five times, and has served as an auxiliary patrol yacht in World War I and an anti-submarine yacht in the Second World War. It carried King George VI (he of *The King's Speech* fame), his wife, and the Princesses Elizabeth and Margaret on a victory cruise in 1945 up the River Foyle in Northern Ireland. More recently, it featured in the television program *Agatha Christie's Poirot* and is one of very few surviving steam yachts.

Even grander was Willie Coats's Queen of Scots, which was a whopping 606 tons, built in 1904 by Fairfields. His son Thomas later sold it to Anthony Drexel, an American millionaire from Philadelphia who used it to take an English expedition to Cocos Island in the Pacific, in what was designated as the first-ever "scientific" treasure hunt. The prize was reputed to be between £12 and £25 million, but they apparently returned empty-handed.

However, the granddaddy of all these boats had already been built some years before. John Clark had Watson design a 700-ton, 215-foot yacht named Mohican, which, apart from being fast—it could do 15 knots—was also really luxurious and easily able to manage a transatlantic crossing, one of which he undertook in 1887.

Unfortunately for the intrepid travellers, they ran into a hurricane some four days into the voyage. They battened down the hatches and anything else that was loose, including themselves, and battled through the weather for forty-eight hours until fortune appeared to shine on them, and the storm blew itself out. Their relief was unfortunately temporary, as it started up again and this time was not so kind, doing serious damage to the upper levels of the boat and severely denting the port bulwarks. The reinforced railings and supports around the deck were twisted beyond repair by the incessant pounding of heavy seas, but the boat limped on and by the following midday was about 300 miles off the Canadian coast.

At this point they came upon a cargo ship, the Lilian, which had lost its main mast and was floating helpless at the mercy of the storm and beginning to break up. All their lifeboats had long since been destroyed or carried off, so the crew of seventeen was stranded and looked as if they were about to sink without trace. Something had to be done, and fast.

The sea was still too rough for the Mohican to get close enough for a direct rescue, and after several hours of trying, it was decided that a small boat would have a better chance. This was launched with some difficulty, but was unable to get close to the stranded vessel, as the waves seemed likely to smash it to pieces on the hull of the larger boat. The only remedy was for each man to jump into the sea, hoping to be picked up by the small craft and then transported across to the yacht, where they had to repeat the process of jumping overboard before finally being hoisted up to the deck. This took hours, during which the Scottish crew were bobbing about in what was little more than a life raft, soaked to the skin, frozen to the bone, and straining to guide their craft back and forth through the storm.

They finally reach Halifax, Nova Scotia thirteen days after setting out from Largs, with no loss of life. The Canadians expressed their gratitude by awarding the coxswain an enormous silver watch for his skill in guiding the rescue and each of the crew a cheque for their bravery and perseverance. After restocking and making some swift temporary repairs, they resumed their voyage to New York, where John Clark was to preside over his first board meeting as chairman of the Clark business in the US.

John Clark would go on to become the commodore of the Royal Clyde Yacht Club in 1889, and this was not because he owned the Mohican, but rather because he was a keen yacht racer, for this was what the club was all about, boasting a membership of about 1,000. Several members of both families belonged and raced against each other.

John had several racing yachts, but two of them were outstanding. The Condor was a 95-footer with a crew of eighteen, which was designed in such a way as to be a successful racer but also a luxurious entertainment centre with a saloon, a cabin for the owner, three other staterooms, and a ladies' cabin with blue silk upholstery. The Vanduara, another Watson design with a steel hull, was large at 90 tons, but reputed to be the quickest in the world, and in 1880 trounced the fastest boat from the previous year by such a margin as to justify that claim. It won eleven of thirteen races entered during the season in the Channel.

Jimmie Coats also had the fastest boat in the world in its class, the ten-ton cutter Madge. This boat once started the Mersey Regatta forty minutes late, but won anyway. In another race, it not only won—it caught the twenty-ton boats that had set out earlier and raced home ahead of Quickstep, a highly fancied yacht from that group. When he took his cutter to race in the US, he was dumbfounded to discover that the US customs were demanding an import duty of 35% on the boat, classifying it as "wooden goods".[5] He refused to

5. There were murmurings that this might have been "organized" by one or another of the American yacht clubs, fearful of the beating they would probably receive at the hands of this notoriously swift competitor.

pay and took the boat back outside US territorial waters, dropped it in the sea, and towed it back in, thus avoiding the duty. Madge ended up competing in the New York Regatta, winning by a phenomenal seven minutes over a thirty-five-mile course. She was equally successful in a series of other challenge races, and her visit was summed up succinctly by the *New York Times* on October 1 1881, "When she made her appearance here it was the almost universal belief that her owner had come a long way for the sake of a bad beating...Nevertheless this little British yacht has beaten our best sloops, and without the least necessity of availing herself of the time allowance to which she was entitled"

By the turn of the century, although Jimmie Coats was still a keen sailor and had several more boats, he had largely given up competitive racing, making way for the next generation. His youngest brother Andrew had found nothing to attract him to the thread business, and his nephew Thomas Glen-Coats (son) was the same, so both had time to enjoy the sport and both owned several racing yachts. Each would find fame as a result of their hobby, in very different ways, described elsewhere.

But before retiring from racing, Jimmie was to have one last epic battle. Kenneth Mackenzie Clark, John Clark's nephew, had largely abandoned the thread business after the merger and decided he wanted to compete in the America's Cup, a serious aspiration of his from 1901 to 1907. To establish his credentials, he challenged Jimmie to a race from Rothesay to Ailsa Craig and back, a distance of forty miles, to see who had the fastest yacht in Scotland. Both boats were big, the Clark yacht Kariad being eighty feet long and Jimmie's Sybarita ten feet longer and therefore subject to an eight-minute handicap. The date set for the encounter was in June 1901 and the purse was £500.

The day of the race dawned with a gale blowing, so both yachts set out with topmasts housed and sails close-reefed, with the smaller boat doggedly tracking the larger one. There was almost nothing to separate them as they rounded Ailsa Craig, now out in the full force of the weather, when the Sybarita briefly lost its mainsail and almost met with disaster. However, she recovered and, obscured from view by a hailstorm, decided to let out an extra reef, a rather foolhardy gambit in such weather. This paid off, for when they both emerged into view, she had a clear lead and went on to win by two minutes and forty-three seconds.

It was a Pyrrhic victory, as the storm had ripped twenty feet of copper sheathing from both sides of her bows, and the Clark factory viewed it as just that. Kenneth Clark was undeterred in his quest for the America's Cup, even if he never managed to compete. The Coatses simply celebrated the win, and Jimmie donated the £500.

So the enmity between the Coatses and Clarks continued. Within the world of textiles it had become more restrained, now that they all worked for the same company, but outside work it had not abated, and they didn't only compete on the sea – their rivalry even extended into the realm of charity.

Chapter 30

Philanthropy

We make a living by what we get. We make a life by what we give.
Winston Churchill

Paisley had come to depend on both companies, and their amazing success was reflected in the fact that it had become one of the fastest-growing towns in the UK, with a population of about 60,000 by the mid-1880s. Over 10% of the inhabitants were employed in the two mills, and the large majority owed their livelihood to thread, in one way or another.

Growth at this sort of pace comes at a price. The town was grimy,[1] the housing substandard, and the sewerage inadequate. Mortality rates were high, illness was common, and disease spread quickly and easily. Government aid was nonexistent, so the two families understood that they had a moral, social, and religious duty to help. They did so, frequently.

It is argued that they had made their money on the back of others' long hours and low wages and that they would have been better distributing their wealth through higher

1. Described in *Scotland the Lowlands* by M. J. B. Baddeley, 1887, as "one of the smokiest in Scotland"

pay and improved conditions. However, there is no denying that both companies paid competitively when compared to others in their (and other) industries, and that to do otherwise would have limited their growth and their ability to invest, expand, and increase employment. Market forces determine these parameters. It is also well-documented that the conditions within their mills were considered excellent for the period. Employee loyalty was a feature of both companies. Carroll Davidson Wright, an American commentator, wrote in the 1880 *Report on the Factory System of the United States* that, "The factories at Paisley are excellent evidences of the good influence which comes from proper interest in employees. The works of the Messrs. Clark and of the Messrs. Coates (sic) are moral establishments..."

Almost all the contemporary commentaries mention their good works. A local poet, who worked as a night shift twiner at Ferguslie, published a book with poems "In Memoriam" for each of Thomas and Sir Peter Coats, including these lines:

> His gifts in secret channels ran,
> Like hidden streams in mountain pass,
> To every scheme, whose object was
> The social welfare of the mass.

about the former and

> Enrich'd by God with wealth immense,
> His goodness had a constant flow—
> The right hand dealing princely gifts,
> Of which his left did never know

for the latter. Not Rabbie Burns, but heartfelt all the same.

In the end, they were wealthy and could afford what they donated, but the fact is that they did give it away, and much of it appears to have been done with no publicity and little desire for recognition. In particular, during the period of the late 1860s some £100,000 was spent by Thomas and Sir Peter Coats on various good works, and although we know of the more obvious ones, described below, there must have been countless others to account for this level of benevolence.[2]

It was natural that when calamity fell upon Paisley, which it frequently did, both families would be at the forefront of those public-spirited subscribers to the relief funds. One of the earliest examples came in 1848, when there were soup kitchens set up all over town, with 7,000 people (of a population of 48,000) dependent on the relief committee for food. J. & P. Coats was still in its infancy, but James, Peter, and Thomas Coats were much applauded when, along with their brother George who had gone into coalmining, they distributed 216 tons of coal to the poor in the West End, giving much needed heat in the depths of winter. Various other considerably more generous examples were to follow and not always locally. Their support of the troops during the Crimean War was but one example.

As early as 1837, at the age of only 28, Thomas Coats was made manager of the Paisley Widows and Orphans Society. He became a Founder Subscriber to the Paisley Society for the Blind in 1859 and was a major supporter of the Storie Street Baptist Church, where he worshipped. He paid all their maintenance and repairs and in 1868 gave them the first pipe organ to be installed in Paisley.[3]

He was a strong proponent of education for all, and supported the Paisley Ragged School and the local grammar school. After the Education Act of 1873, he was voted chairman of the school board. This gave him the opportunity to champion the enlargement of five schools in the area, his intention being to give schoolchildren 50% more space than the government minimum of eight square feet. This was not universally popular, as it was thought it would increase the rates, a real hardship for the less well-off; but after he offered £5,000 to defray the cost, it was established that the rates

2. Estimated from the amount retained in the business for that period, which was far lower than normal.

3. His first cousin (once removed) Jervis Coats was the first organist.

would be largely unaffected, so he got the support he needed.

He is best remembered for two major contributions to Paisley, the first of which was the Fountain Gardens, an area of six-and-a-half acres less than a mile from the centre of town. Created by John Love, a Paisley merchant, in 1797, it was originally known as the Hope Temple Gardens. Love was a keen botanist and had filled it with all manner of exotic plants as well as a museum, greenhouses, and a bowling green. Although ostensibly open to the public, it was seldom used, except by the man himself. He died in 1827 after suffering a reverse over some shady South American deal, so the land passed to his trustees, but continued to get little use.

Thomas bought it in 1866 and converted it into a spacious park for the enjoyment of all, in a town that was rapidly becoming heavily industrialized and built up. The Glasgow landscape architect James Craig Niven redesigned the area with broad walkways leading to an ornate central fountain containing depictions of herons, dolphins, and four life-sized walruses. Iron railings, intricate lamps, ornate seats, drinking fountains, rock gardens, and other decorative items were installed throughout, and the park supervisor had a house by the Love Street entrance with a ladies' sitting room opposite.

The crowning glory was taken from the famous Wallace Oak at Elderslie, which had finally been destroyed in the great storms of February 1856. This tree had reputedly been a hiding place for William Wallace when evading his enemies, and being of almost religious significance, a sapling had been rescued from it, before its demise. Thomas planted this in the northwest corner of the property on March 28, 1868, in a small ceremony involving a few town dignitaries and some stirring patriotic poetry. He had spent at least £20,000 on the project, and on Tuesday, May 26, the newly named Fountain Gardens were formally inaugurated when he handed over the title deeds and declared the park open.

Thomas's other bequest to the town is the Coats Observatory. By the time he started on this project, he was in a wheelchair, though you would find it hard to believe from his portrait in the entrance, painted by Sir Daniel Macnee in 1881 and featuring him standing ramrod straight, with a stylish top hat in his left hand. The building was therefore designed to be one of the first in the world to have access specially designed for the disabled, including a ramped walkway, though this is now described as "unsuitable for wheelchair users". He would no doubt be amazed and disappointed if he knew.

The original intention had been to house a telescope in the Paisley museum built by his brother, Sir Peter. The council of the Paisley Philosophical Society, of which Thomas was a member and former president, had floated the idea in an Annual General Meeting (AGM) in 1880 and he had agreed not only to buy the telescope, but also to pay for a proper observatory to house it. He was an avid astronomer, so the project was close to his heart. A design by John Honeyman, a Glasgow architect (whose employees included Charles Rennie Mackintosh) was chosen and the building was erected for the sum of £3,097. Thomas presented the deed and telescope to the Society at a conversazione attended by 600 people on October 18, 1882.

His original telescope was a 5" "equatorial" model and was replaced by a 10" refractor in 1898, donated by his son, Jimmie. Both are still there. The dome opens and rotates with a rope and pulley system, which is still the same as the day it was inaugurated. The building also includes a working model of the solar system, a small planetarium, and a working seismograph. Thomas was a keen meteorologist, so it was his desire that they keep daily records of the temperature, precipitation, and general conditions in Paisley. This has been done every day since they opened.[4]

4. It seems to rain most days!

The observatory was finally opened to the public on October 1, 1883, and the cost of entrance was two pennies. Only twenty people were allowed in per hour. Thomas, who by this time was confined to his bedroom, managed to visit only once, as he died two weeks later of "an affection of the heart". Over 10,000 people marched in his funeral procession, despite the typically wet autumnal Paisley weather. It is a further measure of the esteem in which he was held that not only Ferguslie, but also Anchor Mills were closed that day, as were the local shops, banks, and schools. Flags flew at half-mast and church bells tolled as a measure of respect. Between seven and eight thousand children from local schools accompanied the coffin, followed by Provost James Clark (of the rival family), the magistrates, the town council, school board members, trustees, and office bearers of the Storie Church as well as church leaders of all faiths. Local businessmen, workers from Ferguslie, some from Anchor and, finally, the general public concluded the procession, with many thousands lining the route, which ran from the town centre to Ferguslie House estate and thence through the gates of nearby Paisley cemetery, where he was laid to rest at 4:00 p.m. by his five surviving sons.

As he had been such a devout Baptist and as the church at Storie Street was in need of a major overhaul, his children decided to build a church in his memory. Known as the Coats Memorial Church, this has probably become his greatest legacy to Paisley, as its imposing size, position, and architecture mean that is dominates the skyline, being visible from most approaches to the town. It has been dubbed the "Baptist Cathedral of Europe".

The redstone building was designed by a French architect in Edinburgh, Hippolyte Blanc, who had previously developed the St. James Church, less than a mile to the north. He originally did models of two designs, one with twin towers, similar to Notre Dame in Paris, and the other—the one they adopted—with a crown tower. Work started in 1886 and was completed for the opening on May 13, 1894.

The layout is in the shape of a cross 165 feet long and 100 feet wide, and the church seats 1,000 people in oak pews. The pulpit is marble and alabaster. The vestibule floor is made up of some 350,000 pieces of coloured marble, and the gilded monograms of Thomas's children are included above the stairs leading to the basement. No expense was spared, with craftsmen coming from as far afield as Italy. The final building is reputed to have cost an astonishing £120,000.

On either side of the chancel stand the 3,040 pipes of the organ. This was built by William Hill & Sons of London and had to be stored by them for three years, as it was ready too soon for the building. It was transported to Scotland on a special train of twelve wagons.[5]

Unlike his elder brother, Peter, Thomas was quiet and modest and therefore underappreciated. When asked to speak at any public function even as the guest of honor, he never took the stage with long rambling speeches to show his own importance. He would say a quiet "thank you" to the attendees and then let others do the orating. It was one of the reasons he never received the recognition he deserved in his lifetime, with titles being bestowed on two of his children as well as his more famous brother, but never on him.

His brother Peter began his own charitable work at an earlier stage in life. He had relinquished his position in the company as far back as 1856 and never worked more than part-time after that. This afforded him more time to redistribute his wealth, about which he said, "I wish to give away my money in my lifetime. It is a great pleasure to me to do it. And it is better, I think, to give it with your own hand, than after you are dead." In keeping with this maxim, he would send money to almost anyone who expressed a need, either individuals or, more particularly, religious institutions, as far afield as Nice, Central Africa, and Cambridge. His support of a variety of charities, particularly

5. It would cost about £1.5 million if built today and is considered to be one of the finest in Europe.

for the blind, was extensive and unsystematic. His major gift to Paisley was the museum and library.

Before 1802, book lending was done by local sellers for a fee and no public library existed. Then the Paisley Library Society was formed as a private, subscription-only institution (three guineas[6] entrance fee and half a guinea per year) and therefore beyond the means of the man in the street. Its membership numbered about 200 at its peak, and others followed but never caught on.

The Paisley Philosophical Society had been established in 1808, with the aim of "self-improvement for themselves and fellow townsmen, through the collection of books and museum artifacts". As their success in accumulating these items grew, so did the need for storage space, and a number of valuable pieces deteriorated over the years as the damp Paisley winters took their toll. A decision was made to start collecting £3,000 to build a museum and small library in 1864, but only about half had been subscribed in the next three years, so Peter Coats indicated that he would fund the whole thing, provided it was regulated by the Free Libraries Act, which had been introduced to Scotland in 1853. It was to provide a free lending and reference library for the townspeople of Paisley.

The foundation stone was laid on April 11, 1869 by the Earl of Dalhousie. The property, which is a single-storey building in the Greek Ionic style, was opened two years later after a fabulous procession of 300 horsemen and followed by a conversazione attended by 600 of the great and good of the town. It received over 7,000 books from the Paisley Library Society, 5,000 from the Philosophical Society, and further volumes were obtained using the original subscriptions that preceded Peter Coats's generous offer.

6. A Guinea was 21 shillings, i.e. £1.05 in modern currency.

He himself donated artifacts from a visit to Egypt in 1867, a volume of Audubon's *Birds of America,* and his *Ornithological Biography,* with a note hoping that they would promote a taste for the Natural History Department "which my townsman, Alexander Wilson, did so much to foster".

The building cost him about £20,000, and when first opened to the public it proved so popular that a ticket system had to be introduced for evening visitors for the first few weeks. The two museum attendants whose job it was to control the entrance had to call the police in to help control the queues.

Further donations followed, and within a decade the premises had become too cramped. An extension was therefore proposed and Peter again picked up the £15,000 bill. It involved a rotunda, the picture and sculpture galleries, and a new reference library. Twelve years to the day after the first property was given away, the extensions were formally opened by the Marquis of Bute.[7]

Peter moved to Auchendrane in Ayrshire in 1877 after his wife Gloranna died, and he erected a church[8] in nearby Minishant in her memory, with a library and reading room. He had been brought up a Baptist, like his brothers, but had decided he preferred the intellect of the Scottish Presbyterian ministers and had therefore made the switch some years before. He later bought a villa out in Algeria, to escape the Scottish winters, which were affecting his health; he suffered from asthma. He built a church for the English-speaking community, tourists, and sailors on the road between Algiers and Mustapha Superieur, where his house was and where he would eventually die on March 9, 1890, after suffering a stroke. His body was returned to Paisley for burial.

7. He later donated two kangaroos to Paisley, but one of them escaped from its place of confinement in Brodie Park and was chased a couple of miles to Ferguslie, where it promptly expired.

8. Now an Indian restaurant!

In his obituary in the *New York Times*, an "intimate friend" summed up his charitable giving by describing him as "...a philanthropist of the wisest and most liberal sort, a giver not through impulse, but on principle". He left about £118,000 in his will, less than 10% of his brother's wealth, and that was certainly in part due to his generosity to others.

Just as they did in thread, the Clarks vied with the Coatses for supremacy in this area as well. George A. Clark was the most conspicuous.

The need for a town hall had first been raised in 1864, but had never been greeted with much enthusiasm. In 1872, James Clark of Chapel was elected as councilor for the fifth ward and immediately set about getting public support for the project and starting a subscription list, with a goal of raising £20,000. By March, the amount raised was near £14,000, but this was frozen when George's will appeared with a bequest of the full amount. It read:

> To remedy a want long felt in my native town of Paisley, I bequeath to the Provost, Magistrates, and Town Council the sum of twenty thousand pounds for the erection of a Town Hall, and, combined with this Hall, a large Reading Room for working men, where they can sit and enjoy smoking, and the room shall be open from five o'clock in the morning until twelve o'clock at night – said building shall be erected in that part of the town called the New Town.

The previous subscriptions were returned to the treasurer, Archibald Coats, who sent them back to the donors. A Belfast architect, W. H. Lynn, was chosen to design the building, which was now going to cost around £50,000, way more than the original budget, but the Clarks, spurred on by George's generosity, agreed to meet any shortfall. After a delay in securing the desired site for another £9,000, construction began in August 1878. A little over a year later, a memorial stone was laid by George's mother and a time capsule placed underneath, containing a curious collection of mementoes: twelve coins of the realm; a biography and portrait of George; an extract from his will; various articles, books, and descriptions of Clark's thread works and processes; a list of town council members; a Paisley directory from 1879-80; various town council accounts; and a variety of current local newspapers.

Old Mrs. Clark died the following May, so did not live to see the hall finally opened on January 30, 1882. As was custom on these occasions, there was a parade, which was over a mile and a half long, with endless floats and marching bands, and 12,000 people—over 20% of the population of Paisley. A grand conversazione was held for 1,000 invitees inside the hall in the evening, and fireworks were let off later from the high church. However, the most amazing sight for the crowd was that of the electric lights blazing outside the front of the hall, blindingly bright to a public more used to gas lamps and candles.

Further celebrations continued for the next two weeks, ending with a concert attended by over 1,700 of the workforce from Anchor Mills. One could be forgiven for believing that the Clarks were once again trying to outdo the Coatses in the ostentatious way they celebrated.

The building itself is located on the site where the Clarks bought their first spools, appropriately within sight of where Anchor Mills stood. It is asymmetrical, with two towers, the taller of which features an octagonal belfry and four clock faces, each with a female sculpture representing one of the seasons. The main entrance to the east is suitably imposing, with six thirty-foot Corinthian columns, whilst the north side is Ionic. The interior includes a main hall with balcony and room to seat 2,000. The original organ, which had just under 3,000 pipes, has since been removed. A connected minor hall with capacity for 300 is to the north side and the promenade, with a vaulted ceiling, was for the town's elite. Other assorted chambers and, of course, a reading and smoking room, according to George's request, complete the interior.

The Clarks made other gifts. George himself left £20,000 to Glasgow University for four scholarships, and numerous other smaller amounts that benefited the town of Paisley. His mother had given extensively, especially to the mission hall for the Thread Street United Presbyterian Church. His older brother, James of Ralston, left money to the Paisley Infirmary.

His younger brother John's will included £70,000 for charity, but his generosity in life was even greater. Some ten years before his death, he moved to Curling Hall in Largs and immediately set about helping his new hometown. He built them a hospital, replaced their inadequate and antiquated United Presbyterian Church and repaired the Esplanade. He would send gifts of food, coal, and money to the poorer families at Christmas and supplied books to local libraries. He took on the whole expense of supplying the Largs soup kitchen, which provided up to 10,000 meals for needy women and children during the winter months. They filled their bellies with soup, bread, and boiled beef, and he paid for a local doctor to keep an eye on them and deal with any medical problems he noticed. The whole enterprise kept people cheered and fed and helped limit infant mortality.

The next generation from both families also pitched in. The reclusive, rather eccentric but nonetheless well-meaning eldest son of Thomas Coats, Jimmie, had an almost single-minded obsession with getting the population of Scotland to read. To this end he sent libraries of books to churches, barracks, remote rural communities, and every lighthouse in Scotland, many of which he visited in his steam yacht, *Glennifer*. He employed an optician to tour the libraries and supply eyeglasses to those who needed them, as well as a lecturer to stimulate the villagers into a desire for literature. Although he was a lifelong bachelor, he obviously cared greatly for children. Not only did he make satchels available to every child in Scotland, but he also supplied books and shoes for the poorer local Paisley scholars for a number of years.

Apart from his generosity to the Alexandra infirmary, "old" Peter Coats (Sir Peter's son) also founded a Mission Sunday School, which he supervised for forty years. When he died, he left his fortune in trust to charity.

The last endowment of major significance for Paisley was a joint effort by the two families—the restoration of the Abbey. This had already been partially achieved in the 1860s, when Thomas Coats proposed the rebuilding of the north transept and other minor work, which he and his brother Peter then largely financed. But by the beginning of the twentieth century, more fundamental work was required, involving the choir vault, the tower, and much of the interior woodwork and furnishings. It was hoped that one person or family would fund the main work, leaving smaller donations to pay for the interior. These prayers were answered by the children of Stewart Clark of Kilnside. He died in 1907, leaving them all very wealthy. They offered £30,000 to the church and, after the detailed design work was done, restoration was finally undertaken as late as 1923 and completed eight years later. The reason for the delay was that the First World War intervened.

Chapter 31

World War I

The more you sweat in peacetime, the less you bleed during war.
Chinese proverb

World War I was hard on all multinationals; Coats suffered, though not as badly as some. Their German and to a lesser extent French competitors were severely hampered, and this allowed the Group to expand their handicrafts business, in particular, much faster than would have been possible without the conflict. In Japan and Brazil, they benefited generally from reduced competition.

The effects of the war were, however, mostly awful. Coats lost complete control of the Witzschdorf mill in Saxony as well as their plants in Austro-Hungary, Poland and Belgium. Ninove was taken over as a billet, but the brass rollers for the twisting machines were buried before the Germans arrived and remained hidden, being dug up and ready for use after the war. At F&FR, the Germans found a boiler mistakenly addressed to "J. & P. Coats, Belgium", so the mill was designated as enemy property subject to expropriation. The managing director, Cumont, fled to England with nothing but the clothes on his back, but Mr. Philippi heard of his plight and took him and his family in, allowing them to stay in the Dower house at Crawley for two years. Ten British nationals were stranded in Pressburg, and others in Budapest, but amazingly were left nominally in charge, working alongside the Hungarians who were theoretically their enemies.

The biggest problems of the war were shortages of raw materials and people, combined with rising prices and taxes. The Germans blockaded Russia and greatly disrupted maritime movement with U-boat activity creating real difficulties, especially from 1916 onwards. Finding space on ships grew increasingly challenging and insurance rates skyrocketed. Coats lost a number of shipments of both thread and raw materials, and these always caused major disruption.

Cotton from America became scarce and the general switch to Egyptian types accelerated. Supply from there was easier, though not without its dangers, and there was a quality compromise involved, as even the best Egyptian was not as long, fine, or strong as the Sea Island varieties. In some places, any cotton was welcome and things became so desperate that experiments were done spinning peat in Austria and paper in Hungary. The cotton price rose to two-and-a-half times its 1914 level, in the case of Egyptian, and three times for American. Yarn prices quadrupled.

Spool wood was a major headache. It was a low value, high bulk item in a situation where cargo space was at a premium. Supplies from Finland, which was part of Russia, became effectively impossible, and getting product from Canada and the US was fraught with shipping difficulties. Local varieties were tried in several places, with very mixed results. Coats bought a Canadian ship to improve their transatlantic supply conduit, and Coats and Clarks in the US lent financial assistance to their two main suppliers and gave them guaranteed long-term contracts. Even so there was an unwilling shift to tubes, and a form of spool with a paper flange was introduced. The number of spool lengths offered in the UK was cut from ten to four, but not for long, as the flow of product rapidly returned to normal in early 1919.

At the start of the war, 80% of the dyestuffs used in Britain (and by extension elsewhere) came from Germany, and the remaining 20% depended largely on German intermediates. Logwood Black, which comes from a tree native to Central America, was used for a time by Coats, but was so filthy that those who handled it were paid "dirt" money. Stocks of all dyes were depleted nationally, and the situation became critical.

The government were persuaded to form British Dyes Ltd.,[1] a company based on Read Holliday & Sons, who, although they made dyes, had been concentrating on explosives, which were also scarce. Financing was both private and public, and the scheme was based on exporting raw materials to Switzerland for processing and then reimporting and distributing the finished dyes, mainly to those companies who had invested in the enterprise. Coats contributed reluctantly; they feared that the company thus created would become a high-priced monopoly after the war.[2] Despite all these efforts, the shortages continued, and prices rose to over three times the prewar levels.

Labour shortages occurred everywhere, but especially in Paisley. With all the losses of capacity from the German closure and the expropriation of mills in occupied Europe, Coats had to depend on Anchor and Ferguslie far more than they had in peacetime. This coincided with a mass exodus to join the armed forces, with 1,600 having left for the front by 1916. By the end of the war, 2,390 had enlisted, 271 had been killed, and 199 were discharged as unfit for active duty. The

1. In 1919 British Dyes of Huddersfield merged with Levenstein Ltd. in Blackley to form the British Dyestuffs Corporation, which later became ICI (Imperial Chemical Industries, now part of AkzoNobel).

2. As a hedge against this eventuality, they also put money into at least one other dye supplier.

girls were also lured away to higher-paying jobs in the munitions factories that had proliferated on Clydeside. All the company plants lost experienced managers, technicians, and operators, whose years of training and knowledge could hardly begin to be replaced overnight. War bonuses were paid, as well as cost-of-living increases for wives and unemployed children, and allowances were given to all those who served in the armed forces. Wages doubled over the war period, and costs inevitably rose, by two-and-a-half times.

Coats had one other unique difficulty, caused at least indirectly by Mr. Philippi. Many of the TCA agencies that had been set up over the years were run by Germans; indeed, a number of the head office employees fell into the same bracket, hired for the same reason: they had a strong work ethic, with good organizational and language skills. The introduction of the "Trading with the Enemy" act, which outlawed any mercantile activity with foreign enemy nationals, meant that these agencies had to be wound up, at least for the duration of the war, and this complicated the company's selling arrangements and tended to raise costs and damage service, which was already suffering due to raw materials shortages.

On top of these pressures, the British bank rate went from 3% to 10% in the first year, and the stock market was closed for a month to prevent panic selling, particularly of multinational stocks. Hoarding was common, and cash grew scarce. James Henderson in Italy had to threaten to close CCC to extract cash from the Bank of Lucca to pay the workforce in 1915. Exchange rates fluctuated, and setting price levels across multiple regions to maintain Sterling earnings became nearly impossible. Prices doubled in the four years of the war, but far from uniformly—in some markets they rose far more. Wherever possible, the company restricted increases to discourage competition, but new challengers appeared anyway, notably in Japan, Mexico, and Holland, as well as Asia.

If all this wasn't enough, the governments of the world had to find a way of financing the war, and so old taxes increased and new ones were introduced. Income tax in the UK went from ½d. per £1 (0.21%) to 6 shillings per £1 (30.0%). Other taxes and tariffs were instituted, but one in particular, Excess Profit Duty (EPD), was introduced in the UK and twenty other countries and caused Coats major problems in Britain after the war, as well as forcing them to restructure their businesses in the US and Canada.

Specific setbacks also afflicted individual markets. Mexico had to contend with the revolution and the associated currency problems. Portugal suffered a drought and chronic water shortages. Neutral Spain had a general strike in summer 1916. Stroppel in Switzerland, which had traditionally exported 75% of its production, saw all imports from Belgium and Germany for the local department stores vanish, and spent the rest of the war trying to replace them. They emerged with almost no export business and a much-enhanced local reputation. Italy ran short of coal and tried burning samsa (olive oil residue) in the boilers. They had to buy a local spool turner to guarantee supplies, but were luckily able to stockpile production and raw materials for the period before Italy entered the war in 1915. They did, however, suffer losses of stocks, goods in transit, and debts from the Austro-German invasion of 1917, as the affected customers lost their businesses. Then, to cap it all, nearly 1 million Italians (including numerous CCC debtors) perished during the Spanish Flu pandemic, which started in 1918. All of Europe was badly affected but Italy was hit particularly hard.

When the US company was faced with the need to raise prices, they baulked after their 1907 debacle and lowered spool lengths instead, to 150 yards in black (and eventually in white) and 100 yards in colours. South America, increasingly supplied from the US as the conflict progressed, was largely unaffected.

Despite all the strictures on the company, they fared reasonably well through the war years. They had entered 1914 with unusually high stocks, not due to brilliant foresight, but rather as a result of the recession of the previous year. By 1916, profits were nudging £4 million and stayed around that level for the remainder of the war. The companies under their control were managing (and being managed) well, with one major exception—Russia.

Chapter 32

The Loss of Russia

Insurrection is an art, and like all arts has its own laws.
Leon Trotsky

In 1914, Coats had over 9,000 people working in the Nevsky Thread Mills, with smaller numbers in Lodz and the Chadwick plant in Strasdenhof, Riga. Their fates took different paths, but they suffered a common demise.

Lodz was commandeered by the Germans and converted to cable making, though the machinery was not destroyed.

The Strasdenhof plant was making about twenty tons a week of knitting yarns and three tons of a Scissor brand six cord article, but the spooling and main office had already been moved to NTM. They had adopted an Eagle trademark from a local German manufacturer who had gone out of business and, as it looked like the eagle on the German coat of arms, they were accused of being pro-German. It took some explaining to show that this was really a single version of the two-headed eagle carried by Ivan the Terrible, but it did them little good. Riga was overrun shortly thereafter, and they were given just three days to get all the machinery out of the plant and moved to St. Petersburg. A superhuman effort allowed them to remove 5,000 twisting spindles, but that was all they could manage and the mill was closed down.

The position of NTM was rather different. The German blockade of Russia simultaneously hit cotton from Egypt and the US, yarn from the UK, and finished product from Paisley. Transport within Russia was dodgy at the best of times but now became virtually impossible. Delivery through Archangel, which was 700 miles from St. Petersburg, was by sledge in winter and was unreliable. Any shipments through Vladivostok had to come even further, by both train and sledge.

The mills managed to partially solve the cotton shortages by making lower-quality articles from Russian varieties and switching others around to preserve the stocks they had accumulated earlier. Although they also suffered from labour shortages, with many employees conscripted into the Russian army and 100 British staff returning to the UK to fight, they managed to get the mills up to near full production after an initial hiccup, and made a small profit in 1915 and 1916.

The first indication of the seriousness of the situation in the lead-up to the revolution was when remittances were all but stopped for everything except for the purchase of raw materials. This prohibition was slightly academic, as any money taken out of Russia at the time would have caused the company what the then-Chairman, Sir Thomas Glen-Coats, described as "a ruinous loss". The exchange had slipped from 9.6 to 15 roubles (Rb.) to the pound by 1916, and the debt owed to Coats had reached Rb. 27 million. The board in Glasgow believed that the money was safe either in treasury bills or lodged with reputable banks and earning good interest, so most of them preferred to wait. The exceptions were J.O.M. Clark and T. J. Hirst, both of whom felt that the debt and therefore the risk should be limited to 20 million. With hindsight they were absolutely right, but the point is moot, as the company was refused any remittances at all at the end of 1916. Faced with this state of affairs they decided to seek an alternative home for their money and began investigating other investment vehicles, but found to their horror that the stock exchange was closed. Alarm bells began to ring.

Back in Russia the winter was proving exceptionally harsh, and the situation deteriorated rapidly. Shortages of food, clothing, and fuel became critical. Transport was chaotic—people could wait at the station literally for weeks to get a train, and when it did arrive it would be packed, with people on the roof, the steps, and even the buffers. Civilian morale reached a very low ebb, and the military were possibly even more despondent. There was general unrest, and strikes were particularly prevalent in St. Petersburg, where NTM were located.

Rasputin's murder was one event that started the first revolution.[1] There are endless myths surrounding his death, but he appears to have been poisoned, shot, clubbed, and then thrown in the river to drown. The discovery of his body in the River Neva is described in the Coats notes on Russia: "The search party...had given up hope of finding the body, when one of the police was attracted to a slight discolouration of the ice. Rasputin's beard had frozen there and the body was secured". Just as well he was hirsute.

Not long after his death, a series of strikes and demonstrations centred on St. Petersburg, combined with extensive looting and arson, led to the closure of almost every manufacturing establishment. Unfortunately for Coats, the Nevsky mill was located right in the centre of all the trouble, near both the revolutionary headquarters and the Duma (parliament), so most marches and parades passed right by their gates. Despite this, there was little damage done, but the plant was stopped and, with shooting quite common out in the street, the British managers often found themselves having to take cover.

1. There were two in 1917.

Coats had three executives running NTM: Boris Mickwitz, the senior director, Neil Buchanan, who was destined to have a long history with Russia, and C. R. Saunders, who had extensive Eastern European experience and had been sent to St. Petersburg with the rather whimsical instruction to "act as a kind of superintendent over all the Russian mills".

The situation for these three men became downright dangerous. One of the favourite ways of disposing of uncooperative managers was for a group of workers to bundle the offender into a sack and then throw him into the river Neva, where he would either drown or die of hypothermia, whichever came first. So it was clear what was on the mind of a group of ten Nevsky mill workers when they pushed their way into the office occupied by Saunders and Buchanan on a Saturday in July 1917, carrying sacks and demanding a 25% wage increase.[2] After an hour's discussion, the delegation left, threatening that if their demands were not met on Monday, the two managers would have to face the consequences. Reports of the incident to the Ministry of Labour had little effect, and it was only the arrival of delegates from other mills on the Monday that prevented the same ten from forcing their way into the office to carry out their ultimatum.

This seems far-fetched, but the Coats files demonstrate that such threats were very real. They tell the story of the director of a nearby mill who was put in a sack and dragged to the bridge over the Neva. The workers were arguing about which side of the bridge they should toss the sack when a military detachment arrived and grabbed it with the intent of throwing it in themselves. The workers wrestled it back from the soldiers and hauled the hapless director, still bundled up, back to the mill. They then took pity and released him "more dead than alive", but he was at least able to report back to the Society of Manufacturers. At their meeting the same

2. The only reason Mickwitz was not there was that he was at home in bed with malaria.

same evening, reports came in that "mobs in the city were quite out of hand" and that "all motor cars were being destroyed in the streets". The unruliness continued for months, and it was only when the Bolsheviks took control after November 1917 that the workers began to show some discipline.

Some claimed that the cars weren't burnt, but were taken by the military to allow them to reach trouble spots more quickly or even to facilitate looting, but whatever the case, the story demonstrates the level of chaos that reigned in St. Petersburg at the time. Unfortunately, it would get worse.

By October the second revolution was in full swing. The workers were now "masters of the situation", according to the British Ambassador, and the Coats board recommended "not risking personal safety by resisting Commissary's control, however distasteful this may be".

The technique employed by the workers' groups was similar in most factories. It involved demands for better conditions or higher wages, citing improvements already granted in other nearby plants, usually fictitious. Colleagues from the neighbouring establishment would accompany the delegation, asserting that these enhancements had indeed been introduced, and this "irrefutable" evidence, combined with threats of violence, would be used to bludgeon the management into concessions. If obtained, these would then be taken next door to seek an ever-escalating wish-list and so on, back and forth. In a similar vein, wage increases would be sought for one group of workers within the mill, and this would then be used to get the same for all other groups, to maintain differentials. It was a never-ending process. What made the workers' positions so particularly intractable was that the agitators were generally the ones with the biggest mouths and smallest intellects who had gained their positions as workers' representatives by making the most outlandish promises. Managing became progressively more difficult.

With the Bolsheviks in power, new Workers' Mill Committees were introduced, and it was hoped that the presidents of these would exert some form of control over their more extremist colleagues. At NTM the reverse happened, as the new president was a particularly obstructive individual named Petroff. His subsequent path to complete power was quite convoluted and is a good example of how Lenin's Decree on Worker Control could be manipulated. Saunders takes up the story (again from the Coats papers):

> Soon after the publication of the Decret, a Commissar from the Ministry of Labour came to our Head Office, along with some five members of each mill committee, to explain the lines on which Control had to be formed, and the role the workers would play in it.
>
> According to his views, the object of the Control was to assist the manufacturers in obtaining the necessary raw material and financial assistance, and to act as a check on abuses. To this we readily agreed, and after discussing the manner of the election of the Control Committee, the workers being quite unacquainted with such procedure, we consented to elect the heads of the mills' offices, chiefs of departments of the Head Office, and a few of their own foremen. The working of the Committee was quite harmonious but, unfortunately, the arrangement did not last very long.
>
> The Nevka Mills President, Petroff, not being elected to the Control Committee, disregarded all their instructions and those of the management and head office, and in consequence of this the Nevka Mills became like a small independent republic. When Petroff was called to explain his behavior, he simply laughed and said that he did not recognize a Committee composed of nominees, and that he would see to it that a new committee was elected with proper and proportionate representation from each mill, according to the number of workers employed. He then succeeded in dissolving the first Committee and in getting a new one elected. He was again left out, so he condemned it and insisted on a third election. This time, he made sure

of the result by getting some of his Red Guardsman friends to intimidate the workers, telling them what would happen to each man individually if they did not elect him this time.

As a result Petroff was elected President, and from that moment onwards the real trouble began.

Workers who had been dismissed years before were rehired and took revenge on the people responsible for their original termination, usually British foremen. Petroff appointed his Bolshevik comrades to the Control Committee, and together they placed a stranglehold on selling, production, finance, and supplies of materials, including fuel, citing the Lenin Decree, which stated that their decisions were final and binding on the owners. The company complained to the Ministry of Labour, who agreed that the Control was informative and not enforceable in the way that Petroff was claiming. They even agreed to send a representative to explain this, but as was usually the case, nobody turned up.

Serious problems soon arose. Cotton supplies started to run out, but Petroff would not allow the management to move product around to minimize stoppages and disruption. Soon the workers from Nevsky were in the Head Office demanding supplies, and a deputation from Beck, who were owed some 1.6 million roubles, was looking for money. They were not the only ones, but, although the company had plenty in the Bank of Moscow and a wad of cash that they had amassed at the Moscow Agency, the Control Committee would only release cash to pay wages.

Then Petroff found out about the Agency cash, which amounted to Rb. 3 million. He decided that he would accompany an armed guard of his choice to collect the money and bring it back to St. Petersburg. Having been persuaded by Saunders to go with several representatives chosen by each mill committee, he set out. In the meantime, Saunders got Mr. Main in Moscow to make up two identical sets of parcels, one with the money and one with cut-up newspaper instead of cash. Petroff was to be shown the original cash but handed the other parcel, and the real money was to be despatched to St. Petersburg separately. As Saunders put it "Luckily both sets arrived safely; the money first and the faked parcels later".

The financial situation became farcical. Banks were all closed whilst an attempt was made to merge them into one. Book entries were made into the wrong banks, and it was said that the mess would take years to unravel. Safety deposit boxes were opened and all cash forcibly deposited in the relevant bank accounts, whilst gold coins were confiscated. When the company lawyer, Mr. Kagan, had his box opened, he noticed that the commissar[3] was putting gold coins in his collar and boots, so the legal eagle managed to save a good portion of his collection by following the commissar's excellent example.

There was a chronic shortage of cash, and lawlessness inevitably followed, with robberies and shootings becoming commonplace, often perpetrated by the Red Guardsmen. One such incident has an element of poetic justice. A Guardsman stopped a British gentleman on a cold winter's night and relieved him of his watch, his money, and his coat. The victim followed his attacker, pleading with him to return his coat, as it was a bitterly cold night. The Guardsman eventually tired of his whining and took off his own rather moth-eaten topcoat and threw it to the ground saying that it should be good enough to keep him warm. The grateful Briton donned the garment and, upon thrusting his hands in the pockets for warmth, was thrilled to find not only his money and his watch, but also another Rb. 14,000.

3. The title "commissar" conjures up the image of a person of great stature, but most were just ex-office boys who happened to work at the bank. Their newfound position allowed them to take bribes of up to 20% of any cheque they allowed to be cashed, as withdrawals were limited to Rb. 150 per week.

By early 1918, the mills had to close due to a combination of excess stocks of thread and shortages of cotton. The German armies were closing in on the area, and some kind of epidemic seemed likely as the streets went for long periods without being cleared or cleaned, and decaying garbage was accumulating, awaiting the spring thaw. It was decided that the few remaining British subjects should be evacuated. Some of the Coats staff got to Murmansk and boarded British ships there. Buchanan had already gone, having been instructed to leave earlier. Saunders remained, but after being rescued from another potential "sacking" by Mickwitz, he too decided that his position was untenable, and he left immediately, also via Murmansk. He was to return only a few months later, as British Consul in Archangel.

The mills were nationalized towards the end of the year by which time Mickwitz had left for Riga for medical treatment. William Beck of the James Beck Spinning Mills was appointed technical consultant to the thread mills group. He closed down Beck and transferred all their stocks to Nevsky Cotton Mills. The Koenig Mill followed in April 1919, with Nevka stopping in October, but the two Nevsky plants struggled on, production fluctuating with the availability of both cotton and fuel, but generally attaining a level some 20% below their expected norm, employing roughly 900 people in each.[4] About a third of the workers would absent themselves daily, feigning illness, since by presenting a doctor's certificate they obtained full wages. Food, boots and clothing were scarce.

The thread mill suffered a seven-month stoppage, but then restarted in 1921 with 1,200 workers and 120 staff. However, there were no spools, so the thread was sold on 400 yard skeins and demand was pitiful. Small wonder, as part was dyed black and the remainder unbleached, with 80% of the production described as glacé, but none of it polished. Buildings and machinery were suffering from

4. This compares to the 9,000 they employed five years before.

neglect, and much of the power supply was out of action. The situation in the Nevsky Cotton mill was similar, but they were still working.

Throughout all this, the board remained surprisingly upbeat, assuming that things would return to normal and that the "funds which we had accumulated there during the last four years...and which are invested in Treasury Bonds, were absolutely safe, and that realisation was only a question of time". This Panglossian view was from the chairman's report to the 1918 shareholder's meeting. As time went on, however, news became more sporadic and announcements less optimistic. Sir Thomas Glen-Coats reported in 1921 that, "...we have no exact knowledge as to whether they are or have been working". A year later he said, "no change in the situation regarding the Nevsky Mills in Petrograd which are working under the control of the Soviet Government".

Coats left about Rb. 167 million in Russia, £17 million at the prewar exchange, and over £4 million at the rate which had reached Rb. 40 to £1 by the end. In round terms, it was split 50% in their shareholdings in NTM and NCM, with 25% in loans, advances for equipment, and materials, and the remaining 25% in Treasury Bonds. These last, which were said to be "safe", were destroyed by a woman commissar before Mickwitz's very eyes, and he only got "a carelessly written, hardly legible scrap of paper" as evidence of this. A claim for the full amount was lodged with the Russian Claims Department in London.

Despite pursuing this over the years, nothing came of it until the advent of "Perestroika", when Gorbachev found himself in need of financing from the West in the late 1980s. To establish his credibility with the International Monetary Fund (IMF) and the World Bank, he came under enormous pressure to settle the question of compensation for individuals and businesses that had lost investments in Russia during the revolution. A solution was needed to allow the restructuring to go ahead.

By coincidence, Czarist Russia had kept a portion of their gold reserves with the Bank of England at the start of the twentieth century. When the Bolsheviks took over, the British Government had frozen these assets, and they had remained that way pending a satisfactory outcome to the situation. They now proved to be a handy bargaining chip.

As so much time had passed, most creditors had either ceased to exist or had incomplete or inadequate paperwork, but this was not the case with the ever-diligent Coats. A deal was struck whereby any British individual or company who could substantiate their claim would be compensated for the full amount, taken from the Czar's gold, on condition that they signed away their right to any further compensation. Whilst this was not a great deal, it was a lot better than nothing, so Coats agreed and finally got all their money back, seventy years late, with no interest.

The Armistice was signed to end the First World War on November 11, 1918 and, although the company had emerged relatively intact, the Russian ordeal and the loss of control in several other countries meant that extensive reconstruction would be needed, and this would be expensive. Wartime inflation had led to higher prices and accusations of monopolistic behavior and profiteering, with Chiozza Money raising his head again, urging the president of the Board of Trade to "exercise the power he possesses to reduce the price of sewing cotton". This was to become the hot topic of the day in the immediate postwar period.

Chapter 33

Mixed Fortunes in Europe

This crash is not going to have much effect on business.
Arthur Reynolds, Chairman of Continental Illinois Bank of Chicago, October 24, 1929

After the end of the First World War, it took no time for the UK antitrust lobby to have their way. The Ministry of Reconstruction set up a select committee on trusts in 1918, and subcommittees were then formed to look into the most successful industries: soap, tobacco, and thread amongst others. Inevitably, Coats, as the largest company in the UK, was the focus of attention in their particular field. They also managed to draw attention to themselves even before the subcommittee had started to deliberate, by increasing their prices by over 100%[1] and then declaring record profits for 1918-19 of just under £4 million, after providing £900,000 for EPD. They then raised their capital from £10 million to £20.25 million by capitalising £7.3 million of the reserves and issuing £2.95 million of new ordinary shares allotted to existing shareholders. This money was sorely needed to finance the replacement of assets and postwar expansion.

1. To 7¼d. from a prewar price of 3d. for the 400 yard spool.

The price hike caused at least one demonstration in Glasgow, and questions were raised in the House. Such was the outcry that the company was compelled to issue a statement explaining the cost increases (which more than justified the changes in price) and, in an unprecedented move, actually showing the cost breakdown of a 400 yard reel. They also pointed out that less than 10% of their profit now came from goods sold in the UK.

Costs had skyrocketed during the war. Coal and wages were up 150% and other raw materials by that much and more, but what had really hit them hard was cotton, where less planting, poor crop outcomes, and a greatly increased demand for the new automobile tyre trade[2] had raised the price by 250%. It would double again in the next year.

Coats had been holding off putting up prices as long as they could, but inflationary pressures were escalating, and a further sharp increase to 10d. for the 400 yard article was announced in February 1920. The press, trade unions, and politicians were furious. It was not so much the size of the increase that caused indignation; the timing of it, just before the subcommittee was due to report, was viewed as borderline arrogant and certainly contemptuous.

The report appeared four days later. Whilst far from a condemnation, it was on balance unfavourable and—on top of the price increase—did nothing to enhance their tarnished reputation. A retort was issued, so well thought-out and clearly presented that it provoked a second statement from the subcommittee, which this time largely vindicated the company position.

Prices were reduced by 20% at the start of 1921, and as is the way with these things, the public, press, and parliament found other fish to fry. Further reductions followed, and substantially reduced profits for that year finally meant that the issue simply evaporated.

2. Each tyre was taking 6 lbs. of raw cotton.

However, EPD hung around and, although supposedly introduced to finance the war, it wasn't abolished until mid-1921. It had reached 80% in the last two war years but was reduced to 40% for 1919 and 60% for the year after. Coats had a long and costly battle with the Inland Revenue over the "standard profit" that was used to calculate EPD and the stock valuation, where Coats used replacement cost, whereas the tax authorities specified the lower of actual cost or market price. This interpretation brought the total EPD liability to £1.5 million and the issue dragged on for years. It was finally resolved in 1926.[3]

The postwar years were pivotal for the Group. The pace of change was accelerating, and their ability to respond was inhibited by their size, complexity, and desire for central control. Ready-made clothing was growing in popularity, with the demob suit being a prime example of semi mass-produced apparel, so the trend towards longer industrial thread lengths accelerated. Bespoke tailoring had become too expensive, but factory produced clothes were relatively cheap and put more garments within the reach of more people. The sale of consumer thread items, particularly the six cord spools, Coats's bread-and-butter, inevitably suffered.

The Depression of the '30s put further pressure on the sales of Coats's traditional high-cost, high-quality spools and opened the gap between them and similar products on tubes in shorter lengths at cut prices. Import duties and currency fluctuations, combined with the inherently high costs in Paisley, which was still the main source for much of their product, simply magnified these differences.

Demand for lighter, more colourful fabrics and lustrous finishes combined with more frequent changes in fashion drove a requirement for a greater number of different

3. Jack Coats managed this in a most extraordinary way. The full story is in the next chapter, pages 333-5.

threads and more extensive colour ranges. Mercerised cotton became popular and rayon (or artificial silk, as it was then known) started to appear, though Coats described it as a "mere bagatelle" in their product range.[4]

Hesitant to go wholeheartedly into three ply mercerised threads for fear of cannibalizing their lucrative six cord market, Coats set about trying to correct their cost base in the UK. They found ways of reducing the number of processes required and automated those they could.[5] They also tentatively began to commit themselves to longer length industrial products, as well as threads for shoes, bags, gloves, and other manufactured items, but they found the increased volatility of demand for these frustrating, and clung doggedly to their consumer spools, still the majority of their turnover.

The increased sale of handicrafts, which had taken place during the war, taking advantage of the absence of the French (DMC) and German (Mez) competitors, now reversed as these two reentered the market, and volumes soon returned to prewar levels. Coats could not match either company for lustre or dye fastness and had to play second (or rather third) fiddle to them.

Then fate took a hand. Paul Mez of Carl Mez & Söhne (CMS) appeared outside the soon-to-be chairman, J.O.M. Clark's office in Glasgow in 1925 looking for "someone in authority". He had come to see if Coats had any interest in embroidery threads, in which case he wanted to work out some sort of deal.

4. Rayon had a greater impact in handicrafts than in sewings, mainly as a substitute for more expensive silk, and Coats started to experiment with this, under a cloak of secrecy. They launched Fibresheen in the US in 1922, followed by Sunsheen three years later, when they also set up an experimental plant in Anchor. Some interest was generated in Italy and Brazil.

5. This included transport of packing cases, well before its time.

CMS was only one of two Mez businesses dating back to 1768, when Carl Christian Mez started up a ribbon factory in Kandern, a village halfway between Freiburg, Germany and Basel, Switzerland. His son diversified into haberdashery, cloth, snuff, and (of all things) banking, but it was his great-nephew who started a silk sewing business, based on a twisting frame he himself designed. In 1864, his sons decided that the now-successful company was too big, so they split off the banking and created CMS and Mez Vater & Söhne (MVS). This division was simple, as their mills were beside each other and their customers were easily allocated (some by drawing lots!), but the two companies later fell out when Gustav's grandson turned MVS over to his brother-in-law. By the turn of the century they were at each other's throats.

When CMS approached Coats, they were effectively bankrupt. They had too much outstanding debt from the war, and inflation was making repayments nigh on impossible. DMC were proving to be a stubborn competitor who kept prices frustratingly low, so CMS found that they needed capital. Coats had this, and could see three immediate advantages to an alliance: it would allow them back into Germany, where they had lost the mill at Witzschdorf, and higher import duties were looming; it would get them into rayon production without the need for further experimentation; lastly, it would give them access to the Mez process for mercerising cotton, so they could hopefully copy the technology and improve their own quality, allowing them to compete with DMC on a more equal footing. After extended talks, Coats reluctantly took a 55% stake in CMS, whose capital was raised from 4 to 6 million Marks. Their reticence was due to not wanting the Mez silk business, as this was not one of their core products and was seen as a distraction.[6]

6. Their interests in silk were destined to expand further when they later acquired MVS, but this would not last, as they did a deal with Gütermann, a competitor in Germany and Brazil, selling them the entire silk trade from the two Mez firms. Coats took a 20% share of Gütermann as part of the agreement.

The new business, now known as Mez AG, proved to be disappointing for the first few years. James Henderson was put in charge of a complete reorganization, during which he rationalised and modernized the Freiburg mill, transferred the remaining machinery from MVS (whom they bought in 1929), and turned their factory in Bräunlingen into a warehouse. Unfortunately, little improvement was forthcoming, and competition from DMC became keener.

The mysterious mercerising process turned out to be nothing more than an absolutely fastidious attention to detail in all aspects of processing the thread through the dyeworks. As such it was relatively easy to understand, though not to copy. Once applied in the UK and US, the effects on quality were noticeable, but it took years to instill the sort of discipline required in the various workforces. It did teach Coats a useful and salutary lesson, and this approach to all aspects of dyeing became part of the company philosophy from then right through to today. It now has fancy names and is computer controlled, but the basic principles are exactly the same.

Anchor also learnt enough from Freiburg to be able to put acetate rayon embroidery on the market in 1927, based on externally purchased yarn, and Pawtucket soon followed. This venture into a new fibre helped to stimulate rumours that Coats was going into viscose rayon production, perhaps in collaboration with Courtaulds, but although they did toy with it for sewings, they were unsuccessful, and it came to nothing. Only the arrival of nylon at the time of World War II would finally allow a synthetic fibre to successfully substitute cotton.

Elsewhere in Europe, a major opportunity was missed back in 1921, when the irksome DMC expressed willingness to sell to Coats, but at a price the latter were unwilling to pay, particularly as they were still smarting from what looked like a total loss in Russia. Prohibitive import duties meant that local production in France was essential, but their offer to take a controlling interest in DMC fell on stony ground. After discussions came to nothing by mid-1922, they opted to buy an unused munitions factory in La Varenne, near Paris, just to get a foothold. By 1926, Agence Centrale & Filteries Réunies SA had started selling spools and made steady progress, only interrupted by a general strike in 1936, after which workers' committees and a forty-hour week became standard for all French factories.

Fabra y Coats in Spain expanded their business through several acquisitions, so that by 1930 they dominated the local market. Unlike the more cautious Coats subsidiaries, they embraced both embroidery and mercerised tubes and were the first in the company to make tyre cord yarns and canvasses for the up-and-coming tyre industry. By 1935, it had become impossible to remit earnings to the UK, so they tried to buy more competitors and even opened a retail store to sell haberdashery.

Then the Spanish Civil War broke out. They lost control of the mills in Catalonia, the British staff left, and the Spanish directors fled to Seville, where they set themselves up in the depot, installing a finishing unit to at least keep some supplies going. One of the Fabras was captured and killed, and the mills were "collectivised" and put in the hands of a workers' committee. All the stocks were sold to help pay wages, and production was limited to official war orders, which in their turn were dependent on availability of materials. The air force dumped 5,000 drums of benzene at Torelló, but through all the turmoil the factories remained largely undamaged, and when the Fabras returned, they found almost no provisions in the mills, a starving workforce, frequent power outages, and transport chaos as the retreating Reds had destroyed all the bridges. Despite all this, they were up and running within the month.

Portugal made fair progress over the period despite a fire that destroyed the finishing department and store in 1922. Further familiar problems with drought meant bringing water from the Douro in wine casks, but they appeared to be getting used to this. Several unexploded shells landed in the mill grounds during a military revolt in 1927, but as the mill was on holiday, there was little damage done, and the government even paid the company an indemnity. This amounted to the magnificent sum of £17.

It took two years to get F&FR in Belgium back into some semblance of order. They had several plants under their control by the time the war started, the last two having been bought shortly beforehand, using a £250,000 loan from Coats. The Belgian Franc went from BEF 25 to 88 per £1 in just four years from 1919, so the added debt burden and the considerable cost of re-equipping overwhelmed the company. The delay in getting up to speed also meant that they missed the immediate postwar boom and, although Coats had tried to preserve the Belgians' export markets by selling their products from the British mills, these efforts were largely unsuccessful.

Despite all this, Coats agreed to help F&FR out. Increased orders, improved costs, and a war damages award of 5 million francs allowed the Belgians to start repaying their debt, and by 1925 it had been wiped out, so a dividend was paid for the first time since before the war.

CCC Italy was much more of a success. With over 3,500 employees, they grew to be the largest Coats company outside the UK and US. This was accomplished by buying up a series of small competitors and expanding their range into longer lengths, mercerised sewings, and handicrafts. James Henderson managed to wriggle free of the centralized control from Scotland, first by taking on his own cotton and yarn buying and then by expanding his product range beyond that which his superiors considered "safe". As this seemed to allow the business to flourish, he met with few complaints.

Problems with government interference emerged. The

authorities were clandestinely opening the incoming mail from abroad and then resealing it, not always as skillfully as they might. To avoid their prying eyes, Coats set up a small office across the border in Switzerland and sent their more sensitive letters from Glasgow there. The hapless James Lamb, Henderson's secretary, would then go and collect the mail and bring it back, but even this was fraught with obstacles, as his bags, papers, and even clothing would be subject to the closest scrutiny. Indeed Henderson himself was strip-searched on more than one occasion when travelling between Milan and Freiburg, where he was a director of Mez AG.

The xenophobic attitude of the Fascists became more blatant. They particularly disliked successful Italian businesses run by foreigners, and CCC was a prime example. To resolve the situation, they hit upon the extraordinary idea of offering Henderson a Senate seat if he would take on Italian citizenship. He refused and was concerned that this might work against him,[7] but was promoted to the main board of Coats shortly thereafter, leaving Italy for the bleaker climes of Scotland, so the problem was resolved.[8]

7. He needn't have worried. Shortly afterwards, he was invited for an audience with Mussolini, who had an enormous, cathedral-like office in the Palazzo Venezia. "Il Duce" complained to him of the abundance of resources the British had at their disposal and challenged Henderson to name a single raw material that Italy had. The Scot replied that their weather was surely their greatest resource and that if you added together the climates of Scotland and Italy and then gave half of the result to each, the tourists would desert Italy and travel north instead. At this, Henderson describes how he "...roared with laughter, slapped me on the back and accompanied me to the door".

8. Luciano Garibaldi, in his book *Mussolini: The Secrets of His Death*, says: "It is very possible that Sir James and Mussolini knew each other from past acquaintance. The Henderson Villa and the offices of the Cucirini Cantoni were located a few dozen meters from the locations where the tragedy of Mussolini and Claretta Petacci [his mistress] took place. However, this could also be a strange but complete coincidence". In the same book he places Henderson in Switzerland during the war, whereas it is clear from Henderson's account that he was in Scotland. He would return to Italy after the war.

In Eastern Europe, the map had been completely redrawn. The Russian Revolution had created five new nations: the three Baltic states of Lithuania, Estonia, and Latvia, where the old Chadwick Mill at Strasdenhof in Riga was situated; Poland, where Coats had the Lodz mill; and Finland, from where spool wood could again be imported.

Although the Riga plant was badly damaged, it was now rebuilt, equipped with spooling equipment from Paisley, and set to work supplying the Baltics grey and coloured thread, mostly from Eagley. The reconstruction of Lodz took longer, due to continued conflict with the Bolsheviks and then through shortages of currency. Barter arrangements were set up, and the mill was repaired and put into operation. However, progress was slow.

Further south, the Austro-Hungarian Empire had broken up. Yugoslavia was created, Hungary declared its independence, and Czechoslovakia emerged with the Coats Hungarian mill at Pressburg rematerializing in this new country. Transylvania became part of Romania, though they still speak Hungarian there to this day, and parts of southern Austria, including Trieste, became Italian. Each of the new countries set about asserting their independence by introducing regulations and tariffs.

The Coats network in the area was totally disrupted. The Hungarian authorities quickly made importing a nightmare, so Coats grudgingly bought some land in Ujpest (now part of Budapest) on the Danube and built a fully integrated mill there. They subsequently also put money into the Mez Hungarian plant in Nagyatad, some 150 miles northeast, near the Slovakian border. Austria was now a relatively small market with overcapacity in Harland and Wilhelmsburg, which was closed.

The machinery from there was transferred to Bulgaria, where Coats bought an old woolen mill at Kazanlik and converted it into a twisting and finishing unit. In Romania,

Mez had a small unit in Talmaciu, and Coats decided to build a fully integrated thread mill there. This took shape over the period between 1935 and 1939 and was about as modern a plant as any in the group, with social amenities and housing for 300 girls included in the program. The total cost was over £200,000 and the final project was similar in scope to the one they had erected in Torelló forty years earlier. They even built a church, and such were the facilities provided for the workforce that they brought howls of protest from other local employers who felt they had set the bar impossibly high.

By the time that Coats had bought a Dutch competitor, J. A. Carp, in 1938 and set up manufacturing in Holland, they controlled mills in every European country except for Estonia and Lithuania (supplied from Latvia), Scandinavia and Eire (supplied from the UK), Greece, which they looked at but decided against, and Russia. With other factories in Canada, Mexico, Brazil, and Japan, not to mention their massive investment in the US, they now had over fifty manufacturing units around the world. TCA were selling to seventy-five countries, and central control in the Philippi mould was no longer possible. Change was needed.

By the end of the 1920s, when the world was in the throes of the Great Depression, there had been several moves at the top of the company. George Coats's (Lord Glentanar's) son, Tom (known as Tom Glentanar) joined the board in 1919, as did Thomas Heywood Coats, Willie Coats's eldest. His younger brother Jack also became a director in 1923, but his heart was not in it and he gave up in 1930.

Sir Thomas Glen-Coats had died in 1922[9] and was succeeded as chairman by William Hodge Coats, one of

9. His son Alexander Harold would follow in 1933, aged fifty. He had fought at Gallipoli and worked for Coats after the war. Renowned for his kindness to all, he was a great promoter of welfare benefits within the company, and was instrumental in developing the pension scheme during its early days.

Archie's twin sons. He only lasted a few years, suffering from ill health for most of his tenure and succumbing in his early sixties. So although Ernest Coats was still there and his son Ian had joined the board in 1931, by the mid-30s there were only four Coatses in the company. It was the Clarks' turn to dominate the conglomerate and J.O.M. Clark, who had been a board member for over twenty-five years became the first non-Coats chairman. This was a significant break with tradition, but there would be others to come, including James Henderson's appointment as managing director of TCA, the first time this post was revived since Philippi's departure, but with one big difference—Henderson advocated decentralization. He would have other allies in this endeavor, particularly John Balfour Clark in the US, who would join the board as well. Before we get to him, the passing of the crown from one family to the other is an appropriate moment to look at some of the Coatses who found fame in other spheres beyond the world of thread.

Chapter 34

Family Heroes, Rogues and Rascals

After all, the wool of a black sheep is just as warm.
Ernest Lehman, American screenwriter

Ten Coatses from the third generation worked for the company, but by the fourth generation only four remained: Ernest's sons George (of whom there is no trace) and Ian Pountney, who was on the board for thirty years; Bill Coats, who would become the last family chairman; and Bill's brother Tim, who ran the business in Spain for many years.[1] Two of Peter Herbert's children, Staneley and Seton, flirted with thread. The former seemingly got involved in something shady and left, and Seton resigned from the US.

However, several of the Coats family had little to do with thread, but found fame for other reasons. The most notorious was Jack Coats, Willie's younger son.

John Alexander Coats (1892-1932), known as Jack or Johnny, was profoundly affected by the early death of his mother,[2] as was his older brother Thomas Heywood. Thomas

1. He was asked to join the board on many occasions, but always refused, preferring to stay in Barcelona.

2. Agnes Coats (née Muir) died in Cannes on March 13, 1894, whilst convalescing after an illness. Jack was less than two years old.

joined the family firm as was expected of him and, although he was a rather shy man, he acquitted himself admirably in his chosen field of finance.

Jack was less able to hide his light under a bushel. He was suave and handsome, had a collection of fast cars, and loved to gamble, spending much of his time and copious amounts of money at the casinos in Monte Carlo and Juan-les-Pins. At one point this got so bad that the family decided to send him on holiday to Europe, as far from the tables as possible. He was physically escorted to the boat, but by the time he reached his destination he owed so much to the other passengers that he was not allowed to disembark until his debts had been settled in full.

He was reckless with his riches in other ways. He apparently offered a particularly beautiful young woman £1,000 to take off all her clothes and dive naked into a swimming pool on the French Riviera; she reportedly took his money. He tipped a barmaid who had wished him luck half a million francs on a night when he broke the bank in a Paris gaming club.

However he was not all frivolity, by any means. At the start of the First World War, he joined the Royal Flying Corps and flew over the front in support of the allied troops. He was promoted to captain but was then shot down and lost a lung as a result of inhaling mustard gas. No longer allowed to return to combat, he transferred to Canada to train their pilots.

At Camp Mohawk in Deseronto, not far from Toronto, he ran into an old friend, Vernon Castle, who was also an instructor. Vernon was an English dancer who had found fame but little fortune in partnership with his wife Irene,[3] first in Paris, and then on Broadway and as a minor film star.

3. She popularized the "bob", the short hairstyle of the flappers that would appear en masse in the twenties.

They were instrumental in stimulating the popularity of the dance crazes to come and opened a dance academy where they gave lessons to the cream of New York Society.

Vernon had returned to England to fight in the war and, like Jack, had been shot down (twice in his case) and then sent to Canada. He and Jack were made for each other—reckless with money, with a passion for fast cars, they cemented their friendship and could be seen around town either in Jack's white Marmon or Vernon's yellow Stutz Bearcat.

Another instructor, Eardley Charles Wilmot, who was a well-to-do native of nearby Belleville with a passing resemblance to Errol Flynn, soon joined them, and the three became inseparable, renowned for their wild lifestyle and daredevil flying. They were famous for "buzzing" the locals in their planes, and Jack had a motor launch that could either be used for pleasure boating or more often to rescue downed flyers from the Bay of Quinte.

It was through one such stunt that Jack Coats was to meet his future wife. Eardley had two beautiful sisters, Audrey and Gwen, and Jack had wanted to meet them for a time, but resolved to make an entrance that they would remember. He therefore ditched his plane in the extensive gardens of Glanmore House, where he knew they would be staying. They came out to see what the commotion was, and there was Jack, literally dropping in for tea, which he was duly offered whilst a manservant was sent off in search of fuel.

Jack fell in love with Audrey and in due course they got engaged, as did Vernon and Gwen, but plans for a double wedding[4] were shelved when the USA entered the war in 1917 and the instructors were all shipped off to Texas to train American pilots.

4. Vernon planned to divorce his wife, Irene, and expected the process to take a year. The double wedding had been set for autumn 1918.

Within a year Vernon had died in a training accident. In a previous crash, a trainee pilot had been killed when sitting in the front cockpit, so Vernon changed positions for all his subsequent lessons. On the day of the tragedy, the session had gone well, and they were coming in to land, but a pilot on the ground had taken off right below them and, although Vernon tried to avoid a collision, at fifty feet in the air the plane never had a prayer. They missed the other aircraft, but smashed nose down into the runway. The trainee, now in the back, was fine apart from the odd bruise, but Vernon never recovered consciousness and died in hospital twenty minutes later.

Jack was devastated and returned to Canada shortly thereafter. Instead of a double wedding, only he and Audrey were married on September 25, 1918 in Belleville. Gwen had been in mourning since the accident, but finally emerged to attend as maid of honor, dressed from head to toe in black satin. The war ended, and Jack left the Royal Flying Corps, by this time a major, with the Air Force Medal and a reputation as a first-class instructor. The couple rented a house near Toronto, and after partying with and entertaining the eligible officers and society debutantes of the area for a few months, they set sail for England. Gwen could find no solace in Canadian society and followed a few months later.

They took a twenty-two-room apartment in Mayfair, and set about ingratiating themselves and Gwen with London's elite. The girls were accomplished dancers and riders and, being feisty and gregarious, were soon well-known and accepted amongst the aristocracy.

Jack joined Coats and split his time between work and fox hunting in Scotland (he became master of the Eglinton Hunt) with side trips to the casinos of the Riviera. He did not enjoy the thread business, but stuck it for seven years, during which time he was involved in one of the most curious incidents in the long history of Coats's relationship with the UK tax authority, the Inland Revenue. Coats had contested their interpretation of EPD after the First World War and the matter had dragged on. By 1925, a resolution appeared unlikely without recourse to the law.

At this point the company began to get cold feet, despite multiple opinions in their favour. Their counsel doubted that the courts would rule for them, and the expense of protracted litigation loomed large in their minds. They suggested a compromise, setting up a meeting to see if an agreement could be reached, with representatives of the Revenue Department on one side, and the company lawyer, their accountant, and Jack Coats on the other.

The protracted negotiations eventually reached an impasse with a difference of £100,000 between the parties. With the frustrated tax team tiring, a Mr. Benstead, head of the Glasgow office of the Inland Revenue, appeared. After analysing the situation, he suggested an absolutely outrageous solution to the entrenched positions of the two sides. He produced a florin (two-shilling coin) from his pocket and made to toss it. The prospect of a gamble was irresistible to Jack, and, with a glint in his eye, he jumped at the chance. With agreement from the other party, the coin was duly flipped and as it rose into the air, the electrified audience heard the flying ace call "heads". The florin fell, the result was uncovered, and they realised that he had called correctly, saving the company a considerable sum of money in less than a minute.

This was not the end of the story. Some two weeks later Jack was sitting in his office dealing with other company matters when he received a call out of the blue from Benstead, who politely but firmly requested his immediate presence at the Glasgow office of the Inland Revenue. Unsure what to expect, he set out.

When he was shown into Benstead's office, the taxman handed him a small presentation box. Inside was a silver florin on a piece of purple velvet and the inscription "To the only man who tossed the Inland Revenue for £100,000 and WON". The wording of this engraving is intriguing—it makes you wonder how often the Inland Revenue did this sort of thing, and how many others had taken a similar wager and lost.

After leaving Coats, his gambling got worse. He had played against a Greek syndicate in the South of France headed by "Nicky the Greek" Zographos,[5] who used to pool their resources, some 1.2 billion French francs, to control the baccarat banks in a number of French gambling centres. The stake for each card in their games was over 10,000 francs, and they said they were good for any bet up to 50 million.[6]

In 1930, when they suddenly ceased operations in protest at a new French tax on large baccarat winnings, the gambling world was distraught. "Dashing Jack" Coats, who was a skilled player, stepped in and took over the bank, saying he would hold it all summer if need be, to "break the Greek syndicate and put Baccarat in the hands of sportsmen who love the game". In an "orgy of Baccarat",[7] people turned up from all over, even dressed in pajamas, and played against him for four days. Although he had just won a million francs from the Greeks, he lost all that and eight million more by the end of the session, the largest amount he ever squandered in a single sitting. He was one of the most skilled gamblers in Europe, but this was hardly the only time he left the casino out-of-pocket. He shrugged off his losses in an almost nonchalant fashion, claiming that his only consolation was that his friends were winning his money.

5. An astoundingly good card player, and cool under pressure, he could memorise up to 312 cards (6 decks) in order.

6. Jack Coats was in good company. Harry Gordon Selfridge, founder of the famous department store, the Aga Kahn, and Baron Henri de Rothschild also used to play the Greeks. André-Gustave Citroën (who started the car company of the same name) was alleged to have lost over 30 million francs to them over a period of seven years.

7. Both quotes are from *Time Magazine* of Aug. 21, 1930.

Audrey, who was turning out to be more of a handful than he had bargained for, had started to drink quite heavily. She reputedly had a fiery temper at the best of times, so their relationship quickly deteriorated. He became deeply unhappy and, like so many war heroes before him, he could find no real purpose to life. Two years after his massive loss at Juan-les-Pins, he had apparently finally stopped gambling, but at the age of forty, Major Jack Coats took out his service revolver and put a bullet in his head.[8] Audrey was in Canada at the time.

He had been a brave pilot and a superb flying instructor, much respected by all his trainees, but civilian life had proved too much for him. To cap it all, it would appear that a part of his losses at the casinos were to a crooked gambling ring, but he was destined never to know that.

As a sad postscript to this tale, Eardley Wilmot was killed at the start of the Second World War, but not in a heroic dogfight or a training accident. By then a squadron leader, he was rushing out to his plane (he was always running late) and ran straight into the propellers of a taxiing aircraft. He had been due to transfer to Camp Borden as chief instructor two days later.

Coincidentally, it is with the 1939-45 war that we associate another member of the Coats family. James Stuart Coats (1894-1966), known as Jimmy, was the grandson of Sir James Coats (USA), but he never had anything to do with the company, being a military man. He had fought in World War I and was awarded the Military Cross in 1918, becoming a major by the outbreak of WWII, during which he was entrusted with a highly confidential task of the cloak-and-dagger variety.

8. Both the *Times* and the *Express* went out of their way to report that his death was due to "natural causes" (heart failure). The suicide theory was based on interviews with his daughter, April Wagrel, for *Dancing in the Sky* by C.W. Hunt, a book about flying aces in Canada; there may have been a cover-up.

One of the main concerns of the British government at the start of the war was how they would protect the royal family if there were a German invasion. A plan was drawn up in 1940 whereby four stately homes in different remote parts of England would be designated as "safe houses" for the royals, and a special company of the Coldstream Guards was made responsible for effecting the required evacuation in advance of the invading enemy forces. Jimmy was put in charge, and the project was known as the Coats Mission.

Jimmy, Captain "Gussy" Tatham, and Second Lieutenant Thompson were briefed on June 27, 1940 and spent the next three days and 900 miles visiting the four houses and planning their fortification, all of which had to be arranged in complete secrecy. The detachment was to consist of five officers and 124 men, tasked with arranging the transportation of the Royals to any one of the designated houses at a moment's notice and setting up an effective defense of said property. A separate detachment (named for Major Morris, who was in charge) had two armored Daimlers at their disposal, so that when the need arose, King George and Queen Elizabeth were to be driven in one of these by Morris, with Princesses Elizabeth (the future Queen) and Margaret in the second car immediately behind. Outriders would stop the traffic and escort them to their safe house. A series of buses containing the troops was to make its way there independently, again with a motorcycle escort, and they were to rendezvous at the chosen mansion. The troops would then set up the defenses and protect the family until they needed to be moved again or were declared safe.

This contingency plan was never put into effect and their only real excitement was when they accompanied the Royal Family to Sandringham, where the officers were invited to go shooting with the King (reportedly an excellent shot), and the guardsmen were employed as beaters. The King, Queen, and even the Princesses would sometimes visit the Mess and have tea with the troops, and there is a story of Princess Elizabeth playing not-very-expert ice hockey with them.

Jimmy Coats left the mission in February 1941, became a Lieutenant Colonel, and retired from the army after the war. He had been a keen skeleton racer—nowadays known as luge—and he competed in the 1948 Olympics, coming seventh. He had the distinction of being the oldest ever competitor in the Winter Olympics at the ripe old age of 53 years and 297 days, but he has recently been knocked into second spot behind a curler (if that can be called a sport) from Minnesota called Scott Baird, who was slightly less than a year older.

The family had another record holder from the Olympic Games. Sir Thomas Glen-Coats (1878-1954) was the son of his eponymous father, who had worked for the company and was knighted during the First World War. He was not a chip off the old block and preferred yachting to thread.[9] At the age of thirty, when he realized that the 1908 Olympics were being switched to London,[10] he assembled a team and had a boat, the Hera, ready to challenge in the twelve-meter class.

Altogether twenty-two nations competed, but given the expense and time involved in moving larger boats around, the entries for the yachting events were limited: there were only two for the twelve-meter class, Sir Thomas and Charles MacIver, a Scotsman from Merseyside, with a yacht named Mouchette. As both competitors were British, it seemed pointless to send them both to Cowes, so they agreed to toss a coin to see where they would race. Sir Thomas won and the event came north, to Scotland and the Clyde.

9. Sir Thomas graduated from St. Andrews University, joined Mylnes to learn marine designing, and became a yacht designer. He also continued to race successfully. He never had anything to do with Coats.

10. The original venue was Rome, but Vesuvius erupted in 1906, and the Italian government had to switch all their funds to dealing with the disaster in Naples and the consequent reconstruction effort.

The title was to be decided by the best of three races, and with the advantage of home waters, Sir Thomas and his crew romped home in both of the first two on August 11 and 12. In the second race, the Merseyside crew had a bit of bad luck, as their way was partially blocked at the start by a steam yacht named Hebe. It was never mentioned at the time or afterwards, but the more observant reader may have noticed that this was the same boat that Thomas Coats, Sir Thomas's grandfather, had bought back in 1877. However, there was never any suggestion that it was put there deliberately,[11] and Sir Thomas became the only Scotsman ever to have won an Olympic Gold Medal in Scotland. This is a record that has stood for over a century and looks likely to endure.

Peter Daniel Coats (1910-1990) was descended from Sir Peter, but was no Olympic hero. His only connection to the thread business was the wealth he enjoyed as a result of the endeavors of his father, Ernest. He became ADC[12] to Lord Wavell during the war, which allowed him access to a large number of famous people, and he met, amongst others, Winston Churchill, Charles de Gaulle, and Gandhi whilst travelling the world. After the war, he reinvented himself as a landscape gardener and went on to create a variety of layouts in places as far afield as Portugal. He also wrote several books about the history and design of gardens.

However, it is his "other" life that gave him a certain infamy. From an early age, Peter, whose nickname was "petticoats", realized that he was gay, and his lifestyle reflected that orientation at a time when homosexuality was frowned upon. In the mid-30s he bought himself an apartment in Brighton that he euphemistically "shared" with Collie Knox of the Daily Mail and then Gerry Wellesley, an architect and brother of the Duke of Wellington.

11. The Hebe by this time belonged to Sir Thomas Glen's father, who cruised the western isles every summer and kept the boat at Greenock. This would probably have been its normal mooring position.

12. Aide De Camp - an army officer who helps one of higher rank.

He then met and fell in love with Henry ("Chips") Channon, who had acquired his nickname when he shared a bachelor pad with a friend called "Fish". Peter wrote in his book *Of Generals and Gardens* of their first encounter, "After ten minutes conversation it was as if we had known each other for years; and indeed it was odd that we had not met, as we had a dozen mutual friends and interests".

Channon was an American from Chicago who had inherited $175,000 from his father and grandfather, so he could enjoy all the privileges of the class society in England. He married Lady Honor Guinness, whose mother stepped down to give him a safe Conservative seat at Southend-on-Sea in the 1935 election. The Channons bought a fabulous house at 5 Grosvenor Square, next door to the Duke of Kent. This was where they entertained lavishly in their silver and blue dining room, which was modeled on the Amalienburg and cost over £6,000. His money was well-spent, as it did "shock and stagger London" as he said it would. It also allowed him to host King Edward VIII and Mrs. Simpson, whom he knew well, at a dinner party on June 11, 1936, only days before the King's abdication.

Channon's political career waned after (and partly because of) this party, but his real gift was as the Alan Clark[13] of his day, for he kept diaries for over forty years, writing prolific amounts about everything from informal get-togethers to Commons debates. He had opinions about everything and, more importantly everyone, describing Wallis Simpson, for instance as, "...a jolly, plain, intelligent, quiet, unpretentious and unprepossessing little woman, but as I wrote to Paul of Yugoslavia today, she has already the air of a personage who walks into a room as though she

13. Alan Clark was a political diarist of the 1980s, whose *Diaries* were described by Adrian Critchley of the Daily Telegraph as "In the same class as Harold Nicholson's or 'Chips' Channon's diaries. They are malicious, lecherous and self-pitying, and they are enormous fun". Coincidentally, Clark was a descendant of the Paisley Clarks.

almost expected to be curtsied to...She has complete power over the Prince of Wales...".[14]

He had affairs with the aforementioned Paul, King of Yugoslavia, and his dalliance with Peter Coats caused the end of his marriage during the war, though it was he who filed for divorce, as she had run off with a Czech airman. He was rumoured to have had a fling with the Duke of Kent and later had a relationship with Terence Rattigan,[15] who dedicated *The Winslow Boy* to Channon's son, Paul. All this added to the fascination of the diaries.

Peter Coats reduced the original thirty volumes from three million words down to half a million in the three years following Channon's death in 1958, and then handed this abridged edition on to Robert Rhodes James, who cut it to readable length and removed most of Channon's early life in Paris, London, and the USA, including such fascinating items as dinner with Proust. This was published in 1967.

The full text is in a bank vault. Rhodes James said that he saw well-connected people go white when informed that Channon had kept a journal, and Channon himself wrote on December 31, 1937 that, "As I re-read my diary I am frequently horrified by the scandalous tone it has. One might think we live in a world of cads."[16] Nancy Mitford was more direct "You can't think how vile and spiteful and silly it is...Chips...was black inside". Peter Coats's view is more sanguine: "Outspoken they were, but not really scandalous",[17] but then he is the only person in the world,

14. Channon's diary entry, April 5, 1935.

15. Crocker-Harris, the schoolmaster in *The Browning Version,* is supposedly partly modeled on Channon.

16. From *The Esoteric Curiosa* entry on Channon at: _theesotericcuriosa.blogspot.com/

17. *Of Generals and Gardens* by Peter Coats, p.287. The quotes in the next paragraph are from the same book.

apart from the author, who has had unrestricted access to them. The current release date for the full version is 2018. Only then will we be able to judge for ourselves.

Poor health dogged Channon during his later life, and he died in a London hospital in 1958 at the age of sixty-one. Peter Coats was at his bedside and described it as the night when "...the corner-stone of my life fell out". He remained a bachelor, dedicating the rest of his life to his gardens "...to brighten what could have been the lack-lustre years of middle age".

Archie Coats (1916-1989) was Peter Coats's youngest brother. He took to the countryside as a boy, and after serving in the Scots Guards in the Second World War, where he rose to the rank of major, he dedicated the rest of his life to shooting Wood Pigeons, becoming one of the best shots in the country. He married twice, once at the start of the war and the second time to Prue Strettell in 1952. She was born in Scotland but had been raised in Buckinghamshire surrounded by horses, before working for the Free French during the war. Their marriage proved to be a match made in heaven, as she was an accomplished cook and developed some fabulous recipes for—you guessed it—pigeon.

Archie wrote what is still hailed as the definitive work on pigeon shooting, which contains straightforward advice without any gadgets or frills on what is considered a difficult sport. Many of his fans express a desire to have known the man, who had a simple charm and a love for his pastime that is positively infectious. He was also rather good at it, establishing the record in 1963 for the number of pigeons shot in a single day. This stood until quite recently at a staggering 550 between 11:00 a.m. and 4:00 p.m., with two excursions back to the farm for more ammunition, and would have been more if he hadn't run out of cartridges and had to take the shell-shocked dog home. In the description of him for his book, *Pigeon Shooting*, he is said to have "shot 70,000 pigeons a year in a tatty old sports jacket".

He wrote one other book on pigeon shooting, but his wife Prue was far more prolific and has published about a dozen cookbooks. Her best recipes still remain the ones developed for the most readily accessible ingredient, the Wood Pigeon.

Andrew Coats (1862-1930) pursued other forms of hunting, for he had the blood of a pioneer and explorer in his veins. Old Thomas Coats's youngest son, he attended Glasgow University, but shunned the thread company and instead became a captain with the Sixth Scottish Regiment, going on to fight in the Boer War. In that period, he trekked 4,500 miles and served at Wittebergen in the Transvaal and Cape Colony. He received the Queen's Medal and the DSO and was promoted to the rank of major.

It was just before going to South Africa that he met William Speirs Bruce, a contemporary of the far more famous explorers, Shackleton and Scott. Bruce was a shy individual, too serious by half, dedicated to and fascinated by the intellectual challenge of natural history, particularly in the wake of Darwin. He did not understand the romance and challenge that polar exploration represented to the public, and therefore found it hard to get funding for his research, which was a real drawback for someone whose life's work depended on the generosity of others.

His first contact with the Coats family was purely by chance and with the most unlikely person. He was studying medicine at Edinburgh University and had been recommended for his first ever voyage of exploration by the recently appointed Librarian of the Royal Geographical Society (RGS), Hugh Robert Mill. The expedition was to the Arctic Circle, leaving from Dundee, and he was to be the surgeon and naturalist.

Mill had recommended Bruce for the voyage and, as he was in Scotland, he decided to go and see him off, taking Andrew Coates, now in his late seventies, with him. Mill was a family friend and knew several of the Coatses. When they got to the dock, there was no sign of Bruce, who "lounged up" half an hour before the ship sailed, declaring that he was all ready. Upon being asked where his bedding was, he realized for the first time that he would need to supply these items. He had no money on him and appealed to Mill, who was unable to help, so Andrew presented him with a £5 note, and he rushed off to get his kit. It was September 1892.

After six more years of exploration, Bruce was back in Edinburgh when he next ran into the Coatses. This time the younger Andrew was organizing a hunting and pleasure cruise to Spitsbergen and Novaya Zemlya and had invited Mill along as naturalist, but as the President of the RGS would not let him go, Mill had offered his place to Bruce, whom he deemed eminently suitable as his replacement.

Bruce joined the trip at Tromsø and spent three months aboard Andrew's relatively luxurious yacht Blencathra, which was specially reinforced to allow it to navigate through most ice fields. Bruce collected samples and data on plankton, salinity, and depth soundings; Andrew and his guests shot birds, bears, seals, and walruses. When they returned to Tromsø, they ran into Prince Albert of Monaco, who entertained them all and then invited Bruce to accompany him back north for a hydrographic survey. Andrew and his guests returned to Scotland.

By 1899, Bruce had gained a wealth of experience and was one of the foremost experts in polar exploration. When he heard that an expedition to the Antarctic was being organized by the RGS,[18] he wrote to apply for a position. Although he received an acknowledgement, he got no firm reply, so he sent a second letter in March 1900 giving references and mentioning that he was, "...not without hopes of being able to raise sufficient capital whereby I could take out a second British ship to explore in the Antarctic regions".

18. This was the Discovery Expedition (1901-1904), lead by Robert Falcon Scott. It also included Ernest Shackleton as Third Officer.

Sir Clements Markham, the president of the RGS, viewed this as mischievous, and an increasingly heated exchange of letters ensued with the result that Bruce turned his expedition into an independent and fiercely nationalistic affair, renaming it the Scottish National Antarctic Expedition.[19]

Bruce had evidently secured his main financing before his latest communication with the RGS. He must have contacted Andrew Coats, who pledged £7,000 immediately and managed to wring £14,000 from his elder brother Jimmie. The remainder came from 170 different companies and individuals, who together gave just over £6,000. Jimmie threw in a further £7,000 the next year to allow the expedition a second winter in the Antarctic and to buy out an American sponsor, keeping the funding in Scotland. He also sent provisions, including Fair Isle sweaters.

Bruce bought a Norwegian whaler named Hekla and then had it completely rebuilt as a custom-made Antarctic research ship, with extensive specialist equipment, two laboratories, a dark room, 36,000 feet of cable to trawl for specimens, as well as sounding and meteorological instruments. The hull was reinforced to withstand the colossal pressures of sea ice, and auxiliary engines were installed.

The expedition set off on November 2, 1902, initially accompanied by Jimmie on the Triton. Although their purpose was largely scientific, they also reached a new piece of land at the southernmost point of their expedition in March 1904. This was named Coats Land in honor of the

19. He flew both the Scottish Saltire and the English Lion Rampant on the ship. When he docked in Funchal on the way out, the Portuguese mistook the latter for a yellow flag indicating plague on board.

main sponsors.[20] They returned in triumph in July, receiving many congratulations, including a telegram from King Edward VII.

It was, "by far the most cost-effective and carefully planned scientific expedition of the heroic age of polar exploration",[21] which spans the years from 1897 to 1916. They collected 212 previously unknown animal species, and the research they did "laid the foundation of modern climate change studies",[22] but Bruce's disagreements with Markham came home to roost, as his work was ignored by the RGS. None of the expedition were awarded much sought-after Polar Medals, which were doled out to the Discovery Expedition as well as to two of Shackleton's Antarctic sorties, one of which was a disaster of epic proportions. Bruce fought in vain to correct this injustice.

In the end, Bruce was probably too good at his job to ever achieve lasting fame. Both Scott and Shackleton became famous on the back of heroic deeds in the face of terrible adversity. Bruce never had such catastrophes, was not interested in the heroics of a race to the Pole, and so died largely unappreciated in 1921. The years spent following his passion, living and working in inhospitable environments had finally taken their toll.

20. The sponsors have attained further immortality, as there is now a Scottish Country Dance of the same name.

21. *William Speirs Bruce* by Peter Speak, p.14

22. *A Diary of Climate Change* by Vanessa Collingridge (for the BBC).

Chapter 35

The Americas and Zippers

The best executive is the one who has sense enough to pick good men to do what he wants done, and self-restraint enough to keep from meddling with them while they do it.
Theodore Roosevelt

The Clarks had taken over in Glasgow, but they also seized the reins of power in the US, and scientific management took a stronger hold after its tentative first steps with the arrival of Mr. Philippi. His success had not gone unnoticed, but his particular form of control could not continue.

Both families had begun to realize that it was not in the best interests of the business for them to monopolize the senior executive roles. To this end, they were progressively recruiting more professional management, and Tom Glentanar and the new chairman were instrumental in starting recruitment of university graduates to fill senior management roles in the long term. The training scheme that they introduced was one of the first of its kind. It endured for sixty years and was largely responsible for the highly skilled management teams that later ran the company.

The very first graduate recruit was a great success. Colin Mackenzie, who had studied economics under Keynes at Cambridge, joined the company straight from university in 1922. His first task was as a member of a team set up to attempt to forecast exchange rates, but with sterling rejoining the gold standard in 1925, this was disbanded. He became a TCA director and then joined the board in 1929, being influential in moving manufacturing overseas, particularly to Asia and South America, and championing improvements in costing techniques, which became so important in the company's development.

Other board level changes followed, so by the end of the 1920s the hands on the tiller were far less sure. The company had become too complex to manage effectively from the centre, and the onset of the Depression only made restructuring more urgent. At the same time, the infusion of new blood was helping to overcome the innate conservatism of some of the older members, who still had emotional ties to their particular UK manufacturing facilities (Coatses to Ferguslie, Clarks to Anchor, etc.). This made it hard for them to address their fundamental problems: these mills had become expensive and were being replaced by local plants abroad; excess capacity was appearing.

The other problem the company had was the vertical nature of the reporting system, where everything related to any one specialist area (manufacturing, sales, finance) was referred to Glasgow rather than being discussed and resolved at a local level. This had been the strength but was now the weakness of the Philippi system and needed urgent reform as the physical and product spread had outgrown it. There was also a sense of frustration at their lack of autonomy amongst the "Number Ones",[1] as best exemplified by younger professional managers like James Henderson.

1. The local man in charge in each market abroad was referred to as the "Number One".

Several changes took place. Production units were split into regions, in five divisions. One of these was "The Home (i.e. UK) Mills", which were almost immediately put together under a new company, United Thread Mills (UTM). This finally allowed the management to begin the long process of creating more specialized manufacturing units and dealing with excess capacity in a rational way. Several small units that had been collected over the years were closed and Meltham Mills, which had become inefficient, was shut down at the start of the Second World War.

Decision-making was delegated to the local markets, each of which would have a local committee made up of a "Number One" and the senior executives from each speciality. These were still responsible to a series of committees in Glasgow, but these now advised rather than controlled. Local autonomy, apart from capital and other major expenditures, had become a reality.

The devolution of power from the centre really started in the US, where the Spool Cotton Company had been under the leadership of Sir Thomas Glen-Coats until his death, when John William Clark had taken over and later joined the main board. The American committee in Glasgow still made the decisions at this point, but they were operating at arm's length, and the US companies clearly needed hands-on management.

The most obvious example of this was when the committee sanctioned the building of a new dye-house in Bloomfield, near Newark, as well as further expansion at Pawtucket, which now had eight mill buildings. John W. Clark disagreed with these investments, as there were already problems of labour shortages and some unrest in the Northeast, but he still lacked the power to stop the expenditure, which was at best poorly timed.

It was no doubt to make their employment offer more attractive that they also built recreation buildings at both

Newark and Pawtucket and supplied land near the latter complex for the employees to do their own gardening. A store was opened, cows were kept to guarantee fresh milk, and, although many sporting and social clubs already existed, the J. & P. Coats Ladies Athletic Association was formed, though the title may have been a misnomer as "One of the most popular features was sewing, crocheting and knitting instruction", none of which have featured prominently in track and field events.

However, the labour situation was serious enough for John W. Clark to raise it at his first board meeting and to recommend that any further investment in the USA be made in the area of Georgia or the Carolinas and not in the Northeast. This was not only driven by the labour shortage and the increased agitation from the unions, but also by cost and the fact that the whole textile industry (and hence a good number of Coats's thread customers) was also moving to the largely non-unionized South. The proximity to the principal raw material, cotton, and the existence of air conditioning, which was now commercially available, helped justify the decision to move, so it is no surprise that the next investment in the US was the Clarkdale plant (named for the Clarks) in Austell, Georgia in 1931. Others would follow, with the Newark plants and then Coats in Rhode Island slowly shrinking.

The fact that the nominal head of the Coats operations in the US was now located there for the first time, meant a natural transfer of power away from Scotland. The US company began to flex its independent muscles by adopting work study and standard costs into their management system and by promoting integration of the manufacturing units, which were still operating along similar lines to those in the UK, with each producing its "own" product lines. The new costing system, unheard of in Europe at the time, would be sold on to the rest of the Group by the US management team and would become a central part of the Coats financial and merchandising methods for years.

But this would come from the next generation, for John W. Clark died in 1928 and, although he had two sons, James Cameron and John Balfour, in the business, it was the younger one who was the real dynamo. John Balfour Clark became both president of Clark Thread and treasurer of Spool Cotton and immediately started to push for even further autonomy, given the size and scope of the American business. He was rewarded in due course by being made president of J. & P. Coats (RI) Ltd. He had effectively become the supremo of all of "Coats USA" and was given a free hand to run the business as he saw fit.[2] As if to cement his independence, he immediately moved their head office into the newly constructed Empire State Building. He also introduced a formal pension scheme in 1932.

Apart from initiating the integration of manufacturing and its migration to the Georgia area, John B. Clark also introduced a very important new product line to Coats—zip fasteners, or zippers, as they are more commonly known stateside.

The zipper was originally patented in 1851 by our old friend Elias Howe, who had made a fortune from his more famous invention, the sewing machine, without ever selling any. It may indeed have been the success of these devices that prevented him from pursuing his "Automatic Continuous Clothing Closure"—not quite as catchy a name as zipper—and becoming the father of the modern fastener. This title fell to Whitcomb L. Judson, who introduced a remarkably similar product to Howe's called the "Clasp Locker" to the world at the 1893 Chicago World Fair. This was initially used for mailbags and tobacco pouches, but he started the Universal Fastener Co. to make and market an adapted version for clothing. Unfortunately, he had little commercial success as the product had one fatal flaw: it tended to come open.

2. Except when he wanted to spend more than $100,000, which required a blessing from Scotland.

However, one of his employees, Gideon Sundback, had risen to the post of head designer and was therefore responsible for fine-tuning the far from perfect, but ingeniously named "Judson Cecurity Fastener". When his wife passed away in 1911, he buried himself in his work, and two years later the modern product emerged. The term zipper was later coined by B. F. Goodrich, who used Sundback's product in their wellington (rubber) boots and wanted a snappier title.

Crown Fastener Corp. was created in 1934 to exploit the inventions of Davis Marinsky and Louis H. Morin. Between them, they had come up with a new method of die-casting the teeth of the zipper directly onto the backing tape. Previous methods involved stamping the individual teeth from wire and then attaching them. The Crown method was quick and created a very sturdy anchor point; the metal used was cheaper, and there was almost no waste, as any rejects could be melted down and reused.

Their initial investment was small and they soon ran into problems with the technology, so they started to look for additional capital. J. & P. Coats (RI) got wind of this and bought a controlling interest, moved the machinery to a larger plant, started tape weaving for them in Pawtucket, and set about developing the business. With largely experimental machinery and little experience, they struggled for a couple of years but eventually got a reliable product. Crown went on to become the third-largest zipper manufacturer in the US by 1941. Coats had again benefited from the entrepreneurial spirit of their American company.[3]

As the Second World War approached, the US continued to suffer from the aftereffects of the Depression. Labour relations in Newark were strained. A seven-day strike and

3. Another notable alliance was formed at about the same time. Coats and Patons & Baldwins, who were destined to join forces in the early sixties, contracted to make and sell wool products through Patons & Baldwins Inc., a US company owned equally by the two parent companies.

union agitation for a thirty-five-hour work week caused John B. Clark (who had by now joined the main board in Scotland) to accelerate the timetable for the move south, and he set out to find a site for a sewing thread finishing mill, this being the optimum way of moving the largest number of workers with the smallest risk to the company products. He eventually found a completely derelict building on the outskirts of Toccoa, in northeast Georgia, about 100 miles from Atlanta. This was, at first glance, totally unsuitable, but as it was near a railway station, and there was abundant labour available, he took it. He then had it cleaned up, and when the finishing machinery was installed and running in summer 1938, the results were so gratifying that they added extensions for dyeing, bleaching, mercerising, and handicrafts.

Further north, Canada remained a small market, beset with the problems of a widely dispersed population. The Montreal mill employed about 500 people at the close of the War, but that number dwindled to 300 as the Depression hit, despite adding silk production to their portfolio.

Mexico also continued to be marginal, but serious competition from one local rival, La Aurora, and a growing wave of nationalism persuaded the company they should augment their local production. They achieved this by removing El Salvador's cotton underwear section and replaced it over the next two years by twisting, renovated bleaching, polishing, balling, and spooling machines. Coats then acquired La Aurora, which they continued to operate as a totally separate subsidiary, not communicating with El Salvador, and selling fighting brands. With the increased production requirement and the typical quality problems of externally acquired yarns, Coats leased La Guadelupe, a small spinning mill in Mexico City, owned by the manager of La Aurora. This mill worked for both companies, and between the three sites they had some 600 employees.

Brazil was far bigger, with over 4,000 personnel by 1930. Capacity in Ipiranga doubled in the early '20s, and further machinery, including mercerising and colour dyeing (both for the first time), followed, as well as twisting machines from Coats's English mills and Wilhelmsburg. More workers' houses were built in 1929.

They invested in a cotton farm, motivated by concerns over the quality of local cotton, which was abundant but totally unsuitable for fine sewings or handicrafts. The government was also promoting local cotton growing and protecting the farms with import tariffs, so Coats hired an American expert, Norman Munro Kerr, to locate suitable land and arrange a purchase. Despite the intention to find something near Natal, and after travelling a grueling 4,100 miles in sixteen weeks by car, train, steamboat, and horse, he plumped for Fazenda São Miguel, some 100 miles farther west. The plantation measured 17,000 acres and was set up as an independent unit in 1925, with CBLC as only one of their customers. They set about finding a way of crossing the local Mocó seed with the longer, finer, stronger Peruvian Pima cotton.

Things did not go well. The experiments showed little promise and the availability of American cotton at decent prices made the economics of the venture debatable. Pests, drought, and, paradoxically, floods on the road to Natal were so bad that by 1929 Coats decided to cut their losses and sell it. However, as luck would have it, they couldn't, and poor American crops combined with improved results locally meant that they started to make a profit. Some tentative expansion followed, but it was only during the Second World War that it really proved its worth.

Coats took a very small share in a silk and rayon production company in the Mocca district of São Paulo, with Lister and Gütermann, but it was their takeover of the Pedra plant owned by the Menezes family that caused major controversy.

This thread mill had been set up by Delmiro Gouveia on the banks of the São Francisco River, near the Paulo Afonso falls, miles from civilization. Some said he did it just to sell it for a handsome profit to CBLC, and he did float the idea from time to time, but its remoteness and relatively small size made it a dubious proposition, so they were not keen. It therefore trundled along as a rather annoying low-cost competitor.

When Gouveia was killed by one of his employees—a jealous husband—in 1917, the mill was bought by the Menezes family, who tried but failed to make a go of it, so offered it again to Coats. By this time the plant's influence on the thread market had waned, and as such its days were numbered. CBLC said they would only buy if the price were low enough, and in due course a deal was struck. The new owners determined that the distances involved made the ongoing transport cost of thread prohibitive, so they decided to close the plant and move only the better machinery to São Paulo to add capacity there, scrapping the rest.

At this point someone blundered. The people contracted to dispose of the machinery decided to break it up and throw it in the river, right in front of the local villagers who had just been made redundant. Such was the negative reaction that a rumour even circulated that Coats had been responsible for Gouveia's assassination a dozen years before.

Not long after this came the Wall Street crash and the catastrophic collapse of coffee exports from Brazil. São Paulo alone saw 579 factory closures and 2 million out of work, but CBLC not only soldiered on, but expanded. As one of the employees at the time said, "In 1932, with the crisis, all the Ipiranga factories came to a halt except the 'English' which was functioning normally. At that time people could not get work, many were laid off, even my father lost his job and I kept the whole family for almost a year."[4]

4. From *Coats Corrente: 100 Anos de Pioneirismo Costurando Sonhos*, A. M. Dos Santos, (Editor), p. 86.

Faced with yarn shortages and the inability to either remit profits to Glasgow or import machinery, the only option left was to acquire a mill, so in 1935 they bought CFRJ (Spinning Company of Rio de Janeiro). This company had blocked Coats's last attempt to import ring frames, so the negotiations were protracted, and they drove a hard bargain. However, the end result was satisfactory, as CBLC got their capacity and one of the two managers, Herbert Pretyman, became the first "Number One" in Brazil. Unfortunately, he was not a great success and was replaced four years later, by which time the company was expanding even further.

Coats had a business, the Imperial Thread Manufacturing Company Ltd. (TSKK), in Japan by this time. They lost a depot and a shipload of goods in the 1923 earthquake, but they had other problems too. A series of structural changes, new competitors, and a growing and pernicious xenophobia, promoted by the government, strained relations with the Japanese partners, the Murais. Machinery was bought to produce local thread as a substitute for unpopular imports, and they modified the ownership of the company to give 51% to the locals, though the articles of association were changed to require a 55% majority for any major decisions. The Japanese kept on insisting that they needed absolute control, but Coats would not budge.

In May 1939, a sort of compromise was reached, and a portion of the Murais' shares was sold to a local spinner, Fujibo, who had a close relationship with the Mitsubishi Bank, as did TSKK. They became the yarn supplier to TSKK, and one of their directors joined the thread company board. However, with the outbreak of the war, the government reorganised the whole industry into large blocks, and the two companies came together, with TSKK obliged to entrust all their interests to Fujibo. The British left the country.

So Coats had increased its market share and expanded its product range with the addition of handicrafts, zippers, and mercerised cotton, not to mention a far more extensive colour palette, but the loss of Russia and mixed fortunes elsewhere had shaken the company. They had been strangely slow to embrace mercerised thread, clinging doggedly and mistakenly to their beloved six cord. Their reluctance with the longer-length industrial products had also hurt them, and these errors of strategy had helped take them from the exalted position of third-largest industrial company in the world to forty-seventh. They had even been overtaken by Singer, who were now one spot above them, though they too had slipped from eighth. The oil, tobacco, chemicals, car, and metal industries were surging ahead, and textiles were struggling to keep up. This trend was set to continue as they entered the Second World War.

Chapter 36

World War II and the Aftermath

War does not determine who is right – only who is left.
Bertrand Russell, British philiosopher

At the start of the Second World War, Coats lost control of most of their European assets. They immediately ceded Mez (in various countries, not just Germany), Harland, Lodz, Bratislava, and Riga. Then the Germans invaded Holland, Belgium, and France and the corresponding mills were also taken. Finally, Hungary and the rest of Eastern Europe succumbed, and they were left with only Switzerland, Spain, and Portugal. The fates of the "lost" mills varied: some converted to munitions production, whilst some were closed and the machinery removed or destroyed. In those where thread production persisted, they were dogged by lack of raw materials and, therefore, poor quality and sporadic production. Egyptian cotton became unobtainable, and eastern units tried with Turkish varieties, whilst others resorted to rayon. In Italy, thread was rationed, but the system never worked and by the end of the war it was being sold by the metre.

The position of the company in Scotland became a matter of concern when it appeared that Hitler might invade after the fall of France. They decided to establish a parallel organization outside the UK, which would be capable of taking control and managing Group trade if the head office came under German administration. The obvious place was the USA, but tax implications made them shy away from there. After toying with Bermuda, which John B. Clark favoured, they settled on the dormant TCA offices in Montreal, where the government allowed them to operate without being subject to Canadian taxes. James Henderson and several senior executives were dispatched to establish the shadow office, and contingency plans were formulated for the production of essential UK articles in the US, in case the Paisley and Eagley mills fell into German hands. It turned out that none of these emergency measures was needed, but it once again demonstrated their foresight.

The consequences of the war were not all bad. The recession immediately before the outbreak meant that stocks were naturally high and the conflict had been well signaled, so some deliberate stockpiling was also possible. Many competitors were taken out of the market, and Coats's wide-ranging locations allowed them to take advantage. Sales of handicrafts benefited, and the war effort meant a surge in demand for industrial lengths where growth was pronounced, particularly for military gear—they sold a lot of khaki thread. The company also opened up two new ventures in 1942: Jumna Thread Mills Ltd. in India, employing about 300 people twisting and finishing local yarn, and the African Sewing Cotton Co. Ltd., which was bought to finish imported thread in South Africa.

The UK mills were on overtime by 1940 as a result of orders for army and navy supply and to supplement thread producers who were short of capacity. Getting sufficient labour was hard, as conscription had started in May 1939, and 500 had already gone to war within a year,[1] not to mention the girls who went off to work in munitions factories on Clydeside. Despite this, the numbers in the two

1. The company made up the salaries of any staff who left to fight.

Paisley mills rose from 7,900 to 9,300 in the period, but that was the peak, and by the end of the war 2,200 had left, 1,786 to fight.

There was extensive government interference in the UK. Exchange controls made transactions between companies both complex and time-consuming. Excess profits tax at an initial rate of 60% went up to 100% once Churchill became Prime Minister. Price controls were introduced, and the new Coats costing methods proved invaluable in arguing their case with the newly formed Central Price Regulation Committee. Use of raw materials (particularly cotton) was strictly regulated, and the Ministry of Labour had the power to redirect the workforce to where it would be most useful, generally making munitions, so it became a priority for the company to persuade the Board of Trade that sewing thread was an essential commodity.

They did this with three main arguments. The first was that it was required (and was already being bought in large quantities) for military applications such as uniforms. These would be needed not only in Britain but also by their allies overseas who depended on the UK for supplies. Second, if there were a restriction on making and buying clothes, which there must be, then thread would be needed in greater quantities for mending. Again, this would be true overseas, so Coats could help with the balance of payments, a real government concern with a war to finance. Lastly, the amount of cotton used relative to the value of their final product was low, so few imports were required to generate high-value goods, both locally and for export.[2] The cotton they used was specialized, and they had the infrastructure set up to buy it cost-effectively.

2. On this last point, the ratio of value output vs. raw material input for sewing thread was recognized by the Board of Trade as being very high, though not quite on a par with handicraft items such as Stranded Cotton, where they considered it to be "the nearest approach to an invisible export they had come across, with Whisky as its only rival".

Their arguments proved persuasive. They were granted what was known as "nucleus" status, but on condition they produced 1,000,000 lbs. of thread per year for other manufacturers. They were also to abandon handicrafts in favour of sewing thread. In exchange, the Ministry of Labour agreed not to call up any of the mill girls, and gave a "protected" classification to TCA (to help with the export effort), as well as the head office and spinning, thus preserving the technical and administrative expertise in the company.

Cotton supplies proved a continuing problem, as they were largely in the hands of the government-run Cotton Control. Even bales belonging to Coats could be redirected to other producers,[3] and the company needed a permit to process each one through their own mills. Misunderstandings led to lost production and some quality issues. Ships were occasionally sunk, but as the Allies' position in the war improved, so did relations with the various government agencies, and by 1944 supplies were plentiful. Coats went on to actively encourage continued control for a time after the war to prevent the sort of price speculation that had occurred after World War One.

Production was not restricted to thread. The government was always on the lookout for additional resources to help with the war effort, and Coats had much to offer in engineering skills and space. The former Nethercraigs bleachworks, which had closed in 1932, was converted to produce cordite charges for twenty-five-pound cartridge cases in 1941. This nonprofit company known as the Fereneze Filling Factory Ltd. had a workforce of 600 (mostly female) and, working three shifts, they turned out 60,000 cases a week for over three years. Production stopped in early 1945, and the company was wrapped up two years later.

3. They lost as many as 9,000 bales in this way in August 1941 alone.

The UK company's war effort did not stop there. The mechanics shop at Ferguslie was converted to producing parts for aircraft, tanks, experimental recoilless guns, and periscope tops for submarines. Anchor did their part as well, with electrical and mechanical parts for range finders, aircraft, gun breeches and gauges, fire control gearboxes, and machine tools; they also assembled servo motors for gun turrets.

The employees themselves organized dances, concerts, and raffles to help the war effort. The workforces of the two Paisley mills contributed a Spitfire aircraft to the RAF in 1941 and, in another highly original fundraiser, war stamps were sold at the mill gates and stuck onto a shell that was later "delivered" to the enemy. Those exempt from National Service established volunteer squads for first aid, incendiary bomb patrols, decontamination squads, and some joined ARP (Air Raid Precautions). A Home Guard platoon was formed, and bomb shelters were dug for employee safety during air raids, which were signaled by the mill siren.

Despite the strains of wartime conditions and the constant changes of routines that resulted, labour relations in the mills were remarkably good. However, a series of minor complaints culminated in an eight-day strike by 2,000 spinners at the end of 1944, demanding a wage increase. This was the first strike in thirty years and was unsuccessful, going into arbitration, where the claim was rejected. But it demonstrated the efforts of the National Union of Dyers, Bleachers and Textile Workers, who were largely unrepresented in the mills and wanted to increase their membership.

This was a minor setback compared to an earlier crisis of a different nature in the US. All direct investments held by British companies across the Atlantic had been registered with the Treasury at the start of the war. By 1941 Britain was struggling to pay for imports, and the question of selling these US assets, worth about $1 billion, to raise dollars to pay for US imports, had become a hot topic. A third of them had already been sold, so the threat was real.

Coats feared that the sale of their US business would simply create a strong competitor who would not only have their manufacturing efficiencies, but also their trademarks, so they could legally sell and export Coats's own products against them. They had warned John B. Clark of this possibility a year earlier and had suggested that they could counter by offering to raise a loan with the American assets as collateral. He had begun discrete inquiries to explore this alternative.

James Henderson and Malcolm McDougall, the company accountant (and a future chairman), were sent to negotiate with the Bank of England and later with the trade delegation in New York. They argued that the loss of the American assets would negatively affect Coats's profits and remittances and, hence, UK tax revenues (Excess Profit Tax particularly) and balance of payments. It would interfere with the group's ability to operate during the war, and the actual value obtained from a forced sale would be far less than its value as security on a loan. In reality, they had little influence on the government negotiators, and the pressure from American officials to do something was mounting. When the US insisted on a gesture from the UK delegation, Courtauld's American Viscose Corporation was sold almost overnight, and this eased the situation.

Coats's arguments prevailed, and when British American Tobacco were authorized a $40 million loan with their subsidiary as guarantee rather than it being sold, the tide had turned. In due course, a general advance of $425 million was granted to the British government with all British assets similar to those of Coats in the US pledged as surety.

Within the US, increased orders for the war effort, and continued labour shortages in the North, particularly in Newark, gave renewed impetus to the relocation to the

South. By 1942, when numerous workers had been tempted away to higher-paying jobs in war related factories, there were too many machines sitting idle, so John B. Clark returned to Georgia to look for another rural mill with an abundant supply of female labour. He found this in Pelham, about fifty miles north of Tallahassee, the state capital of Florida, and by the end of the following year this was up and running with machinery from Newark. Toccoa had been extended, and all three southern mills were running three shifts. The migration of production was quick, as the total employment in Pawtucket and Newark went from 5,300 to 3,350 and, in Georgia, from 1,150 to 1,950 in just 5 years up to 1945. Production remained broadly the same.

Crown fasteners switched all their output over to the more robust zippers required by the armed forces, not only for clothing, but also for tents and other canvas applications. Their most amazing development was a fastener to cover the gun slot for the turrets of combat planes. This zipper opened and closed in both directions and kept the gunner warm, which greatly improved his ability to perform when finally engaged in action.

Pearl Harbor signaled the end of even limited influence on the fate of TSKK, and the Coats shares (and those of their partners) were sold to Fujibo, who took complete control. Coats had also formed the Mien Wha Company in Shanghai in 1934, selling TCA products; it had a finishing plant to process imported thread. Unfortunately, it was located in the Japanese controlled area of China and as such suffered a similar fate, hanging on for several years, but finally succumbing to an impossible situation.

Between the beginning and end of the war, company net operating profits had almost doubled to just over £5 million, but after-tax numbers were very different, remaining broadly unchanged throughout the war at around £1.7 million. British tax was 18% of pretax profit in 1939 and an alarming 64% in 1945, so that throughout the war, despite reduced dividends, 94% of the profits were distributed to shareholders, and only 3½% of the total was retained in the company. This was the subject of vociferous and incessant complaints from the new chairman, Robert Laidlaw, who took over after the war, when J.O.M. Clark, who was sixty-nine, retired.

Clark had quietly steered them through the Great Depression and a world war, but his tenure had not witnessed great advances; rather, it had been more about keeping the great Coats ship afloat in very troubled waters. Although described as "somewhat shy and reserved" it was also said that, "he could not tolerate slackness or loose thinking and the high standard of conduct which he expected of others was rigidly imposed on himself". In short, he was the right person in the right place at the right time.

Laidlaw, although having neither the Coats nor the Clark name, was descended from the latter family, his grandfather being William Clark of Newark. Famed for his "annihilating silences", he had been wounded in World War I and had joined the company in 1923 after a long period of recovery, becoming a director in 1938. His rapid promotion to chairman is testament to his brilliance, and he can certainly be praised for finally embracing the changes that his predecessors had been slow to confront. He was criticized for his conservative dividend policy, but that seems to have been a common theme throughout the company's history.

So, with several new faces in the boardroom, the arduous task of retooling began. Many of the company assets had been badly damaged, dismantled, or destroyed, but these were at least recoverable. Others were not.

The Riga plant in Latvia had returned to the Russians, this time for good, when the Baltic states were overrun in 1940. All the other Eastern European companies were nationalized in the four years immediately following the war, starting in March 1946 with Lodz and Bratislava. This last plant was closed down so quickly that the only asset that could be rescued was a centimeter ruler, which sat on the chairman's desk in Glasgow for years as a reminder.

Then came Yugoslavia, and Bulgaria followed at the end of 1947. The chain of events in each country was similar, and Romania, which came next, was typical. The Red Army swept in and stole absolutely everything they could get their hands on, watches being a particular favourite. They mistrusted everyone and would take pot shots at people who even glanced at them. One of the executives at Romanofir, Valer Tiplic, tells a story of two officers searching his house. When one of them looked thirsty, Tiplic offered him a glass of water, into which he had placed two ice cubes. The Russian seems to have suspected he was being poisoned, so he took them out of the glass and made the Romanian eat them, at gunpoint. "As they were cold I could not swallow easily and was moving them from one side to the other in my mouth, but did not dare spit them out as I felt the point of his revolver against me. I never felt so hot in all my life although my mouth was full of ice".

Fastidious rules were created controlling raw materials and therefore production, the local currency was devalued, numerous crippling and indecipherable taxes were introduced, and to top it all off the factory got a communist union. This combination meant that the business soon ran out of money and had to mortgage the mill at the beginning of 1948. In April, the head of the company, Mr. Stefanescu, was picked up by the Secret Police, never to be seen again, and two months later a team arrived to seal everything up and dismiss all the senior staff. They had been nationalized.

Hungary followed a little over a year later. They had managed to start up soon after the war, but with Russian cotton, so quality was poor, and this damaged their image. Then they were hit by inflation that was so bad they couldn't even send money to pay the workers in Nagyatad, as the 150 mile rail journey was not fast enough to guarantee that the currency would have any value once it arrived. They were raising prices twice a day. The economy converted to bartering, and they managed to exploit this system to import some Egyptian cotton. Despite a lengthy and partially successful intervention by Charles Bell, who had just joined the board, they were only postponing the inevitable, and nationalization followed at the end of 1949.

Coats estimated the total losses in Eastern Europe at £7 million. They sought financial compensation, but the sums obtained were derisory, though the company regained ownership of both Hungarian plants as well as Lodz in the 1990s. These have now been modernized and are flourishing.

The rest of Europe took time to recuperate, with raw material shortages being a common problem. The company withdrew from France, where they had never been anything but an also-ran, but strong recovery in Germany allowed them to expand the plant in Bräunlingen, adding a spinning mill. Faced with the impossibility of supplying the rapidly growing Turkish market with imported goods from Scotland, they bought a corduroy mill in Istanbul that had been built to German specifications at the start of the war, and converted it to sewing thread. The volume required soon outgrew the premises, so a much larger site was acquired in Bursa, on the other side of the Bosphorus, and a brand-new plant was erected there, starting production in 1968.

The steady migration to the South that was already underway in the US accelerated, with the acquisition of Acworth, a plant making tobacco cloth, and two new facilities in Thomasville and Albany, both in the southern part of Georgia. The first two were designed to be grey thread production units, but the last one would process and finish not only thread products but also knitting yarns for both Patons & Baldwins Beehive range, as well as the famous Red Heart knitting products that were originally made by Chadwicks and had been produced in Newark. They are still made in Albany to this day.

Pelham was extended, as was Toccoa, but this site had reached its physical limits, so a new mill was put up nearby. Known as Toccoa No. 2, this was a revolutionary building with no windows. As it was slightly bigger than the original mill, it was rumoured to be a replacement for Pawtucket at the time, but the company denied this. However, the investment did allow them to sell the Newark sites (apart from a small research unit), and they found a buyer so quickly that the move to Georgia had to be completed in rather a hurry. The Coats mill in Rhode Island was downsized in stages and eventually closed in 1965.

Although J. & P. Coats (RI) Inc., Clark Thread, and the Spool Cotton Co. had all been owned by J. & P. Coats since 1896 and had been run as a single business since 1928, the companies had never formally merged in the US as they had in the rest of the world. This had been motivated by a desire to draw as little attention as possible to its size, but as this was no longer an issue, the three companies merged at the start of 1953 and became Coats & Clark Inc. Apart from the neatness and clarity that this created, it also allowed consolidation of trademarks, going a long way to effectively halving the number of items kept on the shelves, with all the associated benefits. It also made life much easier for their customers.

Farther south, Mexico had expanded and now had three mills in both Mexico City and Guadalajara, but increasingly restrictive union activity was starting to take its toll, and Coats would eventually abandon the company there, handing it over to the government. The finance director was the last man out: "he put the safe in his pocket and left" in 1975.

Coats's investment in South America had been limited to the company in Brazil, where the government had placed severe restrictions on imports during the war. Almost no foreign goods had been available, and when these began to reappear, it was as if a dam had burst, and the market was flooded. Their trade deficit left them broke, so a complete import ban was instituted in the early 1950s, and there was a sharp increase in demand for local products, particularly clothing. The thread business thrived, a new plant at Vila Ema was inaugurated in 1951, and further expansion into zippers took place a year later.

Similar restrictions in other South American countries made supply from the UK an uncertain proposition at best, and political uncertainties, periodic inflation, exchange losses, eccentric changes in local regulations, as well as cheap competition simply added to the risks. As the chairman explained in 1956, "...the extent of the barriers raised by foreign governments is often, I feel, not fully appreciated. South America contains eleven Republics. Only in two of these today is unrestricted importation of our products permitted. The other nine have total or partial import restrictions. When licenses do materialize they are granted at infrequent intervals and for values usually very much below normal trading requirements. This induces scarcity in the countries concerned and gives opportunities for local rewinders to produce and sell articles mostly of much inferior quality".

The company's response to this situation was to set up manufacturing plants in Argentina, Chile, Colombia, Peru, Uruguay, and Venezuela over the next decade. These were established in sequence, and the similarity in the layout of each showed that there had been a common touch in their planning and building. Chile was the exception, as it was developed by buying up a series of small competitors until the whole thing was renamed Hilos Cadena (Chain Threads) in 1959. All the other companies in Spanish-speaking South America took the same name. The last to be built, in the quaint little village of San Joaquin, near Valencia, Venezuela, was completed in 1964. The reason they chose this location is unclear, but Heinz had just built a factory there, and the local Polar brewery followed in 1978, so maybe it was a touch of clairvoyance.

The Coats presence in the region was almost unique, as life there was still quite uncivilized, and the risks associated with military coups, corruption, and rampant inflation were almost less worrying than the risk to life and limb from lawlessness,[4] bandits, earthquakes, and situations like "La Violencia" (The Violence) in Colombia, which was at its height when the mill there was being built in the years leading up to 1958. Most multinationals found all this too much and shied away from the area. The intrepid pioneers who put up and operated these production units were made of sterner stuff, and the region became an excellent training ground, particularly for young managers who were thrown in at the deep end, on the sound principle that if they could swim with the Latin "sharks" then they could be said to be ready for almost anything.

The introduction of all this new capacity abroad inevitably put a strain on the mills in Paisley by robbing them of volume, but first they ran into a problem they had only met briefly before, shortage of labour. This was probably caused by a combination of local prosperity, the growth of national insurance, a tendency to marry earlier, and improved education levels raising employment expectations, but the fact was that the mills were no longer the attractive employment alternative they once had been. Turnover reached over 20% and absenteeism 13%. The pressure to reduce the workforce became intense.

By now, much of the machinery in both Anchor and Ferguslie was nigh on thirty years old, and both plants were still operating at least partially as independent units. Both occupied mammoth sites, Anchor covering twenty hectares and Ferguslie thirty-six.

4. In several of these locations you could have someone killed for what amounted to loose change.

A project to reorganize the Paisley manufacturing was put into action. It included a new spinning mill in Ferguslie,[5] a mercerising shed in Anchor, and the movement and purchase of hundreds of machines, so that by 1964 Ferguslie was a grey thread mill, with all other processes in Anchor. The Atlantic and Pacific mills could no longer handle heavy machinery and were demolished.

The opportunity was taken to rationalise the range of products on offer. Although there were 25,000 SKUs (stock items) at the time, the number of standard colours was still a relatively tolerable 354, and this was just before the introduction of nylon, polyester, and cotton/polyester blended threads, at which point the number of articles was destined to skyrocket.[6] Within this total, there were thirteen different whites and a mind-blowing twenty-six blacks, so these were cut to five and ten, respectively. The company also offered 4,000 "special" shades, so this number was slashed by 85%, but the place where changes were most overdue was in the number of spools, where they had exactly 1,007 different types, accumulated over a century. After much soul-searching, this number was whittled down to a more manageable (but still amazing) 219.

Productivity improved, and although any resulting reductions in the workforce were handled by suspending recruitment rather than forced redundancy, there were inevitably a number of disputes, and labour relations in both mills were strained. An air of unease prevailed, even though the demise of Coats manufacturing in the UK was still over thirty years away.

5. It is a poor reflection on the state of British industry at the time that it took over four years to put up this building, yet the new (and much larger) Toccoa property, erected at the same time in the US, was up and running in eighteen months.

6. In the late '90s, there were over 90,000 SKUs in the UK plant, and that was only industrial products—no spools or tubes!

The numbers employed in Paisley had dwindled from a peak of 10,800, to 5,500 by 1960, and the hours each person worked had been reduced, so productivity had doubled. The total cost of restructuring reached a whopping £5.5 million, but with profits after tax in 1960 at almost £7 million, the company must have been well satisfied.

Or were they?

Chapter 37

Diversification

If it ain't broke, don't fix it.
T. Bert Lance, Director of the Office of Management and Budget in the Carter administration in 1977.

By the early '60s Coats had reestablished their dominant position in the world thread market, with fifty-one mills in twenty-five countries, though this was no more than they had before the Second World War. They manufactured in those places with import restrictions and supplied the grand majority of the others from either the home mills, who exported 65% of their production, or from a convenient neighbour. The only countries where they had no presence at all lay behind the Iron Curtain or in Central Africa. They had become what the chairman would describe as "an old and mature group with no territorial markets left to conquer". The company's relative size and importance was continuing to slip, and it had dropped to twentieth in the UK and was no longer in the top 100 worldwide. No amount of cost-cutting would improve this, so they needed to find something else to help generate serious growth.

At the same time, they were feeling increasingly vulnerable to the vagaries of exchange movements, as almost every year there seemed to be an extraordinary loss from somewhere in the world (often South America) due to adverse currency movements. Over 70% of their earnings were derived from overseas, so expansion of their UK assets and income would obviously help. Their only non-thread production was in zippers, where they were starting to find some volume, but this was still limited. The view was that if they were going to branch out, they should stick with textile products, as they would at least have something in common with their area of expertise. They began to search for likely candidates.

The board had changed with the arrival of the new chairman, Malcolm McDougall, who was neither a Coats nor a Clark. He had joined the company at the age of fifteen at the outbreak of the First World War and had worked his way up through the ranks to chief accountant at the start of the Second War and finance director by the end of it. He was then promoted to become the company's first ever managing director in 1953. Several other members of the "old guard" had moved on, including Sir James Henderson (knighted in 1938)[1] and Thomas Heywood Coats, whose son Bill had joined the board shortly after his father's death in 1959.

Bill Coats was a brilliant scholar, who had to forego a place at Oxford University when the Second World War intervened. During the conflict, he became a captain in the artillery in Burma, an experience he seldom spoke of. After a brief spell at Edinburgh University, his career with Coats started at the beginning of 1948. He spent time in Mexico and Italy, but returned to Scotland as a director of the Central Agency, then becoming finance director of J. & P. Coats and subsequently a director of Coats Patons in 1960. He would go on to hold responsibility for the US and Australia for many

1. By this time he was a legend in Italy, having founded and been president of both the British Chamber of Commerce and the Rotary in Italy. He represented the Bank of England there for many years and was appointed Grand Ufficiale of the Order of Saint Gregory the Great, the highest Papal honor to be bestowed on a non-Catholic. A school with his name was founded in Milan after his death, in 1969.

years, before becoming managing director.[2] A bad car crash in the late 60s nearly ruined his career, and he was passed over for further promotion for several years,[3] but he overcame this setback to become deputy chairman in 1979, and chairman two years later—the last Coats (or Clark) to hold that position. A well-respected financial expert with sharp commercial instincts, he did not suffer fools gladly and could be abrupt at times, but like so many of the family before him, this was his way of hiding his basic reserve; he was kindly and empathetic underneath. Almost everyone who met him found him to be a true gentleman.

Another interesting addition was Joe Bullimore, who was not only a close friend of both Robert Laidlaw and McDougall, but also held the chairmanship of Patons & Baldwins Ltd. (P&B), a UK textile company specializing in hand knitting yarns, with whom Coats already had a joint selling relationship in the US.

It was through him that the question of a merger between the two companies was raised. It started with Fleming Reid & Co., who owned or leased some 350 retail outlets known as the "Scotch Wool Shops", which sold knitting wools and knitwear. They also had worsted spinning mill and a hosiery factory, but had become vulnerable to takeover, and P&B feared that the buyer would want them for their real estate rather than their business, raising the real possibility of the loss of a good customer and a large chunk of sales. Coats was sympathetic, and the company was bought, with P&B taking 75% of the equity and Coats 25%. An amalgamation between the two now seemed certain, though strangely it took most people by surprise when it eventually happened.

2. This rapid progress was by no means automatic as it had been in previous generations - he became a company director and then managing director at a young age on merit alone, not because of his name.

3. He used this time of relative obscurity to work marvels with the company Pension Scheme. He instigated the passed dividend (see p.379); he said it was one of his proudest moments.

Patons & Baldwins had their origins in hosiery. James Baldwin came to Halifax in 1785 and set up a wool fulling business, just as Jonas Brook had done only fifteen miles away some ten years earlier. Baldwin's son joined him, and they expanded into carding and spinning, moving to Clark Bridge, where they would stay for 150 years.

Then John Paton began wool spinning and dyeing in Alloa, Scotland. His son Alexander joined him and recruited his brother-in-law and a nephew to help carry on the business when John died in 1848. These two, neither of whom was called Paton, changed their name by deed poll to preserve continuity of the family name—this turned out to be a wise decision, for by the end of the nineteenth century their factory covered the whole town as old John knew it.

Both companies decided independently to switch production from hosiery to wool for hand knitting. This had been performed exclusively by men for centuries, but by the mid-1800s it seemed doomed to extinction, as there were already 40,000 knitting frames in Britain, and more than enough mule spinners were available to feed them. The days of the wife spinning yarn for her husband to knit at home were long gone; by the 1890s, women had started to knit.

They both produced their first pattern books—the *Patons Knitting and Crochet Book* with 125 designs in 1896, and the *Baldwin's Universal Knitting Book* with six pages of babies' and ladies' wear some three years later. Patons charged the rather magnificent sum of one shilling for theirs, whereas the Baldwin book cost but a penny. They were the progenitors of this highly effective form of advertising which was to develop over the next century.

They amalgamated in 1920 and, although they concentrated production in Alloa to begin with, they acquired a whole series of smaller sites and were manufacturing all over England by the start of the Second World War. Immediately after the war, they built a huge facility in Darlington, county Durham, along with a modern office block and sixty acres of sports facilities and consolidated all the English worsted production there. By the time they got together with Coats, they had further units in Tasmania and Toronto, and would also expand into Randfontein, South Africa shortly after the merger. A large factory that they built in Shanghai, China in 1934 went the same way as the Coats investment in that country.

Although the most logical way to merge Coats and P&B would have been for the much larger Coats to take over P&B, this was never going to be acceptable to Joe Bullimore, his board, or his shareholders. He insisted and kept reiterating that the arrangement was a "marriage of equals", even if it was blindingly obvious that one of the "spouses" was more of a heavyweight than the other. So the Coats shareholders ended up receiving 79% of the equity in the new holding company and P&B the rest. McDougall was chairman, with Bullimore as his deputy, and the board consisted of four executive directors from each company and two non-executive directors from Coats. The sensitivities of P&B were such that, although the head office for the new group was in Glasgow, board meetings were alternately held there and in Darlington.

The name of the new company was initially J. & P. Coats, Patons and Baldwins Ltd., but this did not last long as the City and financial press, who love their acronyms, had neither the time, the patience, nor the space for such a mouthful. Eventually, the *Daily Express* offered a bottle of whisky to the best suggestion sent in by the readership and, although such ingenious ideas as Patwinco, Woolcoats, and Cottonwools Ltd. were floated, the final choice was the rather boring, conventional, but practical Coats Patons Ltd. It stuck.

It took time for the management of the two companies to get comfortable with each other, and this was particularly true of the two main players. In one of their early meetings, it was revealed that McDougall had decided on a particular course of action without consulting with the deputy chairman. Bullimore was incensed and insisted that this marriage of equals (he kept repeating this phrase) meant that he must always be fully briefed before any decisions were taken. Eventually John B. Clark, who was over from the US and sitting beside him, leaned over, put his hand over Joe's, and in a wonderfully laconic American drawl came out with the immortal line, "You have to remember, Joe, that in any marriage, somebody's got to get screwed". Joe's reply was not recorded.

Despite these minor spats, the relationship worked well, and for the next seven years the newly formed group went on a shopping spree. They bought Pasolds, who specialized in children's clothing under the famous Ladybird brand; William Briggs, makers of embroidery kits and iron-on transfers; Bellman, a chain of ninety-two shops selling clothing and knitting wool; and Jaeger, the luxury clothing retailer. All these companies were based in and had the vast majority of their sales in the UK.

They also made a start into the zinc moulding business. Crown Fasteners in the US had developed their zipper in conjunction with Gries Reproducer Corp. of New York, who made small precision parts in both zinc and plastic. After an association that had lasted thirty years, Coats & Clark finally acquired their assets in 1964, so they became a subsidiary of the company in the US. J. & P. Coats (Canada) then bought Dynacast, a company in Montreal that made and sold die-casting machines. With both these companies on board, Coats Patons created Dynacast International, which manufactured and sold precision parts, mainly in zinc, but also in plastic. End uses included spark plugs, locks, record players, cassettes, lighters, cameras, and electronic components. They also made non-precision items such as umbrella tips, coins, and medallions for giveaways (fifty million for one petroleum company in France alone). They operated throughout Europe, Brazil, the US and Canada.

Charles Bell took over from Malcolm McDougall as chairman in 1967, but the philosophy remained the same. UK sales and profits needed to increase, not only to minimize the effects of exchange fluctuations but also because the introduction of Advanced Corporation Tax (ACT) made UK earnings and cash flow all the more vital to be able to pay for this new levy. The UK acquisitions continued. Laird Porch & West Riding Worsted were both involved in ladies' fashions, and by 1970 Coats Patons had added another eight knitwear, yarn, and fabric companies in England to their growing portfolio. That year they also bought Davidson Industries, makers of plastic dye springs for the Group, but also suppliers of garment labels and cellophane.

Another non-textile, but very thread related acquisition followed. The firm was Needle Industries, whose origins could be traced back to Henry Milward & Sons of Redditch in 1730, exactly 100 years before the formation of J. & P. Coats. They had been producing sewing and knitting needles and had steadily absorbed many of their competitors in the area, taking on the current name for the first time in 1946. Their products were complimentary to both the Coats and the Patons businesses, so it was a very natural fit. Coats had already sold their needles in the US and other parts of the world.

Coats Patons now began operating as two divisions: thread, and everything else. Despite all this activity and an increase in turnover from £130 million in the early '60s to £487 million in 1975, the percentage of the profit earned in the UK stubbornly refused to shift from between 15 and 20% and the profit itself couldn't keep up with inflation, which had skyrocketed in the mid-1970s. The cash flow became so bad that they passed on their final dividend for 1974, which caused a scandal in the City, as they were not in serious financial trouble at the time. The company pointed out that inflation had meant that they had put an extra £37 million into working capital just to maintain the same level of business, and they wanted the government and the City to better understand the evils of inflation—this was one of the most effective ways to do it. Instead of a 4% final dividend, a scrip issue (the equivalent number of shares) was given out. This annoyed just about everyone, as pension funds could not legally sell shares to pay pensions and small investors incurred unreasonable expense if they sold the few shares they got for cash. However, it made a point and helped protect the Coats Pension Fund for the longer term.

With the move into UK-based textiles delivering neither the desired growth nor UK profit, it was now determined that what the Group needed was new products with a competitive edge in just about any field. Bill Henry, who took over as chairman in 1976 wrote that, "We are...willing to assess the viability of any idea or product, if its development would involve our existing technological and management skills".[4] As much as anything, this change of strategy had been encouraged by the success of the Dynacast zinc die-casting business, which now formed a part of a division of Coats known as Engineering.

A "New Ventures" Group was created and embarked on projects in several different fields. They formed a transport company, Scorpio, integrating all the different distribution companies used within the UK and offering out the spare capacity to third parties, to make the enterprise profitable. It was not a success and was sold off within two years.

The thread part of the business already supplied surgical sutures, so there was some logic in making and selling medical products. Through several different parts of the group, they got involved in heart pacemakers, syringes, knitted vascular grafts, and equipment for occupational and physiotherapists.

4. *The News Reel* (Coats company magazine) Summer 1978, p.22.

More esoteric ideas would follow. Eel farming was looked upon as a possible way of making use of hot effluent from dyeing, as warm water was needed to get the elvers to grow quickly. In the end, as Bill Coats, who became chairman in 1981, so succinctly put it, "the little blighters refused to cooperate" and the scheme was abandoned.

Although a handful of these and other initiatives showed promise, the company abandoned the strategy after seven years, as the successes had been few, the failures expensive, and finding fruitful projects had not been easy. Bill Coats summed up the situation: "we have found by experience that it can take much longer than originally thought to get worthwhile ideas off the ground".[5] He had always expressed the view that the company needed to find goods or services similar to sewing thread in the 1830s: new products based on new technology where the company could get a jump on the rest of the world and then use their global spread to generate growth—Dynacast was a fine example.

They decided to target established businesses of this type instead of starting from scratch, but events were to conspire against them and they never got to implement this new plan.

In 1984, Bill Coats proudly announced that turnover and profit before tax had hit two major milestones, £1 billion and £100 million, respectively.[6] Despite this, the company's languishing share price made them vulnerable to takeover and rumours that the Hanson conglomerate, who had acquired Barbour Campbell Threads, were gunning for Coats became serious. The company prepared a document known as Project Dunkirk as a guide on how they should react to such a bid. They also ran an exercise to look at their future as a company, during which they considered several takeover possibilities, amongst them Dawson International, the

5. Ibid Summer 1983 p.6.

6. To put this in perspective, the profit just before World War I was around £3 million, the equivalent of about £130 million in 1984.

knitwear group most famous for their Pringle trademark. A possible bid for them was rejected, given the relative share prices of the two companies and the fact that Dawson was highly dependent on cashmere. Coats did not want a business that relied on China for its raw material.

Internal discussions followed about the possibility of a merger with various candidates and, as a result, an approach was made to Sir Christopher Hogg in 1985 to investigate the feasibility of an arrangement with Courtaulds. A series of meetings ensued, but they could not agree on a price and the whole thing had stalled by the end of the year.

Then Sir Bill Coats, who was knighted in the 1985 New Years Honours list, resigned. He said that his sudden decision was in part for health reasons, but it may be that he expected a takeover of Coats Patons and, as his dealings with the possible suitors had left him unenthusiastic, he decided to move on. He stood down as CEO, but stayed on as chairman, awaiting the inevitable. He had become disillusioned with the way commerce was conducted; "There are no gentlemen left in business any more" was his lament. It is rather poetic that just as Coats became the prey rather than the predator for the first time, the last of the family should leave the board.

He then got a call from Ronald Miller, the CEO of Dawson International, who wanted a meeting with Coats for a general discussion. As Dawson was small, it never crossed Bill's mind that they were contemplating buying Coats Patons, given their relative sizes, but this was a time when minnows could bid for sharks using their inflated p/e ratios[7]

7. For the non-financial reader, the p/e ratio is simply a measure of the share price of a company compared to its earnings. A high p/e ration means you are paying a lot for the shares relative to the company's profits and is usually an indication that the company is expected to increase these significantly in the near future. A p/e ration of about fifteen is "normal", but during the dot-com boom, many companies would reach numbers well over 100!

and it subsequently transpired that this was effectively what Miller was after. Bill passed the message on to his replacement, Jim McAdam.

A series of meetings followed and the press were informed that a bid was in the offing. Speculation about the mystery bidder centred on Vantona Viyella, Courtaulds, and BTR, who were cash rich at the time. Dawson was hardly mentioned, but despite that, their offer was finally approved at a board meeting on Friday, January 24, 1986 subject to agreeing the terms of the press announcement. The mood was resigned, as Coats did not relish the idea of being taken over by Dawson, but were at least pleased that they had managed to talk the price up a little. A press conference followed on the Monday to announce the terms of the offer.

Almost immediately David Alliance of Vantona Viyella appeared on the scene and started to make overtures, trying to push Coats to accept a rival bid. He had apparently been "thinking of a tie-up for months" but he and his chairman, James Spooner, had only met with Bill Coats a couple of times for general discussions.[8]

Although Alliance's advances were initially rebuffed, he eventually struck up a deal that improved on the Dawson offer of £700 million by £34 million.[9] The view of the company and the City was that this was a better fit with

8. As with Dawson, he didn't consider them as a potential predator. They were two-thirds the size and made half the profit of Coats.

9. Or at least that is the official version of the chain of events. It is unclear at what point discussions with Alliance started, what stage they had reached, how detailed they were or who was involved. Some believe they had been going on informally for some time, but without Bill Coats, possibly as far back as when the negotiations with Courtaulds came to nothing. Whenever it was, Bill may have found out, but wanted no part of a deal with Viyella and resigned. This would explain his unexpected decision to leave a job he loved at the relatively young age of sixty-one. It would also make the rejection of the Dawson bid for a mere 5% more understandable. However, it is pure conjecture, and somewhat academic now.

Coats than Dawson. It also benefited the Coats team, as they would have more representation in the boardroom than they would have had with the previous deal, and it probably didn't hurt each individual financially either. However, everyone expressed surprise at the extraordinary volte-face by Coats, and Dawson were understandably "astonished" at being rejected. One of their advisers was stupefied at Coats "deserting the bride at the altar for only a 5% price improvement",[10] whilst others saw the move as more akin to making love with one partner only to leave them to sleep with another who seemed prettier, in the next door room.

So Coats Patons became Coats Viyella (CV) in early 1986. Alliance proudly announced that, "the days of job losses in the British Textile Industry are now over".[11] How wrong he would prove to be.

David (formerly Davoud, now Baron) Alliance grew up in Iran and came to the UK in 1951 at the age of nineteen with a family background in textiles and nothing in his pockets. He started by selling clothing off a barrow, but soon acquired a series of minor textile firms, and by 1968 had taken control of Spirella, a publicly traded company that would form the backbone of his budding empire. This was divided into three groups: foundation garment manufacture, textile merchandising, and spinning and household textiles. Further acquisitions followed, until he made his first "reverse" takeover, when the relatively tiny Spirella successfully bid £5 million for the much larger Vantona Ltd.

The newly formed Vantona Group was now the third largest producer of household textiles in the UK, but still small in the overall industry. This made his next takeover of Carrington Viyella all the more astounding, as the target was eight times the size of the bidder. Not everyone could see the wisdom of this deal, as the "troubled giant" was carrying a

10. *Glasgow Herald*, February 11 1986.

11. Ibid.

mountain of debt. Alliance had trouble raising the £50 million financing he needed, but he got his money in the end, and Vantona Viyella was created in 1983. It not only gave him a foot in the door of garment manufacture, home furnishings, and carpets, but also such well-known brands as Dorma, Van Heusen and of course Viyella.[12]

Two years later, Vantona Viyella absorbed Nottingham Manufacturing, a hosiery and knitwear supplier to Marks & Spencer run by another self-made textile magnate, (later Sir) Harry Djanogly. As before, this company was capitalised at a higher value in the market than Vantona Viyella, and was rolling in cash. It was just the shot in the arm that Alliance's empire needed to embolden him for his bid for Coats.

The great hope for CV was that the global reach of thread could be used to increase the sales of the other textile businesses, but the way this potential synergy was approached was, at best, half hearted. Most of the UK management had enough of their own problems to deal with without gallivanting around the world, dealing with unfamiliar cultures and languages, and insufficient resources were made available to the thread management to have them develop the markets for these other products. As Coats had found out before, this type of cross-fertilization takes a great deal longer to bear fruit than you would think, and neither the stock market nor the new management had much patience. Coats Viyella appeared in the FTSE 100 index after the merger, but had dropped out within three years.

12. This name dated from 1894 and was derived from the Via Gellia, which runs from Cromford to Grange Mill, near Matlock. Henry Ernest Hollins of William Hollins & Co. had bought a new mill in 1890 and transformed the company by doubling its output. To commemorate this achievement, he adapted the name of the road that ran past this factory—now less romantically part of the A5012—as the trademark for their high-quality cloth.

Another casualty of the merger was the Coats management system. The training and recruitment schemes that had been started back in the 1920s and had produced a series of articulate, self-confident, and numerate managers were dismantled. The expatriate teams that had dealt with places like South America and Russia when times were tough were systematically returned to their home countries or let go. The culture was frowned upon as being too comfortable[13] and too expensive, but by the time it had disappeared, it was being talked of wistfully as an intangible that had been lost. By then it was too late.

For the first couple of years, not a lot was expected of the new CV Group, and things progressed nicely. Then the 1988 profits were announced as £135 million, lower than the two companies had declared individually (Coats £102 and Viyella £52 million) four years earlier. All was not well.

In April 1990 CV bought Tootal for £241 million after a protracted fight. Their original bid the year before of £395 million had lapsed and when they renewed at a much lower level Tootal baulked, behaving like "a dowdy Jane Austen heroine: desperate to wed but equally desperate not to look too keen".[14] For the first time in his career, Alliance launched a hostile takeover and eventually had his way.[15]

Slowly but surely, things deteriorated from there. Neville Bain and Michael Ost came and went as CEOs, but could not halt the slide. By 1998 CV only made £52.9 million profit and one-off items took a further £19.6 million off that rather measly figure. They decided to de-merger the clothing and

13. It was referred to as an "old boy network", but in its heyday was also known as the "Scottish Diplomatic Service" due to its spread and the multiplicity of languages and cultures the team members were able to handle with apparent ease.

14. *Daily Telegraph*, January 15 1991.

15. The reasons why this was such a good deal for the thread business are revealed later.

home furnishing businesses and the following year sold off precision engineering (basically Dynacast) for £322 million to reduce group debt.[16]

With hindsight it is easy to see that David Alliance and Coats were not a good fit. He was an expert dealer and a brilliant trader, but less of an inspirational leader for such a large, diverse group, and his cold, steely, piercing gaze and sometimes impenetrable English accent[17] didn't help him to transmit his vision with much success, particularly to a company with so many employees who spoke English as a second language. He retired shortly after the Dynacast sale, leaving Sir Harry Djanogly to take over as chairman. Martin Flower, an experienced thread man, became CEO in 2001, and the company name was changed to Coats plc., signaling a focus almost exclusively on the core business, thread. The disposal of Viyella dragged on over several years. Fashion retail (essentially Viyella & Jaeger) was sold in January 2002. The last non-thread business, bedwear, finally went in early 2005.

The share price had gone from 240p. at the time of the Viyella takeover to a low of 20.5p. at the end of November 1998. However, it steadily recovered, and in February 2003, a consortium led by Australian investment conglomerate Guinness Peat offered 58.5p. a share for the company, which was duly accepted. Coats exited the London stock market for the first time in over 100 years.

16. This was a shame, as the business had been the one bright spark in the whole conglomerate, making 23% of the group profit in 1997. It had only been 6% of the much smaller Coats Patons group in the late '70s.

17. This could cause inadvertent misunderstandings. Many years ago, when the author had just undergone knee surgery, Alliance stopped him on the stairs in head office in London and appeared to ask "How is your ankle?"

"No, Sir David, it's my knee" was the natural reply. He then repeated the question several times, eliciting a similar response on each occasion. Finally it twigged that he was actually enquiring into the health of the author's uncle (Tim Coats), who had been hospitalized with a brain tumor. "He died" was the unfortunate (but accurate) conclusion to the exchange.

The Group had returned to its roots, bringing a forty-five-year distraction to an end. It is easy to be wise after the event, but it is evident that the numerous diversifications undertaken were poorly timed. Coats had become a dumping ground for the disappearing UK textile industry, no longer able to compete with South East Asia. The complications this caused had prevented the company from taking full advantage of their better, non-textile businesses such as Dynacast, but at least the original thread business was intact and had not been standing still.

Chapter 38

Back to Basics

The men who have succeeded are men who have chosen one line and stuck to it.

Andrew Carnegie, Scottish-American business magnate

Whilst Coats was buying up the ailing UK textile industry and taking their eye off the ball as far as thread was concerned, a quiet revolution was taking place in their main trade.

When the first merger of this era, with Patons & Baldwins, was being contemplated, synthetic fibres had not only been invented, but were being commercialized, with huge implications for the sewing world. First came nylon, which, in its bonded continuous filament form,[1] was a stronger, smoother, better wearing alternative to polished cotton, and became the accepted standard for sewing all leather goods, particularly shoes.

1. Bonding with resin cemented the filaments to each other and stopped the thread from unravelling. Many applications for leather stitching involved twin needles and, being on opposite sides of the sewing machine, one of the threads would untwist during the sewing process if it weren't stuck together in this way.

However, the real game-changer was polyester, both filament and fibre, which Coats started to spin in the '60s. Polyester production really hit its stride some ten years later, largely replacing cotton, particularly for fine threads in light sewing applications such as shirts. It was less expensive than cotton and much easier to dye, and, being a manmade fibre, did not suffer from the problems of bad harvests, pests, and the other complications associated with vegetable fibres.[2]

Next came cotton-covered corespun, a thread made up of yarns with a polyester filament core wrapped in a cotton sheath. This construction gives it great strength from the filament, which is up to four times as strong as its cotton equivalent, but protects it from needle heat with a wrapping of cotton, so it will sew heavy fabrics at high speeds without breaking. The increased strength meant that a much finer thread could be used, saving cost and making a neater seam. The fashion for jeans was crying out for a thread like this.

It had one drawback. It had to be dyed twice (once for the cotton and again for the polyester), so it was expensive and difficult to process. There is no better thread for tough sewing jobs, but where possible it was substituted by Poly-Poly, a polyester core wrapped with polyester fibre. This has several of the advantages of cotton-wrapped corespun, but dyes quickly as it is all made with the same material.

A variety of textured products were also developed, simulating yarns spun from fibre using a variety of technologies. This introduced inexpensive threads that did not require major infrastructure to produce, and opened the doors to a whole new group of competitors. As processing machinery became better and more reliable, it was soon clear that almost anyone could make a good sewing thread, and Coats's quality advantage quickly eroded. They had always

2. It is petroleum based, so the cost (and by implication, price) does depend indirectly on OPEC. There are times when this is a decided disadvantage.

spent significantly on research, with a large laboratory having been established in Anchor Mills back in 1932, so in the 1970s they decided to concentrate on two areas where they felt they could gain a technical advantage: lubrication and colour measurement.

Up to then, lubrication was rather crude, with the thread being dragged over blocks of wax (usually beeswax). As sewing machine speeds increased, this became totally inadequate, so Coats developed their own proprietary lubricants, which were applied in emulsion form very much more accurately. This allowed higher sewing speeds to be attained without thread breakage. Specialized formulae were established for each thread type and were a closely guarded secret.

In the early days of Coats, most thread was sold in white or black, but the twentieth century brought more demand for colours. The salesman would offer a range that he presented on colour cards, from which customers would choose the shade that came closest to the cloth they were sewing. In exceptional circumstances, special dyeings would be carried out for colours that were nothing like any of the standard shades on the colour card. The application of colour was really more of an art than a science, and a dyer would have to guess what combination of dyes he needed to make a particular shade, based on the recipes he already had for the stock items. Good experienced dyers were quick and accurate and were worth their weight in gold, but even so the delivery time on these "specials" was long when compared to products taken from stock, particularly if the customer was a long way away from the production site. As the century progressed, standard colour ranges grew but so, paradoxically, did the demand for special shades.

Dyeing itself became more sophisticated, with open vessels and manual steam valves being replaced by pressurized vats and accurate temperature controls. By the 1960s the dye cycle could be predetermined, and the dyer became less of a magician and more of a loader and unloader, with instruments controlling the actual processing of the thread.[3] Unfortunately, colour matching and any adjustments were still being done by eye, so that part of the dye-house continued to resemble early alchemy. Comparisons made by dyers in the same factory varied greatly—between dye-houses and countries the variation was worse.

As the world shrunk, a new phenomenon known as the Global Customer appeared. These are large international retail companies like Gap and Adidas, who have no manufacturing, but send out specifications to multiple contractors for them to produce garments or shoes. Cloth is dispatched to the producer, who only buys the thread once the fabric has arrived, as batch colours vary, and they want an exact match. They also want it quickly, so they can cut and sew the finished product and send it out with the appropriate label. If a batch of shirts is being made in three different plants, the thread for each has to be the same, for obvious reasons. Yet Coats could be producing them in three different dye-houses and countries. Keeping consistent standard shades and dyeing and matching everything uniformly had become essential.

Coats realized that they needed some way of automating colour measurement, so the research department made this their goal. They first found a way of expressing colour in three dimensions (called Colour Space), so that any one shade could be accurately defined by a set of three numbers. This also gave them a numerical way of expressing the difference between two shades, but these numbers had to be adjusted, as the human eye, which can detect over 10 million different hues, sees colour in a non uniform way.[4]

3. Computers simply improved on this so that the modern dyeing process is completely automatic.

4. For instance, humans are very good at detecting minute differences in shades of grey, but can tolerate quite large variations of red without noticing them.

To further complicate matters, each of us sees colour differently, so a standard observer had to be developed. Finally, allowances had to be made for metamerism, the quality of some colours that makes them appear different under different light sources.[5] Thousands of samples were viewed and measured and the necessary corrections made. The result was a way of measuring colour differences scientifically and establishing acceptable objective tolerances. The days of colour being a matter of opinion were over, with Coats Research having been at the forefront in developing the basic systems. These techniques are still the foundation of the science of matching textiles to this day.

Many further advances have been made since then, and Coats has now reached the stage where they have mobile spectrophotometers (instruments that simulate the human eye) available. These can measure and transmit the required colour to any factory in the world, where they can be in production within minutes without anyone there ever seeing the sample. They also have an electronic colour card that will suggest the nearest colour to any sample from within their standard range. They are getting really good at dyeing; they produce a mind-boggling 160,000 different shades every year, and they've been at it a long time.

What has happened to their global spread? Throughout the '60s and '70s, Coats invested in thread production plants in the Philippines and Indonesia, both joint ventures, and in Venezuela, as previously mentioned. There were no other moves into new countries, but additional capacity was added in India and a fine spinning mill was bought in the north of

5. Bill Coats told a story about the difficulties of metamerism. In the late seventies, Marks & Spencer (M&S) developed a low-energy light for their stores (the precursor to the successful TL84). Coats found that some of the thread sewn into M&S garments changed colour completely when placed under this light—the stitching looked horrible. The research boffins were stumped until a Coats director asked innocently whether the light affected any other products. It turned out that fresh red meat turned a rather nasty shade of grey under this special illumination, so the light was withdrawn and Coats breathed a collective sigh of relief.

Brazil, both in 1979. Other investments concentrated on modernizing, introducing synthetic threads and reducing cost in the existing mills, but with so much activity taking place in the non-thread part of the business, the international part of Coats was left treading water.

In the UK, however, there was serious "trouble at t' mill". Short time working became common in Anchor and Ferguslie, with both plants suffering the effects of the severe decline in the UK textile industry, which had become uncompetitive and was being replaced by imports. Mills in Lancashire were closing down at the rate of almost one a week. With less UK production, there was naturally less demand for Scottish thread. By the early '80s, too much excess capacity existed in Paisley, so the company invested £5 million in relocating all production to Anchor, and Ferguslie was closed.[6]

Elsewhere, free trade was the watchword, and treaties such as NAFTA and the EU were not far away. The Multi Fibre Agreement was supposed to protect the developed countries from cheap imports, but, particularly in Europe, it was largely ineffective. Coats did not want to be caught napping. Their experience in overseas expansion gave them a distinct advantage, and they already had extensive capacity in developing countries, particularly India, where by now they had three factories. In 1987 they invested in China, building two state-of-the-art spinning mills in Tianjin and Guangzhou. This was the start of a decade that saw a major geographical shift in the Coats thread world.

Production was started in Mauritius (an important centre for garment assembly), Morocco, and Vietnam. The company was also invited back to Hungary, where manufacturing resumed in Ujpest and later in the old Mez plant at

6. It has now been demolished, with an old gatehouse remaining as the only evidence of its former glory.

Nagyatad. They would also return to Lodz in Poland in 1995, by which time they had restarted sales in the Baltic states.

However, it was the acquisition of Tootal that gave them complete world coverage. There was a very good reason why this was such a good fit for Coats.

English Sewing (ESC) and American Thread, both of whom had formed after the Coats/Clark merger of 1896, persisted through thick and thin, and, just as Coats had done, ESC expanded overseas, but largely in Asia, an area where Coats was less strong. American Threads were a spirited competitor to Coats & Clark USA, and Dewhursts (arguably the founding company of ESC) were a worthy opponent in the UK. In almost everything, ESC complimented Coats; in a takeover they would fit like a glove.

The Tootal that Coats absorbed incorporated ESC, American Thread, Tootal Broadhurst Lee, and others. The non-thread parts of the business were integrated with Viyella and sold off, but several important additions were made to the Coats portfolio overseas, in places where they had yet to establish a presence. These included Bangladesh, Sri Lanka, South Korea, Malaysia, France, and Finland. Their domination of the UK market was going to be such that Coats was required by the Monopolies and Mergers Commission to sell off their consumer business there, as well as their share in Gütermann, but the industrial part was given the all-clear.

More capacity followed in India, China, and Vietnam. The company began their quest to create a seriously low-cost base, but they understood that this was not just a case of making everything in South East Asia. If a customer wants bright pink thread to sew up a new batch of cloth into flowery shirts, which just happen to be the latest thing, he is not going to wait while the product arrives from Shanghai or pay for it to be flown over. The fashion world had evolved to a point where there were four seasons (and changes of style) every year, so quick turnaround was as important as low pricing.

The best of both worlds, they realized, would come from making the bulk items inexpensively and keeping small, fast response units near to the customers for those last-minute orders so vital to many businesses. Spinning and twisting grey thread was obviously a mass production operation, so this was separated from the dyeing and finishing as an independent business, and either moved to low-cost locations or terminated and substituted with externally purchased product, as Coats had done for much of the nineteenth century.

Mills in Western Europe that were engaged in this part of the manufacturing operation were shut down over the next decade, and product was brought in from Hungary, Turkey, and Asia. US capacity was also closed, but with Mexico[7] and Central America supplying what could not come from the East. South America was rationalised, with production concentrated in Colombia and northern Brazil.

The principle was extended further. Black and white were still the most popular colours and, together with a few other high-volume shades, the same logic applied, i.e., they could be dyed in bulk in a low-cost region for distribution elsewhere.

Coats was not the only company deserting the western nations. Many of their industrial customers were doing the same, so that nowadays less than 5% of the clothing sold in Europe and the USA is sewn there. Further closures of factories in the developed world followed, and although Coats still has seventy-three manufacturing facilities around

7. Coats had lost their Mexican business to the government in the mid-1970s after the union situation became impossible, but bought up a local competitor, Hilos Timon, in 1993. They then bought and converted a spinning mill outside Puebla to supply the USA and Mexico with corespun thread and built a mammoth dyeing and finishing plant in Orizaba three years later in 2004. Another spinning mill was later built in Honduras.

the world, on six continents, very few of them are in high-cost countries, and those that are make little or no industrial garment sewing thread.

This raises the question: what do they make? Some are involved in consumer thread and related products—for instance, the incredibly popular Red Heart brand of knitting yarn is still made in Albany, Georgia. Others are manufacturing zippers, which Coats made only in the US and Brazil before 1960. Since then, the company has bought Lamprom in Italy, the global number two Opti in Germany, and started production in Estonia and Poland; capacity in China and India was added more recently.

The latest thread companies to come under the Coats wing are Hicking Pentecost and DMC Industrial. The latter was a relatively minor deal, but the former involved many new products where Coats had limited experience.

Hicking Pentecost were the owners of Barbour Threads, who specialized in making products with unusual applications such as meat tying, baseballs, pool cues, dental floss, mattresses and airbags. The main interest in the company was in the US, where their bonding process was seen to be vastly superior to anyone else's. Indeed it was Coats's main US competitor, American & Efird, who felt the same way and made the first tender, at £1.75 a share. After a bidding war, the final price reached £2.40, which shows how desirable this technology was. The company turned out to be a bit of a hotchpotch, selling minute amounts of tens of thousands of products. However, the bonding secrets were invaluable, some intriguing new products were introduced to the range, and with the migration south of the apparel thread trade, this business became the mainstay of US industrial thread manufacturing. It is also the launchpad for many exciting new Coats products like antimicrobial and security threads. They are even talking of it being possible for thread to replace barcodes in garments of the future.

Although Coats are now better placed than any of their rivals to compete in the world thread market, it is a very different company from the one that the Jameses Clark and Coats created two centuries ago. Anchor Mills went the way of Ferguslie and never made it through their second century. April 2, 1993 was the day the last worker clocked off, production having been transferred to the two Tootal plants in Lisnaskea, Northern Ireland and Newton Mearns, near Paisley. These have since been closed as well, largely replaced by a new mill in Romania.

Head Office in the iconic building at 155 St. Vincent Street (and half a storey down in Bothwell St.) in Glasgow moved temporarily up the road to a new glass monstrosity, but was taken to Saville Row in London in 1993 and then out to its current location by Heathrow Airport.

Many years ago, one of the descendants of Sir Peter Coats started his autobiography in fairy tale style with "Once upon a time, in Scotland, there lived a family of rich thread-manufacturers called Coats. Once upon a time—because today the family is not particularly rich, and comparatively few of them live in Scotland."[8]

How appropriate to end in similar vein.

There is no longer anyone from the family working for Coats.[9] It is not really a Scottish company and has no production (and few sales) in Scotland. However, it carries in its DNA the philosophy on which its founders based their success. A high-quality product, scrupulous honesty, hard work, fair treatment of others, and a sense of adventure took them a long way, and these attributes served their successors well. As long as the people entrusted with the ongoing success of Coats remember this, it will surely be a case of "and they all lived happily ever after."

8. *Of Generals & Gardens* by Peter Coats, p.1. Peter ("petticoats") was a great grandson of Sir Peter.

9. The author was the last one. He left in 2004.

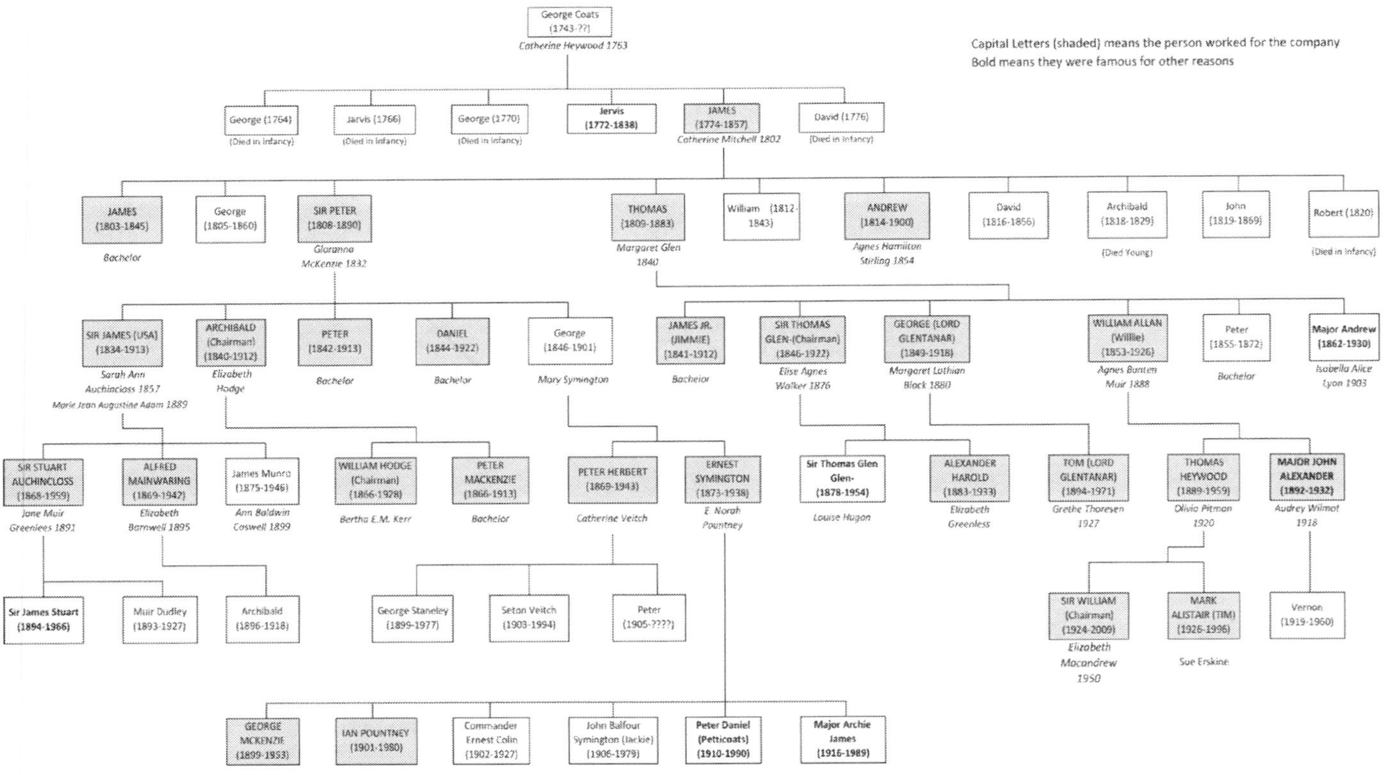

COATS FAMILY TREE
Capital Letters (shaded) means the person worked for the company
Bold means they were famous for other reasons
George Coats (1743-??)
Catherine Heywood 1763
George (1764) (Died in Infancy)
Jarvis (1766) (Died in Infancy)
George (1770) (Died in Infancy)
Jervis (1772-1838)
JAMES (1774-1857)
Catherine Mitchell 1802
David (1776) (Died in Infancy)
JAMES (1803-1845)
Bachelor
George (1805-1860)
SIR PETER (1808-1890)
Gloranna McKenzie 1832
THOMAS (1809-1883)
Margaret Glen 1840
William (1812-1843)
ANDREW (1814-1900)
Agnes Hamilton Stirling 1854
David (1816-1856)
Archibald (1818-1829)
(Died Young)
John (1819-1869)
Robert (1820)
(Died in Infancy)
SIR JAMES (USA) (1834-1913)
Sarah Ann Auchincloss 1857
Marie Jean Augustine Adam 1889
ARCHIBALD (Chairman) (1840-1912)
Elizabeth Hodge
PETER (1842-1913)
Bachelor
DANIEL (1844-1922)
Bachelor
George (1846-1901)
Mary Symington
JAMES JR. (JIMMIE) (1841-1912)
Bachelor
SIR THOMAS GLEN-(Chairman) (1846-1922)
Elise Agnes Walker 1876
GEORGE (LORD GLENTANAR) (1849-1918)
Margaret Lothian Black 1880
WILLIAM ALLAN (Willie) (1853-1926)
Agnes Bunten Muir 1888
Peter (1855-1872)
Bachelor
Major Andrew (1862-1930)
Isabella Alice Lyon 1903
SIR STUART AUCHINCLOSS (1868-1959)
Jane Muir Greenlees 1891
ALFRED MAINWARING (1869-1942)
Elizabeth Barnwell 1895
James Munro (1875-1946)
Ann Baldwin Caswell 1899
WILLIAM HODGE (Chairman) (1866-1928)
Bertha E.M. Kerr
PETER MACKENZIE (1866-1913)
Bachelor
PETER HERBERT (1869-1943)
Catherine Veitch
ERNEST SYMINGTON (1873-1938)
E. Norah Pountney
Sir Thomas Glen Glen- (1878-1954)
Louise Hugon
ALEXANDER HAROLD (1883-1933)
Elizabeth Greenless
TOM (LORD GLENTANAR) (1894-1971)
Grethe Thoresen 1927
THOMAS HEYWOOD (1889-1959)
Olivia Pitman 1920
MAJOR JOHN ALEXANDER (1892-1932)
Audrey Wilmot 1918
Sir James Stuart (1894-1966)
Muir Dudley (1893-1927)
Archibald (1896-1918)
George Staneley (1899-1977)
Seton Veitch (1903-1994)
Peter (1905-????)
SIR WILLIAM (Chairman) (1924-2009)
Elizabeth Macandrew 1950
MARK ALISTAIR (TIM) (1926-1996)
Sue Erskine
Vernon (1919-1960)
GEORGE MCKENZIE (1899-1953)
IAN POUNTNEY (1901-1980)
Commander Ernest Colin (1902-1927)
John Balfour Symington (Jackie) (1906-1979)
Peter Daniel (Petticoats) (1910-1990)
Major Archie James (1916-1989)

CLARK FAMILY TREE

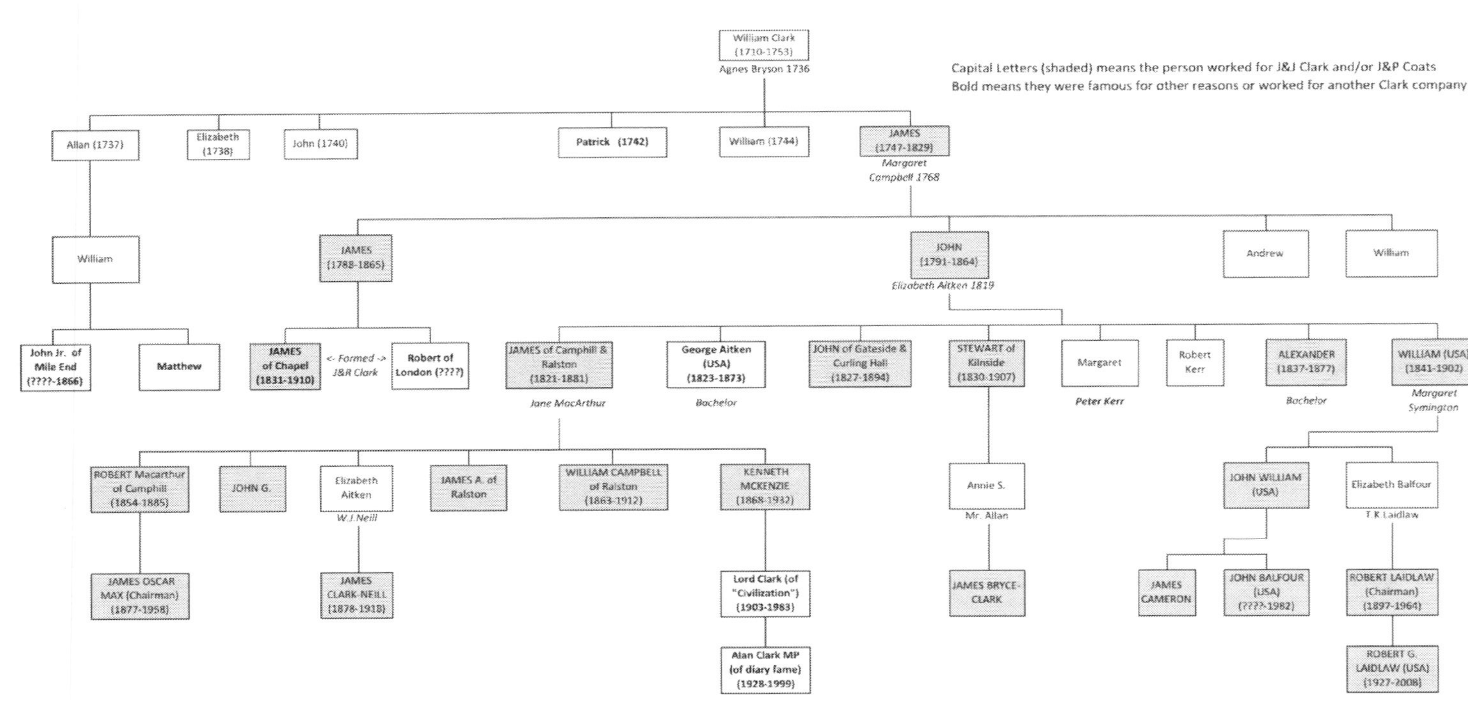

Selected Bibliography

Unpublished or for Private Circulation

The August Cruises of the SY Zara, Paisley, 1910

Bell, John, *Two Great Names in Thread: History of J & P Coats, Clark's and Affiliated Companies,* New York NY, 1957

Campbell, David A et.al., *Six Cord Thread,* 1994

Coates, Andrew, *From The Cottage to The Castle,* Perth, 1890

Coats, George H., *Rambling Recollections,* Paisley, 1920

Conant, Frederick Odell, *A history and genealogy of the Conant family in England & America,* Portland ME, 1887

Hunter, J.B.K., *History of J&P Coats,* Glasgow, 1951

In Memoriam Andrew Coates, Perth, 1900

The Inauguration of the George A. Clark town hall, Paisley, Paisley, 1882

Keir, David, *The Coats Story,* Glasgow, 1964

Photographs & Brief Description of the Establishment of the Conant Thread Co., Pawtucket RI, 1878

White, George Savage, *Memoir of Samuel Slater,* Philadelphia PA, 1836

Published Books

Bissell, D., *The First Conglomerate: 145 Years of the Singer Sewing Machine Company,* Brunswick: Audenreed Press, 2010

Blair, M., *The Paisley Thread Industry & The Men Who Created It,* Paisley: Alexander Gardner, 1907

Clark, Thomas D., *Pills Petticoats and Plows,* Indianapolis, 1944

Coats the Threadmakers, *The Technology of Thread and Seams,* London: Coats, 1995

Coats, P., *Of Generals and Gardens*, London: George Weidenfeld & Nicholson Ltd., 1976

Dos Santos, A. M. (Editor), *Coats Corrente: 100 Anos de Pioneirismo Costurando Sonhos,* São Paulo: Alexandre Dórea Ribeiro, 2007

The Draper and Clothier, Vol. 1, London: Houlston & Wright, 1860

Espinasse, F., *Lancashire worthies, Volume 1*, Manchester: Simpkin, Marshall & Co, 1874

Factories Inquiry Commission: Supplementary Report of the Central Board Volume 2, London: House of Commons, 1834

Farnie, D.A. & Jeremy D. J. , *The Fibre That Changed The World,* Oxford: Oxford University Press, 2004

Fowle, Dr. F.A., *Impressionism and Scotland*, Edinburgh: National Galleries of Scotland, 2008

Fowler, G., *Fowler's Paisley Commercial Directory*, Paisley: G. Fowler, 1845

Fox-Davies, A. C., *Armorial families,* Edinburgh: T.C. & E.C. Jack, 1905

Gibson, C. R., *The Romance of Modern Manufacture,* Philadelphia, PA: J.B. Lippincott Co., 1910

Golden, E., *Vernon and Irene Castle's ragtime revolution,* Lexington, KY: University Press of Kentucky, 2007

Homans, I. S., *Hunt's Merchants' magazine and commercial review, Volume 43*, New York, NY: Freeman Hunt, 1860

House of Commons, *Papers By Command Volume 23*, London: H.M. Stationary Office, 1920

Howard, M. & Sparrow, J. , *The Coldstream Guards 1920-1946,* Oxford: Oxford University Press, 1951

Hunt, C.W., *Dancing in the Sky*, Toronto: Dundurn Press, 2009

Irwin, M. H. et al., *The Royal Commission on Labour Reports on the Conditions of Women*, London: Eyre & Spottiswoode, 1893

Knox, Dr. W.W., *Hanging By A Thread*, Preston: Carnegie, 1995

Macdonald, C.M.M., *The Radical Thread,* East Linton, East Lothian: Tuckwell Press, 2000

Macrosty, H.W., *The trust movement in British industry*, London: Longmans, Green & Co., 1907

Metcalfe, William M., *A History of Paisley 600-1908*, Paisley: Alexander Gardner, 1909

Millar, John, *A History of the Witches of Renfrewshire: Who Were Burned on the Gallowgreen of Paisley*, Paisley: J. Neilson, 1809

Oliveira Santos, Carlos, *Coats & Clark: Uma Linha de Vida - Cem anos duma empresa em Portugal*, Vila Nova de Gaia: Companhia de Linha Coats & Clark, 2005

Parkhill, John, *The History of Paisley*, Paisley: Robert Stewart, 1857

Schmitz, C.J., *The Growth of Big Business in the US and Western Europe 1850-1939*, Cambridge: Cambridge University Press, 1995

Seacrest, Meryle: *Kenneth Clark: A Biography*, New York, NY: Henry Holt & Co., 1985

Shaw, William H. (compiler), *History of Essex & Hudson Counties, New Jersey, Volume 1*, Philadelphia, PA: Everts & Peck, 1884

Singleton, John, *The World Textile Industry*, London: Routledge, 1997

Slaven, Anthony & Checkland, Sydney George, *Dictionary of Scottish business biography 1860-1960*, Aberdeen: Aberdeen University Press, 1986

Speak, Peter, *William Spiers Bruce: Polar Explorer & Scottish Nationalist*, Edinburgh: National Museums of Scotland Publishing, 2003

Wilkins, Mira, *The History of Foreign Investment in the United States to 1914*, Cambridge, MA: Harvard University Press, 1989

Wilson, James Southall, *Alexander Wilson, poet-naturalist; a study of his life with selected poems*, New York, NY: The Neale Publishing Co.,1906

Articles

Binfield, Clyde, *The Coats Family and Paisley Baptists*, The Baptist Quarterly, January & April 1995 Volumes 36.1 & 2, pp.29-42 and 80-95

Clark, James, *The Origin of Spool Cotton Thread,* Textile World Record, March 1904, Volume 26, pp.85-88.

Kim, Dong-Woon, *From a Family Partnership to a Corporate Company: J. & P. Coats, Thread Manufacturers*, Textile History, Autumn 1994, Vol. 25 No. 2, pp. 185–225

----------------------, *J. & P. Coats in Tsarist Russia, 1889-1917,* Business History Review, Winter 1995, Vol. 69 No. 4, pp. 465–94

----------------------, *J. & P. Coats as a Multinational before 1914,* Business & Economic History, Winter 1997, Vol. 26 No. 2, pp. 526–539

----------------------, *The British multinational enterprise in the United States before 1914: The case of J. & P. Coats*, Business History Review, Winter 1998, Vol. 72 No. 4, pp. 523–52

Kininmonth, Kirsten W, *The growth, development and management of J. & P. Coats Ltd, c.1890–1960: An analysis of strategy and structure*, Business History, Oct 2006, Vol. 48 Issue 4, pp. 551–579

Kininmonth, Kirsten W. & Sam McKinstry, *Stitching it up: accounting and financial control at J & P Coats Ltd, c1890–1960,* Accounting History, Oct 2007, Vol. 12 Issue 4, pp. 367-391

Lorraine Peters, *Paisley & The Cotton famine of 1862-63,* Journal of Scottish Historical Studies, Nov. 2001, Vol. 21 No. 2, pp. 121-139.

Patsy Richards, *Inflation: the value of the pound 1750-2001,* House of Commons Research Paper 02/44, July 11 2002.

Paul Stokes, *Rich man, richer man? The 'missing' wealth of a Victorian manufacturing millionaire: The case of Thomas Coats,* Glasgow University Dissertation for MPhil in History, Sept. 30 2004.

Samuel P. Orth, *Germany & England's Attitude Toward Trusts,* The World's Works, 1913, Vol. 25, pp. 679-84

William S. Bruce, *With The Yachts "Blencathra" and "Pricesse Alice" to the Barents and Greenland Seas*, Scottish Geographical Magazine, 1899, Vol. 15, pp. 113-126.

Manuscript Sources

Coats & Clark USA, Greer/Charlotte - Miscellaneous papers
Glasgow University Archive Services, Thurso St., Glasgow
  Records of Coats Viyella plc, thread manufacturers, Paisley, Renfrewshire, Scotland.
Paisley Central Library
  Clark & Co. Miscellaneous Files
  J&P Coats Miscellaneous Files
Paisley Museum - J&P Coats Collection
Private family papers

Newspapers & Periodicals

Atlantic Monthly
Bystander
Daily Express
Daily Telegraph
Draper's Record
Economist
Evening Post

Evening Times
Fibre & fabric: a record of American textile industries …
Field & Stream
Forest & Stream
Glasgow Herald
Independent
Journal of Mercantile Law
Journal of the Society of Arts
Life Magazine
Manchester Guardian
New York Times
News Reel (Coats Internal Magazine)
Observer
Paisley Daily Express
Scientific American
Scotsman
Stock Exchange Times
Textile World Record
Time Magazine

INDEX

ABOUT THE AUTHOR

Brian Coats was educated at St. Andrews University and then obtained an M.A. in Business Management from Brunel University. He worked for the Coats group's Thread Division for thirty years, spending most of his time in South America, but ending his career as a surprising number of his ancestors did, in the USA. When he left the company in 2004, he was the last Coats to ever work for them, marking an end to the family dynasty.

This is his first book, but he has written several articles for newspapers and magazines, mostly about cinema, which is one of his great passions; the other is golf. He is married with two children and lives in San Diego, California.

Made in the USA
Lexington, KY
18 December 2013